THE TALE OF A CITY
RE-ENGINEERING THE URBAN ENVIRONMENT

BY TONY O'DONOHUE, P.ENG.

THE DUNDURN GROUP
TORONTO

Copy-Editor: Cy Jamison
Design: Andrew Roberts
Printer: Webcom

Library and National Archives of Canada Cataloguing in Publication

O'Donohue, Tony, 1933-
   The tale of a city : re-engineering the urban environment / Tony O'Donohue.

Includes bibliographical references.

ISBN-10: 1-55002-556-2
ISBN-13: 978-1-55002-556-9

   1. Urban ecology. 2. Urbanization--Environmental aspects. I. Title.

HT241.D65 2005   307.76   C2005-901798-8

1   2   3   4   5   09   08   07   06   05

Conseil des Arts du Canada   **Canada Council for the Arts**   Canada   ONTARIO ARTS COUNCIL CONSEIL DES ARTS DE L'ONTARIO

We acknowledge the support of the Canada Council for the Arts and the Ontario Arts Council for our publishing program. We also acknowledge the financial support of the Government of Canada through the Book Publishing Industry Development Program and The Association for the Export of Canadian Books, and the Government of Ontario through the Ontario Book Publishers Tax Credit program, and the Ontario Media Development Corporation.

Care has been taken to trace the ownership of copyright material used in this book. The author and the publisher welcome any information enabling them to rectify any references or credit in subsequent editions.

J. Kirk Howard, President

Printed and bound in Canada.
Printed on recycled paper.

www.dundurn.com

Dundurn Press	Gazelle Book Services Limited	Dundurn Press
3 Church Street, Suite 500	White Cross Mills	2250 Military Road
Toronto, Ontario, Canada	Hightown, Lancaster, England	Tonawanda NY
M5E 1M2	LA1 4X5	U.S.A. 14150

THE TALE OF A CITY

DEDICATION

To planners, engineers, politicians and community leaders: that they may be able to overcome their addiction to squandering the planet's non-renewable resources.

To all those addicts of the "not in my backyard" or NIMBY syndrome: that they will see the bigger picture and that the "big pipe" will take all their wastes and the wastes of others to the treatment plant.

To politicians everywhere: that they may speak with clarity, act wisely and do what has to be done to care for our small blue planet.

TABLE OF CONTENTS

ACKNOWLEDGMENTS

I am thankful for the assistance and advice given by many people — engineers, planners, journalists, community activists, monitors of the urban scene and politicians — in the preparation of *The Tale of a City*.

This book would not be possible without the help of Toronto historian Mike Filey, the Toronto Archives, the Municipal Reference Library and clippings from the Toronto daily papers over the years — the *Globe and Mail*, the *Sun*, the *National Post* and the *Star*. I owe a special thanks to the reporters and columnists from these papers. Their articles helped fill in the gaps of memory and added to the fullness of the book.

When I needed to confirm or add to the technical details of the many subjects, I had a very helpful group of professionals — engineers and planners — who were anxious to make sure that these details were correct.

I am particularly thankful to Garry Reid for his knowledge on the Port of Toronto and the waterfront; Doug Floyd and David Kaufman for their help on transit and transportation issues; Don Roughley for his advice on sewers and wastewater management; Patrick Nowland for setting me straight on Toronto's water supply; Brian Howieson for adding to my knowledge of environmental assessment and regulations; Angelos Bacopoulos for providing waste management and recycling information; Earl Burke for helping with the details of electricity; Arnold McMillan for filling in the gaps in waste heat recovery; Danny Harvey for his advice on global warming; Jack Gibbons for comments on fossil fuels and Phil Jessup and Richard Morris for their work on energy efficiency and energy conservation.

I enjoyed the inspirational writings of Thomas Moore's *The Re-enchantment of Every Day Life*.

I used many books on environmental issues, which were of great help to me in my work, including Rachel Carson's *The Sea Around Us*; Morris Cohn's *Sewers for Growing America*; Merrill Denison's *The People's Power*; Joel Herlgerson's *Nuclear Accidents*; Konrad Krauskopf's *Radioactive Waste Disposal and Geology*; Nigel Henbest's *The Exploding Universe;* Margaret Cheney and Robert Uth's *Tesla*; Gerald Foley's *The Energy Question*; Michael Guillen's *Five Equations*; Canadian Public Works Association's *Building Canada.*

My thanks, also, to the many municipal and provincial engineers and planners for all their advice and assistance. The many technical papers of engineers and scientists on energy and environment issues helped reinforce my understanding and commitment.

My thanks to Cy Jamison for editing and technical advice in the world of print. Also thanks to Mark Mandel for the cover design.

And of course, my wife Aldona and family friends, who helped me along when I needed a little push. Without their encouragement this book would not be possible.

FOREWORD
by Frank Stronach

The world is full of critics, but there are very few individuals who will take the time and effort to come up with constructive solutions, and then submit those solutions to public scrutiny.

Tony O'Donohue, whom I have known for nearly three decades now, is one of those rare individuals. In *The Tale of a City*, he tackles some of the central problems facing cities today, with a particular focus on the City of Toronto. Chapter by chapter, Tony puts forth clear-cut, practical solutions to a number of the critical issues confronting urban centres — not only here in Canada but around the world — and he shows how we can make our cities work better for all citizens.

The Tale of a City is ultimately about re-engineering the urban environment, and few people understand the mechanics and workings of municipal infrastructure better than Tony O'Donohue. He has served as an elected councillor in Toronto for more than a quarter of a century and, as a civil engineer, he has hands-on experience in the construction and delivery of municipal services — everything from energy and transit to water supplies and waste disposal. As a result, Tony is able to call upon a wealth of experience in analyzing problems and then suggesting workable solutions in simple language that any citizen can understand.

Like Tony, who has devoted many years of service to the people of Toronto, I have a particular affection and concern for this great city. It is here in Toronto that I settled after immigrating to Canada in 1954 as a 21-year-old tool and die maker. And it is here that I got my start in business after opening a one-man tool shop in a rented garage at the corner of Dufferin and Dupont streets. It was a time when Toronto was growing and modernizing and beginning to finally come of age as a truly world class city. And it was a time when the signing of the North American Auto Pact would help turn Toronto into one of the world's major automotive centres. Today, the Greater Toronto Area produces more vehicles than even Detroit, and the automotive industry generates about one in every seven jobs in Canada.

The automobile has played a great role in the development of Toronto as well as most other modern urban centres. The rise of automobile ownership has gone hand in hand with the growth of cities and the spread of municipal infrastructure — roads and highways, sewers and electrical lines. And automobiles continue to be a key component in the working of major cities, carrying people to and from the many factories and offices and shops scattered across the metropolitan core, and serving as the wheels of commerce, moving goods and services around the country and around the clock.

When discussing automobiles in the context of our cities, two issues immediately come to the fore. The first is municipal planning in regards to transportation. The second is the issue of dwindling fossil fuels.

In regards to how cities manage their transportation systems, we must recognize that there is a great desire in humans to have individual transportation. Public transportation systems — everything from buses and trains to underground subway systems — provide a great service to society, and are an efficient and economical means of moving people across the city and throughout the wider region that rings most urban centres. But people will always crave the individual freedom and mobility that personal transportation brings. In other words, people will always aspire to own and drive automobiles. That is why any politically feasible plan for dealing with urban transportation must take this reality into account.

The second issue that we as a society must come to grips with is our reliance on fossil fuels and the exploration of alternative energy sources. Fossil fuels power our vehicles, feed the engines of our industries and heat our homes. But at current rates of consumption, they are simply not sustainable. You do not have to be a great scientist to figure out that our oil and gas supplies are being depleted at a rapid rate. The amount of gas that is consumed around the world every day, from Los Angeles and Shanghai to London and Rio de Janeiro, is the equivalent of a huge river the size of the St. Lawrence emptying into the ocean — and it is not difficult to realize that this river will soon dry up.

That is why it is crucial that we put more money into research to come up with alternative fuels and alternative energy strategies. Governments have a great responsibility in this area and need to take a greater leadership role. We not only require a local strategy but a national strategy as well. And, in this increasingly interconnected world, we will also eventually need a global strategy.

According to projections by the United Nations, the world's population will increase by about 3 billion to 9 billion by 2050 — most of it taking place in developing countries, which can ill afford such increases. This will require a new approach to sharing the resources of our planet and preventing the destruction of its natural environment.

The key to our future must lie in our ability to provide a basic education in science and technology for the youth of the world. This should help them understand the finite resources of the planet and the most effective way to use these resources sparingly.

Frank Stronach
February 2005

Frank Stronach is founder and chairman of Magna International Inc., one of the world's largest autoparts companies, with its headquarters located on the outskirts of Toronto.

INTRODUCTION
A City Moving through Crisis

Cities, by their very nature, are confining and tightly packaged environments. In early modern times, the city was a walled community and the bastion of power in much of the world. Indeed, the city-state was the dominant structure throughout the Middle Ages. But as modern democracy took root, the elected legislatures of nation states, or the ultimate rulers of even broader territories — empires, commonwealths, federated states — began to take on the role of governing and protecting the city and its hinterland. It was a balancing act — finding the best structure to govern and administer a land where the population might share basic roots, but where competing interests vied for power, funds and services.

In the modern application of democracy, cities are the driving engines of the wealth of nations. But cities, on the road to universal suffrage, have ended up as very junior partners in sharing the enormous wealth generated in large urban areas. In consequence, the gradual siphoning of taxes, with little in return to urban centres, has led to the slow decay of cities. Gone are the days when the city-state dominated the political and business structure of a country. The new concept of democracy has pushed the city out of the decision-making role and boundaries of the country and its sovereignty.

It is hardly the decline and fall of ancient Rome, but Toronto's world-class aspirations are at grave risk if protective measures are not taken. On an annual basis Toronto contributes more than $35 billion in taxes to the federal and provincial treasuries. Of that amount, about $20 billion is returned to the city in services. Over the years the senior governments, while increasing the tax take from the city, have gradually withdrawn funding for many major infrastructure capital projects. At one time, the federal government contributed two-thirds of the capital costs for sewage systems and the provincial government contributed up to 75 percent of the capital costs of rapid transit. These governments have now withdrawn from these programs.

Others may be better prepared to detail the case for a larger share of the tax pie from the senior governments. I have only touched on it. But I do not have to be an economist to realize that the active participation of the federal and provincial governments is a key component for the economic health of the city. Although municipalities, constitutionally, come under the jurisdiction of the provincial government, the Ontario Legislature has all but abandoned the city's needs in many of the servicing areas where Toronto alone cannot carry out its mandate of effective government within its own tight boundaries.

Take the example of waste disposal. As a civil engineer, with the early responsibility for the Keele Valley landfill site — before Metropolitan Toronto acquired it — I could feel the local opposition to Metropolitan Toronto using its power outside its political boundaries. When the site closed on December 31, 2002, the shortcomings of the political criteria had a crippling effect on the City of Toronto. I knew the long-term problem of waste would have to be addressed in a more comprehensive way and with the help of the province — which has not arrived. If it was not for the availability of a landfill site in Michigan (and the rules of NAFTA), Toronto would have been in dire straits.

Ontario has twice taken on the task of "aiding" Toronto with waste management and spent $253 million between 1985 and 1995 in developing detailed plans. But, with the election of the Conservative government, these plans were cancelled in 1996. Toronto was told to manage its own waste and to find a "willing host." The Liberal government, after the defeat of the Conservatives in 2003, has chosen to follow the same path, with little attention or help for waste disposal in the province. Because of the cumulative neglect of the province, and the chaos at City Hall, Toronto taxpayers are now paying a minimum of $42 million per year to haul garbage to a landfill site in Michigan.

In this book, I have attempted to cover the major services that every city or community needs. They include electricity, energy, water supply, sewage treatment, transportation, waste disposal, recycling, environmental issues, etc. These are all part of the urban landscape and will always be essential wherever large numbers of people live and work. But the vast majority of people, perhaps as high as 99 percent, have no idea how these everyday services work and what they cost. Flick the switch and the light comes on; turn the tap and the water is there; flush the toilet and the sewage disappears; put out the garbage and it is picked up and hauled away. We have taken all these services for granted. We ask questions only when something goes wrong — and recently much has gone wrong. We have had a serious electricity blackout, garbage disposal chaos, water problems, overflowing sewers, sludge mess, filthy beaches, smoggy skies and traffic gridlock. Even our elected representatives know very little about the workings of those basic services or how to improve them. True, they are not very glamorous, but they are part of the package of costly ingredients which every city needs and which the taxpayers pay for.

Any city with a nuclear power plant on its doorstep has an additional cause for concern. The eight aging reactors of the Pickering nuclear power plant, begun in 1972, are like a festering sore on our eastern border. This plant will not improve with age. It will only get worse and will be a menacing problem for generations to come. As a city, it should be our number one priority. Although it is a provincial responsibility, we cannot duck this one: we do have a stake in it.

The lack of knowledge, the absence of any clear plan, the probing at a distance, the secrecy, the unknown magnitude of coping with unrecognized or unseen defects — these issues have challenged all those assigned to "fix" the reactors since they were closed for repairs in 1997. But then again, there is no manual on "fixing" reactors. Of the 400-odd reactors in operation now in the world, most are past middle age and showing signs of wear. They were supposed to have a maximum life span of about 40 years. Imagine the nightmare legacy we are leaving to our children as these first generation reactors sputter to the end of life and their final resting place in a yet-to-be-located nuclear graveyard!

Nuclear power, electricity, energy and environmental concerns are all part of this book. It is meant to provide a very basic primer for all who are interested in the workings of a community or a city. I hope it will help planners, politicians and all those interested in the way we live and use our resources. Catering to an increasingly fragile environment will require a lot of attention as more of us crowd the planet and strip it of its green mantle — all the time adding to the pollution of the thin band of atmosphere surrounding us.

In an attempt to chart the road ahead for the next and future generations, in the last chapter of this book I have focused on developing a standard education package for the youth of the world who will inherit a deeply wounded planet. Recognizing the mistakes of the past, and the corrections that must be made, will require a basic understanding of our fragile planet and how it can be nurtured back to health. This may take many years to achieve. But, through environmental education, it will attract people who can make a difference. And it will encourage many of them to run for public office.

As a professional engineer with nearly 50 years experience, I know at first hand how difficult the task is. And as a former Toronto city politician, with more than a quarter-century of service, I know how tough it is for an elected politician to make a difference in the turmoil of local politics.

I hope this book will be helpful in challenging all to improve our relationship with our engineered and our natural environments.

CHAPTER 1
The Re-engineering of a Modern City

The flight of rural people to cities and towns is not a new phenomenon. Human beings, naturally seeking close relationships, have always had a tendency to avoid living in isolation. It has been a mark of human existence since our ancestors evolved into *homo sapiens* a mere thousand generations ago. And indeed, there has been remarkable continuity across the centuries in the concept of the city, not only as a locus of power and wealth, but as a centre of culture and civilization. So, too, there is continuity in the notion that to be urban is to be urbane (both have their roots in the Latin *urbs*, or city). Big cities are seen to be chic and "cool" environments, places of glamour, a major draw for the Hollywood elite at events such as the Toronto Film Festival, held every September.

But great cities are also prone to calamity — as evidenced by the 9/11 terror that hit New York in the World Trade Center attacks; by strange diseases such as the SARS outbreak that rocked Toronto in the spring of 2003; or by the blackout that plunged 50 million people in parts of eastern Canada and the United States into medieval darkness at 4:11 p.m. on August 14, later that summer. Cities can also be devastated by plague, economic catastrophe, drought, storms, wars, fire and earthquakes. And they can be affected in more mundane ways by the corruption and mere incompetence of their city leaders.

The ancient world had many great cities — and some, like Athens and Rome, continue to flourish. Others, like Carthage and Babylon, lie in ruins or under mounds of sand. By the beginning of the Dark Ages, Athens was all but forgotten and Rome had fallen to the Visigoths. The cities of the classical world were in trouble. Civilization shifted to the periphery of Europe, where for 500 years or more, beginning in the seventh century, Celtic monks planted the seeds of a modern enlightenment. They built churches and centres of learning around which towns developed. Many of these exist today as bustling towns and cities in countries such as France, Britain, Germany, Austria and Switzerland.

Throughout the Middle Ages, many Christian religious orders built monasteries, which attracted people to live and work in their communities. Paris, for example, had the great medieval monastery of Cluny. Monks led structured lives and helped develop crafts and industries for their communities. It was the monk Dom Perignon, the abbot of Hautvillers, who discovered how to make wine sparkle — and the bubbles led directly to the huge champagne industry and to the growth of cities like Rheims. Local people also felt protected and helped by the more erudite monks, who established schools to educate the populace — especially teaching children from the earliest years.

The Normans depended heavily on monasteries to develop centres of learning and commerce. Once the development and integration of the urban system had taken place, a structured form of self-government became possible. Most European cities, including the great city-states of the early modern world — like Venice and Genoa — still have some historical links to the monastic past and to the work of the Christian church. After the confiscation of church properties and the closing of the monasteries by Henry VIII in the 1500s in England and Ireland, accompanied by the turmoil of the Reformation all over Europe, wars and revolutions caused many problems for local communities. The crafts and trades that had developed around the monasteries struggled to survive. But ordinary people, not wanting to lose community-based industries and schools, produced civic leaders who took a more active role in the development of their communities.

In other cultures, beyond the reach of the Western churches, towns developed primarily for the same reasons. The leader of a group selected a site, which could first and foremost be protected from enemies. It was then the responsibility of the leaders to design and build the town and its fortifications. A well-fortified town usually had a moat and sturdy walls around the perimeter — all designed to ward off marauding bands of bandits or the hostile armies of rival chieftains.

Leaders emerged as a result of conflict. The new chieftain was often a military conqueror, like William of Normandy in England when he defeated the Britons in the Battle of Hastings in 1066; or Brian Boru when he beat the Norsemen in the Battle of Clontarf in Ireland in 1014. And most of the great monarchs and emperors of the day simply established their right to rule through bloody battles, accompanied by indiscriminate human slaughter. Most victors were strict and cruel tyrants — ruthless with the people they were supposed to protect. Kings ruled by "divine right." Citizens were subjects of the monarch and the sword was the law. There were no elections — and on the death of the king, his eldest son succeeded to the throne. It was an "all in the family" hereditary system, unless some upstart tyrant defeated the king and established his own dynasty. Ordinary people accepted this system and looked to the king as protector and provider.

All of the prevailing dynasties, especially in Europe, can trace their roots to intrigue, skullduggery and bloody battles where people were used as the cannon fodder to enrich the monarch. Wars were waged to subdue more people and control more lands. Even in the years after World War II, a ruthless dictator like the Soviet Union's Joseph Stalin could oust people from their lands because of their religion or ethnic origins and replace them with loyal supporters of the Communist way of life.

Feeling guilty for the plight of the Jewish people and the terrible genocide inflicted on them by Nazis in World War II, the United Nations, at the instigation of Britain and its Allies, decided that a space or a homeland in Palestine would be created for them. In the process hundreds of thousands of Palestinians were ousted to make way for the State of Israel. These actions and the further occupation of more Palestinian lands by Jewish settlers have caused enormous problems of terror and hatred between the Muslims and Jews in that area. It is an expanding cauldron of bloodshed and tears, not only for Arabs and Israelis, but for all civilized peoples. And there is no end in sight.

About 1,000 years earlier, the Crusades of the eleventh century, organized by European Christian kings to oust the Saracens or Muslims from the Holy Land (Palestine), achieved little and succeeded only in laying the foundation for centuries of bitterness and violence between Christianity and Islam — which exists to this day. And the splits in the Christian religion added to the carnage and breakup of many peoples all over Europe. But the "togetherness" of a common religion in those times did offer a certain amount of security — inside the old protective wall or moat. Cities such as Rome, Mecca and Constantinople (now Istanbul) are examples of the powerful impact of religion on the history and life of cities. Great religious centres have also tended to see themselves as golden cities at the heart of the world. When the Pope gives his apostolic blessing, it is delivered *urbi et orbi* — to the city and the world.

Religion also played a dominant role in determining who should stay in the city and who should be banished. Monarchs and emperors fought to preserve or restore their particular brand of religion. Many bitter and bloody battles were fought between city-states in the name of religion. The winning side, after these battles, would invariably draft laws that imposed their religion on the losers and had to be obeyed under penalty of death or dismemberment. The idea of civility suffered, too, when sectarian violence became part of the landscape and the religion of the losing side was outlawed.

Most of these religious laws are now part of the junk heap of history. But, sadly, the odd law still survives. It reminds us how difficult it has been to adhere to the basic principles of the democracy we so loudly proclaim. As an example of the latter, the Act of Settlement 1701 is included in the Canadian Constitution — the Canada Act 1982. It spells out clearly that no Roman Catholic, or anyone married to a Roman Catholic, can become monarch of Britain or her possessions (and that includes Canada). It makes a farce of the Canadian Charter of Rights and Freedoms — also part of the Constitution!

All monarchies and kingdoms began through bloody battles and not through the ballot box. Democracy was just a word at the time (the voice of *demos*, the crowd) — although the ancient Greeks in the millennium before the Common Era had done their best to use it as a foundation for government. But it was not fully understood or desired by the kings and rulers of the time. It did not take root until much later, when education and the idea of civic responsibility brought the franchise and the freedom of the city to all people.

The beginning of the industrial revolution in the mid-1850s, following the development of the steam engine (and railroads) and the discovery of oil, sparked the increase of country folk moving to towns and centres of industry. Indeed, the industrial revolution led the modern rush into cities. Farm mechanization required fewer farm workers, and factories were built to mass produce goods in the urban setting.

But an increasing world population has shown a worrisome acceleration of the movement of peoples in all countries to towns and cities. Population projections for the twenty-first century are alarming and disturbing: alarming, because of the need to provide so much more food and shelter; and disturbing, because nearly all of the projected population increases will occur in Third World countries — countries that cannot handle their present numbers, let alone an increase in their overall population.

If good urban planning is crucial to the successful city, the more immediate reasons for early man to come together were safety and security. And once the most desirable location was found, work began to build the fortifications. The great old cities of the world owe their existence and survival to the foresight of their first inhabitants. These cities were usually situated on a prominent location at the mouth of a river with a sheltered harbour. The river provided the freshwater needs and the port helped develop trade and commerce. Water played the key role in the development of every city. If there is no water there will be no life. Every living thing needs water to survive, so towns and cities would only flourish if water was available. Some towns and cities, as populations grew, had to import additional water — a costly and necessary element for the life of a city. Las Vegas, the modern gambling town in the Nevada Desert, is one such example. There, all the water needs are carefully monitored and water conservation is an integral part of survival. Its future survival depends on its ability to maintain that constant supply of water.

The Romans were great urban engineers. Their ability to forge a relationship with the natural environment was superb. After 2,000 years, we can still see the aqueducts and bridges they built in many old European towns and cities. Many of these structures are still in use today. The survival of peoples and cultures throughout the short existence of the human species has depended on their intelligence and adaptability. All the historical evidence shows that the old civilizations — Greeks, Romans, Persians, Incas, Aztecs, etc. — built and used water systems to sustain them. They had to be urban planners. And with the discovery of America in 1492, Europeans began to import their developed urban skills to aid in the building of the New World and its cities.

But there is no clear way to calculate accurately the pressures of population on cities around the time of the great explorers. The world's population would not have been much greater than 500 million, five centuries ago. The planet, at that time, was much more in harmony with all the living creatures it nourished. The tools of man had not yet begun the destruction of the natural environment. That came much later with the industrial revolution, when the world population reached an estimated 1.2 billion in 1850. A century later, by 1950, the world population had doubled to 2.4 billion. By 1988 it had reached five billion; and in October 1999 it passed the six billion mark. Sadly, population increases have taken place in the poorer countries — in places that could ill afford to feed and house so many additional people.

Before the discovery of the New World, the Americas were vast, wild, open spaces — home to a host of nomadic tribes whose existence scarcely made a dent on the land. They had a different concept of life than Europeans. They worshipped the sun and other gods and made human sacrifices to satisfy their deities. Mostly nomadic and living inland, away from the ocean, some aboriginal people developed towns that are almost forgotten today. They lie in ruins, consumed by jungles and forests over the centuries. A few town sites have been discovered and attempts have been made to understand life in these towns and why they were eventually abandoned. The ruins of Copan in Honduras, Chichen Itza, Uxmal and Tikal in Mexico and Machu Pichu in Peru provide a glimpse of what life was like for those earlier inhabitants.

As wave after wave of immigrants arrived, after the discovery of the "new world," the landscape began to change. Land was cleared for farming and trees were logged to build homes. Soon the landscape began to show the same type of scars as the "old country." The northern European town soon found its roots in areas that attracted Germans, Swedes, Ukrainians, Polish, Irish, English, French and other immigrants from countries with colder climates. The streets were planned and laid out with a little more controlled planning — with a wider, grid-like street pattern. The centre was the area catering to the commercial and shopping needs of the people. It included government buildings, churches, small parks and at least one main street. People lived on the upper floors of commercial buildings and added to the vitality of the inner-city community.

As new people arrived, the residential characteristics began to change. Houses were built on large lots in the suburbs or out-skirts of the city — most times in a haphazard sprawl of subdivisions. These developments consumed vast tracts of farmland outside every city, giving an ugly, disjointed appearance to most modern cities. Spanish and Portuguese settlers built towns and urban centres — replicas of the towns and cities in their home-lands. The broad square or plaza in the centre, surrounded by the major government buildings, stores, hotels and the church or cathedral, was the focal point of every town and city. High walls — to guard the privacy of the inhabitants — surrounded court-yards and dwellings. Location was important, and towns and cities were built wherever the first immigrants found a site that was easy to defend, with a protected, safe harbour. The old colonial towns and cities of many Latin American countries have retained the charm and character of Spain and Portugal. But the stifling humidity of the tropical climate along the coast had a dampening effect on the vitality of these Hispanic towns. Later on, many towns were built in the mountains where the climate is more moderate.

By the beginning of the twentieth century, the expansion of Third World cities has scarred the planet in many ways and has dramatically pointed to the division between rich and poor. The enormous extent of the poverty, despair and ugliness illus-trates what such cities can do to people. The population explosion and lack of employment has caused many of the poorest unskilled peasants to flock from rural to urban areas. The haphazard shantytowns and *favellas* give testimony to the plight of the poor and the difficulty of eking out a living.

In North America, the aboriginal Indian tribes fared no better than Central and South Americans with the arrival of the white man. The Indian and Inuit peoples were nomadic and paid little attention to permanent structures. There were no towns or cities — only encampments that could be moved as the need arose. Their mobility was restricted, as even the horse was not known to them at that time. Although the aboriginal peoples were peaceful, it soon dawned on them that they were losing control of their territory as more and more immigrants began to clear the land and build towns. It also became apparent that the white man was staying. The aboriginal peoples were considered savage and a nuisance to the immigrants. As constant battles erupted, the superior weapons ensured that the white man would win. Eventually the Indians were rounded up and moved to reservations. Some tribes supported the Spanish, some the French and some the British. And many stayed neutral. But it did not matter who won — the aboriginal peoples would lose in the end.

At one time, British administrators thought of the Indian chiefs as a mere nuisance to be wiped out. They invited the chiefs of all the tribes in Upper Canada to a council meeting. Most of the chiefs, suspecting treachery, did not attend, but sent delegates. When the delegates were leaving after the meeting, their hosts sent presents to the chiefs as a sign of friendship. The presents were carefully wrapped with clothing material taken from victims of the cholera virus!

Immigrants adjusted more easily to their new surroundings but were always fearful of Indian attacks. Business and farming reflected a continuation of old country life with that extra drive to succeed in the new country. This was a land of opportunity — a land where a better life was available to all. A little hard work and the door opened to that life. As the chuckwagons full of immigrants moved west, the spirit of adventure was part of the challenge of this new land. And then, the linking together of rivers and lakes with canals became the challenge of the expanding population after the American War of Independence and the founding of the Republic in 1776.

The European battles between Britain and France spilled over into Canada. The battle of the Plains of Abraham in 1759, in Quebec City, led to the Treaty of Paris in 1763, which gave Canada to Britain. The British government passed the Quebec Act in 1764, which permitted the French-speaking population in Quebec to follow French civil law and allowed Roman Catholics to practise their religion. British forces then proceeded with the building of Canada, modelled after the English or British system of government.

By the early 1800s many canal works were underway and continued over the next 150 years to the opening of the St. Lawrence Seaway in 1958. These canal works were labour-intensive. Towns developed at the most favoured locations along the routes, as the movement of goods by river and canal became the transportation of choice. The development of the steam engine led to the building of the railroads, which began in the 1850s and continued at a furious pace for the rest of the century. Railroads had a devastating impact on the canals. The railroads not only opened up the age of passenger travel but for the first time linked towns and cities together to move goods and open new markets to manufacturing businesses. By the time Canada became a dominion in 1867, the building of the railroad was well underway. In 1885 the Canadian Pacific Railway reached Port Moody on the Pacific coast of British Columbia — duplicating the link-up of the Atlantic and the Pacific coasts in the United States in 1869.

To many planners, the separation of the town's waterfront from the centre of the town by a few railroad tracks seemed to clutter up the urban landscape. Many towns have earned an ugly reputation because of the clumsy way the railroad invaded the town. But there is no denying that the railroad became the lifeline of towns and cities across the land. It also meant that any city with a deepwater port and a railroad to the port was guaranteed success. Old cities had to change to make way for these railroads, while new cities included the railroad and its "Union Station" as a vital hub for commerce and business.

As towns and cities expanded with each wave of new immigrants, and advancements in technology boosted business, the needs of the newcomers and the younger generation began to change.

Their expectations were different from those of the old city dwellers. They wanted a rural-like setting — more grass and trees, less density and more breathing room. They saw themselves as benefiting from the best of both worlds, as citizens of the New World. After the end of World War II in 1945, the two-car garage became their symbol. This meant the building of more roads and highways to accommodate their vehicles. Rail and public transit systems were regarded as obsolete.

But as the cities of the First World flourished, the cities of the Third World — or to use the more politically correct label, "developing world" — made desperate cries for help. Water supply, sewage treatment, education, housing, health services and an adequate supply of energy are some of the basic needs — and they are often sorely needed. The exploding population of these cities — through migration from the countryside and increased birth rate — adds to the poverty and continues to eat away at their viability. On the other hand, the cities of the developed world continue to grow at a slower and more organized pace. But there are still pockets of poverty, unemployment and homelessness. There is always a quest for a better life in any city. And no matter how hard a municipality tries to "house" and help the homeless, the poor will always be there, either by circumstances or by choice. As St. Paul said, "The poor will always be with us."

As we ponder the economic divisions on our planet, the developed world has to reach out to bridge the great divide between the poverty of so many cities and the affluence of others. That helping hand may not come during our lifetime. It will only become a reality when there is a vastly increased flood of refugees putting ever greater pressure on the more prosperous cities and towns of the developed world.

THE CITY OF TORONTO

When the British army staked out the Town of York in the 1750s, it never envisioned the city of 2.4 million people we now call Toronto — or that the Greater Toronto Area, with close to 5 million people, would be the fifth-largest megalopolis in North

America. As was the custom of the time, the streets were laid out in rectangular fashion, beginning along the shore of Lake Ontario, between the Don River and the Humber River. The wooded land gently rolled to the lake as it carried water runoff in the many little streams, gullies and seasonal ditches. Although the town was not in a windswept location, a few small islands just offshore offered added protection to the little budding hamlet. The land was fertile, with many varieties of wild fowl and animals and plenty of water — all ingredients for the beginnings of a new town. Since most of the early settlers were from the British Isles, the town followed the pattern of "old country" towns — down to the naming of streets after dignitaries and sovereigns.

Since the British and French were the two major colonial powers in the northern half of North America at that time, it was only natural that their way of life predominated in the towns they developed. The native peoples were easily subdued and had to conform to the new system of government and the European way of life. When Canada became part of the British possessions, the British North America Act of 1867 established it as a colony, with limited powers. The act allowed the French to maintain their culture and language and participate with the British as a junior partner in the colonial rule of Canada. The two official languages — English and French, with French mainly in Quebec — made Canada a bilingual country. Earlier, after the American Revolution and the Declaration of Independence in 1776, many British loyalists who fought to maintain the status quo and retain George III as their king moved to Canada. Many of these loyalists settled in the Town of York, while others settled in rural Ontario.

Toronto grew slowly from its humble beginnings. It did not register as a city of any significance until the influx of new immigrants after World War II, between 1947 and 1972. Those 25 years of immigration turned the city into a modern cosmopolitan centre to rival many of the fine cities of the world. It brought prosperity and a new life to a city that some said "just woke up." For the first time, local governments were not accustomed to dealing with the vast increase in the numbers of immigrants, most of whom wanted to go to work immediately and make a new home. Government infrastructure — mainly provincial and municipal — was not in place to handle the integration of the newcomers and prepare for the orderly expansion of Toronto. And immigrants had visions of a better life, after six years of war in Europe and the Far East, which had brought nothing but hunger and misery. Toronto was the place to make a new start and build a permanent home.

Toronto developed like most other cities in a hurry — with a simple plan for modest development at first and a hurried plan for expansion as more people arrived. Planning for expansion was mostly politically motivated and depended on how the majority of the electorate reacted. Rarely would a politician lead if the plan would cause major dissent or the prospect of not being re-elected. The politician usually tried to get a snapshot of what would be acceptable and then present it as a proposal for acceptance to the municipal council — with support from hired professional planners.

Toronto, from a planning point, has been — and still is — a city in confusion. Its true planning vision has a lifespan of only one or two terms of council — three or six years. The only real vision it has shown, and it is recalled often, is the Bloor Street viaduct, which provided for the future Bloor/Danforth subway line. All other plans, which over the years have cost in the tens of millions of dollars, have achieved little. Yet, planners are always coming up with ideas — many at the request of politicians and many in response to plans or ideas submitted by interests outside of politics.

THE MODERN PLANNED CITY

But at least Toronto does not have the sanitized, sterile look of modern planned cities, such as Brasilia, Brazil, which was developed, as an example of a modern administrative capital, by planner Lucio Costa and Oscar Niemeyer — a respected architect. The open spaces and modern buildings, without a compact "people" centre, provide no warmth or personality. It is a kind of plastic place — in sharp contrast to Rio de Janeiro or even Sao Paulo. But there are many modernists who love Brasilia, and it has become a tourist attraction.

Two other cities of note — Mexico City and Paris — had major planning facelift programs in the nineteenth century. These introduced broad, tastefully laid out new streets in the downtown areas — changes that have made a delightful impact. But there are few other similarities between Paris and Mexico City. Paris is a First World city with a river link to the sea and a healthy air shed that easily ventilates the city. It has strict planning laws and a superb system of public transit — both surface and subway. It has an adequate supply of water and wastewater treatment. As a member of the European Union, it has much expertise available to ensure that it meets all the planning and environmental standards of the EU.

Mexico is different. When Hernan Cortez reached the Mexican coastline of Vera Cruz on March 4, 1519, he scuttled his ships so that his small force of 600 soldiers and 18 horsemen could not return to Cuba. The native Indians saw horses for the first time and looked on Cortez as the promised "fair god from the east." Eight months later, on November 8, 1519, Cortez reached what is today Mexico City. The old Aztec city, in a valley surrounded by mountains, sat in a beautiful location. It was built on many islands with causeways and drawbridges.

Montezuma, the Aztec chief, thought that Cortez was a god. Aztec folklore had promised that, one day, a fair-skinned man would come from the east and he would be a god-king saviour. The natives had never seen horses before, and that reinforced their conviction that Cortez and his small group were indeed the promised saviours. The Spanish took over all of the city's key locations before Montezuma realized that Cortez was very human. But it was too late. Terrible battles raged across the city. Montezuma was seized and was later executed. Cortez and his small band of soldiers eventually got the upper hand as the city lay in ruins. Its stone structures, culture, government buildings and places of sacrifices were destroyed as the conquistadores took over.

Napoleon III, after invading Mexico in 1862, installed Austrian Archduke Ferdinand Maximilian as emperor of Mexico in 1864. He proceeded to redevelop the centre of Mexico City with parks, wide boulevards and tree-lined streets to mirror Paris. He was later executed by a Mexican firing squad in 1867. With Maximilian dead, the city's European facelift program came to an

31

end. When I visited Queretaro City in 1977, I went to the last place where Maximilian stayed and where he was executed. I listened to the sad story of a very simple and vain man. He gave a silver peso to each member of the firing squad so they would not shoot him in the face. His wife, Carlotta, ended up in a mental institution in France after the execution. Maximilian's body was returned, years later, to Vienna.

Very little of Aztec Mexico remains today. The modern Mexican capital is a sprawling, heavily polluted city of more than 18 million people, with no access to the sea, trapped in a bowl that provides conditions for a constant air inversion. By mid-morning every day the air above the city becomes warmer than the air at ground level, trapping an obnoxious yellowish-brown mixture of air pollution from factories, cars, trucks and buses. This smog, shrouding the city, is a terrible health hazard. The city's water supply is also in a critical state as the aquifer beneath the city cannot meet the needs of the people. Wastewater treatment is almost non-existent. Some have recommended that as a capital it should be abandoned and a new city built on higher ground, where the quality of life would have a chance to improve.

Sadly, there is no single political framework in the Americas, like the European Union, to help developing countries and their cities. As more and more *campesinos* move to the already crowded cities, creating enormous poverty and housing problems, the real problems of the third millennium will become the plight of the millions of refugees from these developing countries.

Meanwhile, we live in a fair amount of affluence — smug and comfortable. The gap between the haves and have-nots in developing countries is great. And yet, we cannot see the looming crisis that will eventually engulf us unless we reach out and offer a helping hand.

Toronto is probably close to the maximum ideal size for a modern city. Situated on a large body of water, with adequate natural resources within easy reach, it moves along in a casual, lethargic way. The downtown is compact and livable.

The automobile has made an impact, but has not taken over completely as it has in many U.S. cities. But the core of the old city has been hit hard by the spiraling cost of doing business, bloated and ineffectual government bureaucracies, as well as general neglect by the provincial and federal governments. The survival of Toronto and other Canadian cities depends on a new understanding by provincial and federal governments of the major needs of cities. If that does not happen, the cities will decline and lose their vitality. A city like Toronto can get better as it gets older — or it can die of neglect. Whatever happens, the decline or fall of Toronto would be tragic for Canada as a whole.

The ills of our city begin with the minimal financial support coming from the federal and provincial governments. It is as if the Canadian Constitution has an unwritten section that promotes the financial rape of cities. Toronto provides $35 billion annually to the federal and provincial coffers — about $15 billion more than is returned to the city in services. And these meagre financial crumbs have only a little impact on the needs of the city. Projects such as the rail link to Pearson Airport and beyond, funding for subway construction, the development of Downsview airport lands, municipal infrastructure improvements, etc., are dusted off before federal elections and repackaged as projects to be funded. But nothing ever happens. Ottawa terminated its aid to municipalities for sewage treatment in 1982. Since then, it has been mostly "take a lot and give back a little."

And the provincial government has abandoned the capital of Ontario. The garbage dilemma is an obvious area where Toronto needs help outside its boundaries. Provincial aid in this area has been an embarrassment. The province decided, in 1981 and again in 1990, to help find a site for Toronto's waste processing and disposal. Both attempts were cancelled by 1996 after Queen's Park had spent $253 million. And Toronto was then told to find its own "willing host" for its garbage. In the early 1970s, Ontario Premier Bill Davis had a program of 75 percent capital funding for transit in Toronto. That disappeared a long time ago.

Cities need constant attention and re-engineering to maintain livable urban environments. Our dependence on funding from senior levels of government is part of the formula for a healthy, active and workable city. Sadly, Toronto and other cities are now playing the role of beggar to get back a fair share of what they have contributed.

CHAPTER 2
Governing a City: The Perils of Amalgamation

What is the ideal size of a city so that it can be governed effectively and efficiently for those who live and work there? There is no easy answer to that question. Attempting to manage a city as if it were a large company does not fully address the question. Linking together individuals and neighbourhoods, in developed relationships under the umbrella of a town hall, is the cornerstone of its survival. If changes are contemplated to expand the boundaries, it is wise to consult the people who are affected. The Ontario provincial government found that out in 1997 when it announced its intention to amalgamate the old City of Toronto and its five surrounding municipalities into one big city.

Sometime in the fall of 1996, Ontario Premier Mike Harris told a cabinet meeting that the six municipalities of Metropolitan Toronto were to become the new, larger City of Toronto. He gave the order to Al Leach, his minister of municipal affairs, to begin the amalgamation process for one level of local government and for the November 1997 municipal election. I was pleased, as I thought it would lead to a more practical, efficient and workable form of local government — which was sorely needed. How wrong I was! After two terms or six years of the amalgamated Toronto, it has proved to be a disaster for the people of the city. I had expected so much from the new city. I believe it could have worked — and worked well — if the newly elected city politicians, bureaucrats, and provincial politicians had worked together on a practical implementation plan.

If blame is to be allocated, it has to rest squarely on the shoulders of those who had the opportunity to make it all happen — the politicians — but failed miserably. The provincial government is first in line for blame for introducing a half-baked amalgamation proposal. Throughout 1997, those who opposed amalgamation — especially local politicians and their friends who did not want change — were successful in changing and scuttling some of the key elements of the plan. When Bill 103, the provincial legislation that introduced amalgamation, became law on April 21, 1997, there was barely enough time for the November municipal election. The final bill was a shadow of what the original legislation had proposed. The government had caved in to the many demands of local interest groups and municipal politicians who saw their influence and numbers being drastically reduced. What should have been an easy and practical introduction of a unified City of Toronto turned out to be a public relations disaster for the Harris government.

Leach, former general manager of the Toronto Transit Commission (TTC), stumbled his way through the amalgamation proposal. And Dave Johnson, the former mayor of East York, who was the provincial minister of education, ripped the guts out of the original legislation. He insisted that the old municipal identities, in some form, should be retained, with the introduction of local community councils. Instead of harmonizing the municipal boundaries with the federal and provincial boundaries as originally planned, which would have given 22 wards, the province decided that the 28 old Metro wards would be retained, with two councillors from each ward. This set the number of councillors at 56 — an extremely high number of unaligned politicians in a system without a party structure. The whole idea of amalgamation was to streamline local government, to make it more efficient and more helpful for the taxpayers who pay for it. But it did not work out that way. As time has proved, it went terribly wrong.

Although a five-person transition team was appointed by the province to oversee the implementation of amalgamation, the team had very little power. That proved to be one of the major failings of the amalgamation plan, as once the municipal election was over, the work of the transition team was relegated to a minor role and it then melted away.

A strong implementation committee, with a clear mandate and real authority, was sorely needed during the first term of the new council to make amalgamation a success.

The downloading of services to the municipalities was lumped together in presentations that were confusing and seemed to be part of the amalgamation plan. And no attempt was made to develop a specific "critical path" process, the cost of implementing amalgamation, or how it would enhance the new city. There is no doubt that the sloppy way amalgamation was presented contributed to its failure and the resultant decline of the city.

Clear rules and guidelines on wage harmonization for city workers should have been laid out from the beginning. The whole idea of amalgamation was to provide a leaner, more effective and more efficient work force to give good value to taxpayers. It was not to squeeze more money out of the taxpayer by topping off wages to the highest bracket.

The surplus city halls and other properties should have been disposed of or rented within a specific timeframe, much as any normal business would deal with such matters.

Municipal politicians should not have been allowed to set their own salaries and office budgets. This should have been done by the implementation committee.

Amalgamation should have been easy for Harris. Instead he failed the City of Toronto and let it stagger and stumble through a process that lacked the common sense he constantly preached.

The new city council had its inaugural meeting at Metro Hall, on King and John Streets, on January 6, 1998. It was like all other inaugural meetings, only bigger and a little more confusing as the 56 councillors met for the first time and began to get to know each other. Inaugural meetings are more formal and ceremonial and a time when committees are appointed and schedules for future meetings are set. It is also a time when liaisons are made and there is a "feeling out" of the ideas of others.

In the beginning of the new city, the politicians dusted off the election debris and prepared for work. But although they accepted amalgamation, many were still reluctant participants. The hostility remained for a long time. The dedication was not there when the hard work had to be done. And it began to show as the new council got down to business. At the first regular meeting, the matter of assistance for councillors was discussed. Tom Jakobek, as budget chief, led the move to give each councillor an annual office budget of $237,000. It was far in excess of what was recommended by the transition team. It was presented as a fair amount, as the newly elected politicians saw their new role as most demanding, with a heavier workload. It set the pattern of how the new council would work — and also its priorities.

The first real indicator that amalgamation would provide inferior services to the people of Toronto surfaced when the politicians addressed their new salaries, which they raised above the highest of any of the salaries paid in the councils they replaced — all on the basis that their workload would be horrific.

Councillors staffed their offices in such a way that a councillor had two assistants for research and much of the contact work with the electors. It seemed to be designed to make it more difficult for a taxpayer to contact or meet a councillor. And an assistant usually dealt with taxpayers' inquiries.

In earlier times, local and metropolitan councils and committees met every two weeks. That was adjusted later to a meeting every three weeks. Now, with amalgamation, council decided one monthly meeting was enough. That provided very poor service to taxpayers and slowed down the process of decision making.

The direct telephone line was replaced by an answering system most of the time. It was difficult to talk to a councillor unless one was privileged enough to have the unlisted cell number. And the telephone caller ID system shielded many politicians from their constituents. Although the mayor, in this election campaign, promised that people would not end up talking to machines in his administration, it turned out to be the opposite. Taxpayers would indeed end up talking to machines in the new Toronto.

To cap it off, amalgamation produced Mel Lastman as mayor. Most people saw his first three-year term as a training time for the new mayor. And he began the term with high expectations. He made a few big gaffes, but many of his supporters, and some constant media backers, urged that he be given a fair chance. People were forgiving and hoped he would improve, if given a second term.

Mel Lastman got the second term as mayor, but it merely showed he was unable to head a great city. His performance, at times, was embarrassing and demeaning to the city. His administration introduced a new level of cronyism and appallingly poor administration. Many people, in the end, wished that he would just stay away from City Hall and spend most of his time at his condominium in Florida — or resign. The computer leasing inquiry indicated how inept the administration was and how little the mayor knew about the state of city governance. The sad thing for the taxpayer was that the inquiry itself would end up costing about $20 million — just to show how incompetent the administration at City Hall had become.

There is no doubt that the mayor was a great salesman when he built his Bad Boy appliance stores into a multi-million-dollar business. But he sold the business just before it went bankrupt — leaving many creditors in its wake. The fear of the same roadmap for the City of Toronto suddenly dawned on many in Toronto. Whatever happened at the end of his term, the taxpayers would have to foot the bill. They would be left "holding the bag." In the end, Lastman left the city in a mess. It would take a lot of housecleaning to bring back order and some semblance of good government.

Lastman had many headline-grabbing ideas over his two terms: the bid for the 2008 Olympics, the $12- to $17-billion waterfront plan, bringing the army in to clear the snow, the moose program. The plastic moose proved to be most positive of all his efforts. Although it did not mean much, it was a fun thing and it raised money for some charities. Don Wanagas, a City Hall columnist for the *National Post*, wrote that when the citizens elected Lastman, they thought that they were getting a mayor, but ended up "getting a municipal mascot." That, probably, is a more accurate description of Lastman as mayor.

Many of the senior bureaucrats and managers of the old amalgamated municipalities were jostling for the top positions in the new city. They were preoccupied with their own careers and their future in the new administration. Consequently, infighting and bickering sapped a lot of the enthusiasm that comes with setting up a new corporation.

As competition and lobbying clouded the jockeying for top jobs, the effects of infighting showed up in many places. As an engineer, I had two contracts with companies doing work for the city. Both were begun before amalgamation and both bore the marks of the turmoil of amalgamation.

The first contract was to build a detention tunnel and three shafts to hold 85,000 cubic metres of wastewater after heavy rains in the Western Beaches area of the city. It was a major undertaking by the former City of Toronto and it took many years to get to construction, primarily because of the cost. When the city originally called for tenders, the lowest bid was $74 million. In that design, only the tunnel would be used to contain the desired volume. The price tag was more than the city could afford.

One of the bidders, C&M McNally, suggested that the specifications should be broadened to allow builders to present their own proposals through a design/build bid process that met the requirements of the city. Eventually, with some funding from the federal infrastructure program, the decision was made to re-tender the project. McNally had the ideal tunnel-boring machine sitting idle in its yard and won the bid. A $59.5-million contract was awarded in 1997 to McNally-Frontier Inc. — a joint venture with a U.S. construction company, Frontier Inc. McNally-Frontier had considerable experience in construction. The two principals, Mike and Chris McNally, both professional engineers, had a hands-on role in ensuring that the detention system was properly constructed. The tunnel project began with few problems.

McNally-Frontier Inc. submitted a lump sum price for the contract, with two prices for the disposal of about 85,000 cubic metres of excavated material. One price was to haul it to the Leslie Street Spit — about five kilometres away. And the other was to provide additional land for a proposed aquarium, on the east side of Ontario Place — right next door to the project. The difference in cost for excavation disposal was substantial — primarily related to the longer haul to the Spit area.

In meetings between the city, McNally and Ontario Place, it was agreed that the material should be used at Ontario Place. My role was to obtain all the approvals from the various government agencies to allow for the excavated material to be used to provide additional land for the eastern section of Ontario Place. That took about five or six months. In the summer of 1997, officials from Ontario Place, McNally-Frontier Inc. and the city engineer, Werner Wichmann, met at City Hall to finalize the details of hauling the fill to Ontario Place. It was then that Ontario Place asked the city to pay $2 million extra for dumping the excavated material to provide the additional land. The city could offer only the difference between the two haul and dump prices, as per the bid. But Ontario Place would not agree to anything less than $2 million. And Ontario Place had other financial demands of the city for encroachment and services to the tunnel.

At that time, Premier Harris was talking about provincial downloading and the need for the province to cut back on spending — especially spending that might be to the benefit of municipal governments. I could understand that. But I did not think that it would reach into a project like the Western Beaches Tunnel. But relations between Ontario Place and the city's Works Department deteriorated to the point that the city and McNally-Frontier Inc. eventually decided to relocate the eastern end of the tunnel outside the property boundaries of Ontario Place, so that there would be no more contact or conflict with Ontario Place. With Ontario Place out of the picture, work proceeded on the tunnel without any further financial or relocation problems.

But the impact of amalgamation was just around the corner as the senior management positions were about to change. Wichmann, the city engineer, and other senior staff from the old City of Toronto, were lumped in with their colleagues from the other amalgamated municipalities. When the dust settled, Wichmann was no longer in charge of the Western Beaches Tunnel. And there were other changes that caused much upheaval and confusion, not only in the construction of the Western Beaches Tunnel, but throughout the civic administration. It hurt the morale of all staff and permeated every corner of every department of the new city.

The selection of senior staff for the new city was supposed to be above politics. But it did not happen that way. Politics was very much a part of the process. Many were appointed because of their political contacts. And others lost out because they had no experience in lobbying politicians. Admittedly, it was a difficult task to choose from this vast pool of talent. And the process dragged out too long as appointments had to be filled down the line after the senior positions had been filled.

In my other contract with Harbour Remediation & Transfer Inc. (HR&T), which had a five-year contract with Metro

Toronto for the lime and heat treatment of 10,000 dry tonnes per year of sewage sludge (about 36,000 wet tonnes), I saw the other changes that amalgamation would bring. The new amalgamated city inherited the HR&T contract and the odour problems it had brought outside the Ashbridges Bay Sewage Treatment Plant to 127 Commissioners Street. All this happened under the old Metro government.

The newly appointed works commissioner and his deputy decided not to spend any more money on odour control at the HR&T plant at 127 Commissioners Street and to cancel the project entirely. After all, none of this happened under their watch. It appeared that they wanted a clean slate. HR&T negotiated a contract termination agreement with the city, which paid HR&T for some lost profits over the five-year term of the contract. The termination agreement also indemnified HR&T from any debts incurred through contracts they had with other individuals or companies.

Armed with support from citizen activists in the area, local politicians and consultants, City Works management unveiled a $72-million program in February 1999 to convert the sludge into usable and saleable "biosolids." They also committed to closing down the incinerators at the plant by the end of 2000. But by the end of 2002, the sludge project was in tatters and two of the incinerator units had been demolished to make room for the new sludge handling facilities. By the end of April 2003, the city had spent about $89 million on new installations for the handling of sludge and the construction of a pelletizing plant, which was still not in operation. And any sale of the pellets looked doubtful in the foreseeable future. A few months later, on August 14, 2003, the pellet plant conveniently burned down.

The haul and spread contract with Terratec Environmental was also in tatters as the province prepared to introduce new guidelines for the application of sludge and farm manure on agricultural lands. As 2003 dragged on, it looked like the sludge would end up going to Michigan with all the rest of Toronto's garbage after the closing of the Keele Valley landfill site. And the sludge handling and pellet plant will match the MFP computer contract mess for things that go wrong! How did it all happen?

That's another story.

But there are more visible examples of why amalgamation has failed:

- The old inner City of Toronto — the city I believed should be the nucleus of the new Toronto — has been eroded bit by bit by a new structure that has shown little understanding of the need for a lively and livable downtown core.
- Ugly, costly, dangerous and pollution-causing speed bumps began to spring up like mushrooms on many of the city's residential streets. Instead of being helpful to residents, they prevent police, fire and emergency vehicles from giving fast, effective, life-giving services to area residents. And they are costly to maintain — especially during the winter months.
- Street parking rates began to soar. In many downtown streets the rates increased as much as 400 percent in the first three years of amalgamation. And the rates have been extended from 6 p.m. to 9 p.m. daily — and on other more lucrative streets, like the restaurant area on King Street West, to 10 p.m. It is like an extortion racket, but legal — to collect from the customers and penalize the stores of the old city.
- For the first time, charges for street parking on Sundays were introduced. They have placed a burden on cafés, local stores and strip commercial streets. Even the deserted core of the city has a noticeable number of Green Hornets trying to squeeze out a few extra dollars from unfortunate customers who might venture downtown. Amalgamation has brought a new level of gouging as street parking has been recognized as a new source of revenue. It appears that the system is designed and determined to destroy the downtown.

The demise of the downtown business community is a major casualty of amalgamation. Merchants and small business are unable to combat the constant demands for more taxes, increasing street parking rates and inferior services. And the burden of all these is so noticeable.

The new city bureaucracy is already staggering under its own weight and confusion. More than 1,000 additional employees have been added to the city's payroll. Amalgamation was supposed to provide a less costly, faster and more effective service to the taxpayer. The cure has become worse than the disease!

The city's homeless problems have become more noticeable as downtown streets become sleeping areas for many who prefer the streets to shelters. As usual, the cry "homes for the homeless" is probably one of the most used political phrases of our time. Our new democracy has given street people the freedom to freeze to death. That is some freedom!

The corners of downtown streets are increasingly used by panhandlers. Local politicians occasionally offer pious regurgitated statements now and again about the need to help them and build houses for the homeless, who have become the untouchables of our time.

Many American cities have gone through the same type of downtown decay. Small businesses and merchants had little say. Crime slowly became a way of life, as low-cost inferior housing was built. Many businesses closed as merchants boarded up their stores and moved away.

Suburban shopping malls — probably the greatest enemy of the old cities since they became fashionable in the 1950s — contribute to the draining of downtown business. The malls provide a safe environment and free parking. Malls are privately owned and operate as profitable businesses. Consequently, competition for the shopper's dollar is the incentive to provide the best service possible. Assuming that most people have to use their car for shopping, it makes little sense to patronize downtown shops or department stores and pay a high parking fee when a trip to a suburban shopping mall is less troublesome and parking is free.

Cities in the United States have shown that shopping malls located outside the core of the city have siphoned off much of the business and left downtown streets deserted. St. Petersburg, Florida, is a good example of that. Downtown St. Petersburg now has two-hour free parking on its main street — Central Avenue. But it is too late. The malls have captured all the shopping business. The new shopping patterns of the people have been set. It is almost impossible to win back the shopper to the downtown stores. It is a lost cause, as many stores are boarded up and few people walk the sidewalks.

The demise of the Toronto downtown is also a foregone conclusion unless politicians recognize that changes have already begun to divert much of the shopping from the old city. Business in the old city cannot survive unless its special needs are addressed — not burdened with additional city costs and taxes. That has not been understood by the amalgamated city council.

Modern cities have little regard for their own endurance. The life expectancy of a modern building is probably 50 years, and in some cases, perhaps 100 years. And its capital cost can be recovered in about 25 years. It has what is called "built-in obsolescence" — it is not meant to last too long. It really is a disposable city, where the word "permanent" has little meaning. Modern cities cater to the whims of changing societies where the wrecker's ball has more clout and as much relevance as construction cranes.

The era of the stonemason, and of buildings with strong, stout stone walls, is gone. And building codes reflect guidelines that regulate structural stability, health and fire requirements. The building code requirements for any structure dictates its final cost and of course its life expectancy.

But it would be unfair to long, nostalgically, for "the good old days" that left us many monuments in solid stone, erected with meticulous skill. Modern technology has also provided many improvements for a better life. These have been incorporated into our less-than-permanent structures. The life of a city is always a struggle for balance — building on what makes the city work and caring for its roots and foundations.

Still, there is no escaping the heartbeat of a city — it is the core. Destroy it and the city dies. Is Toronto headed that way?

CHAPTER 3
Lights Out: When a City Fades to Black

The massive electricity blackout that hit Toronto, New York and other major cities on the afternoon of August 14, 2003, showed very clearly how flipping a switch is so fundamental to modern life and urban living. But without some understanding of the discovery, development and use of electricity, we risk taking it all for granted. And if we get sloppy about it, we can literally fade to black in the modern city. But do we want to return to the darkness — where we can really see the stars in the nighttime sky?

In 1831, Michael Faraday discovered that electric voltage could be generated across the ends of a wire by moving it through a magnetic field. This was the first step to establishing that mechanical movement could generate electric current. And it established, for the first time, the interrelationship between electricity and magnetism. Faraday's definition of the phenomenon of electricity was clear and crisp: "Whenever a magnetic force increases or decreases, it produces electricity; the faster it increases or decreases the more electricity it produces." He developed the first dynamo as a way to make electricity. He found that when a shaft was rotated and placed between magnets, an electromagnetic field was developed. This produced a flow of electrons that could be carried in conductors, like copper wiring. It provided the key to unlock a new future for mankind. There was little understanding of magnetism, and the introduction of electricity with magnetism further confused the magic of it all. The unknown powers of electricity and magnetism needed the help of many.

James Clerk Maxwell (1831–1879) is recognized as one of the giants of physics. He formulated the four equations that predicted electromagnetic radiation, which are among the fundamental equations of physics. All electromagnetic radiation obeys these equations.

Before the development of the dynamo, many communities and towns developed on the banks of rivers, where mills could be built using the head of water to turn great circular blocks of stone to mill corn and other grains. After it was discovered that falling water could produce electricity from the turning of a shaft, a new era for the use of water helped many riverside communities. Rivers became the prime locations for the production of electricity — hydroelectric power.

As electricity had to be used where it was produced, these river towns became the centre of activities. Lumber and grain mills would later facilitate the introduction of other industries. These riverside plants continued to dominate the countryside as the nineteenth century capitalized on the advent of the industrial revolution. Turning a shaft in a magnetic field became the key to providing a constant supply of electricity. After the development of hydroelectricity, the windmill and the steam engine followed. More than 95 percent of the electrical needs of the planet today use water — from the flow of water, burning fossil fuel or nuclear fuel — to produce steam. In a way, the use of water, with its own miraculous qualities, has become the catalyst for creating electricity.

ALTERNATING CURRENT (AC)

Nikola Tesla was born in Croatia, the son of Serbian parents, in 1856. He is the unsung hero of the use of electricity in North America. As a young man he was fascinated with science. He had mental visions of how things should work and was able to transfer the technical details to precise drawings to make it all work. He had a vision of going to America one day, when he was shown a drawing of Niagara Falls. His dream was to capture and use the energy of the water flowing over the falls.

With the help of his uncles he began to think of improving his education. At the Polytechnic School in Carlstadt, he immersed himself in mechanical and electrical engineering. When he was shown how an electric motor operated on direct current (DC) using a commutator to reverse the flow of the current, he saw the possibility of improving on the process. He attracted widespread attention among his engineering colleagues because of his belief in alternating current. Many other engineers were also fascinated with the idea of using alternating current and began to experiment on their own.

Meanwhile, Thomas Edison and his associates in New York were making great strides with the invention of the incandescent light bulb in 1879 and the use of electricity. Tesla admired Edison and his work. He sought out an Edison company, which had just been hired by the Hungarian government to build a telephone exchange in Budapest. For a while he worked there as a draughtsman, impressing management with his skills — especially his ideas for alternating current. But he was not making much headway on his proposals. So, he decided to go to America and seek out Thomas Edison.

Tesla did not discover alternating current. It was a European engineering application that was under investigation by many engineers but not fully developed when Tesla left Europe for the New World. But its use, development and application, in America, was led by the drive of Tesla. Engineers in Europe had already begun to experiment with alternating current about seven years before its North American introduction in 1893, at the Chicago World Fair. At least two major experiments were carried out during that hectic time in Europe. In 1884, Gaulard and Gibbs built a 40-kilometre demonstration AC transmission line from Lanzo to Turin, in Italy. And in 1891, 300 horsepower was transmitted at 30,000 volts of three-phase AC for more than 160 kilometres — all part of a demonstration for the Frankfurt Exhibition. It was the standout attraction at that fair.

Armed with an introductory letter to Edison from the manager of the Budapest company, Tesla arrived in New York in 1884. He was determined to develop his ideas for alternating current and convince Edison to abandon his direct current applications. That was a bold step, as about 20 electric light and telephone companies were in competition for New York business and all were using direct current, with Edison the driving force. Edison admired the brash young man's challenging spirit and gave him a job. He proved to be a real asset to Edison and very soon was solving many of the electrical problems in the

Edison shop. But Tesla would not forget the plans he had for alternating current.

At that time, New York was the invention capital of the world. Edison had dozens of patents and had attracted the major financiers of the day — men like J. Pierpoint Morgan, Cornelius Vanderbilt, John Jacob Astor and others.

The relationship between Tesla and Edison became more strained as time went by. Edison had built all his plants to use direct current, while Tesla was now actively proclaiming that his ideas for alternating current were far superior. But Edison would not support Tesla and his ideas.

All electric motors, both AC and DC, use the same principles. A magnetized rotor turns and aligns itself to a stator, which is also magnetized but is fixed and does not move. They are both electromagnets. Direct current flows in one direction only. Alternating current, on the other hand, changes its direction of flow.

The electric power transmitted over a line is simply a product of voltage and current if the load is a resistive one. This is true of AC or DC. The advantage of AC is that the voltage can be raised and lowered easily by transformers. When the electricity is transmitted over longer distances the voltage is raised as high as required. The current can then be lowered by the same amount and still transmit the same power. Since the current is so much lower, the size of the conductor can be much smaller and much cheaper.

It was inevitable that Edison and Tesla would part ways. When Tesla became convinced that he needed help to develop alternating current, George Westinghouse of Pittsburgh arrived unannounced at his testing laboratory. Westinghouse bought all of Tesla's AC patents and proceeded to compete with Edison — a competition that became bitter, vicious and uncompromising. It was known as "the War of the Currents."

One of the most bizarre pieces of dirty work concerned the decision to change the penalty for capital murder from hanging to electrocution in New York State. Edison provided a friend, Harold Brown, with a research facility in New Jersey. Here Brown experimented with the electrocution of animals. He convinced New York State prison officials to try electrocution on a human being. A law was passed in New York State, in 1887, to use electrocution in future instead of hanging. Brown wanted to use alternating current to show how deadly it could be. George Westinghouse would not provide the equipment and refused to play this morbid game. Brown, however, was able to buy used AC equipment from another source, and on August 6, 1890, William Kemmler, who had murdered his wife, was electrocuted in Auburn Prison. It was a messy affair. It took several electrical jolts and several minutes for Kemmler to die. According to Harold Brown, Kemmler was "Westinghoused" — a term Westinghouse did not appreciate.

Tesla, with the sale of his patents to Westinghouse, had some money for the first time in his life, which he invested in his laboratory and research. He was preparing for the Chicago World Fair of 1893, which called for proposals for power and light. Although the fair had many proposals, it turned out to be a battle between the Tesla/Westinghouse team and Edison and his partners. More specifically it was a battle between AC and DC.

General Electric (Edison and his associates) bid $1 million to provide power and light. Much of that money was used to pay for the enormous amount of copper wire for the DC system and two sets of lines — one for motors and one for lighting — that were needed to provide a different voltage level. Westinghouse and Tesla proposed an AC system. It amounted to almost half the price of General Electric. It would be a single system for power and lights and less cumbersome. Westinghouse and Tesla won the bid. Their work at the 1893 Chicago World Fair exceeded all expectations. It was the highlight of the fair. In hindsight, the Chicago Fair — celebrating the five-hundredth anniversary of the discovery of America by Christopher Columbus — launched electricity as the ultimate discovery for the betterment of life and living. It pointed the way to the future.

In the meantime, Niagara Falls, New York, had attracted many financiers — all searching for a key to harness the power of the falling water of the famous falls. In 1890, Edward Dean Adams, a business financier and president of Cataract Construction Company, decided to visit Europe with engineer Dr. Sellers to have a look at electricity development. Adams, while in London, set up a consulting group called the International Niagara

Commission. The group included the famous English physicist Lord Kelvin, as well as the finest scientists and engineers of the time. And of course, the attraction and grandeur of the falls on the Niagara River were known all over the world.

There was much confusion on how to get international interest in harnessing the power of the falls. Eventually, the call went out for proposals, with a grand prize for the winning bid and smaller prizes for other engineering innovations. Of the many proposals submitted, none were deemed to be worthy of the grand prize. But one proposal, using alternating current, was submitted by the Westinghouse group. It was approved by the selection committee.

In 1889 Tesla was employed by the Cataract Construction Company of Niagara Falls, New York, as the consultant to harness the power of the river and transmit the electricity to Buffalo, 22 miles away. If all went well, it would be the first hydroelectric plant with the capability to deliver electric power anywhere.

The Niagara hydroelectric power plant would be the real test of Tesla. If it worked according to plan, it would be 75 megawatts and provide AC power to Buffalo. In 1893 the Niagara Fall Commission awarded the contract to build the powerhouse to Westinghouse to contain the ten 5,000 horsepower dynamos designed by Tesla. General Electric was awarded the building of the transition lines to Buffalo using Tesla's polyphase AC designs.

On November 16, 1896, Buffalo's Mayor Jewett threw the switch and the city received its first electricity from Niagara Falls. Few people were in attendance at that historical event. Many thought it could not happen — among them even some of Tesla's most ardent admirers and financial supporters. As the electricity began to light up Buffalo, even his detractors could not contain their jubilation.

There were so many cities, towns and villages in need of electricity. There was now real proof that electricity could be delivered anywhere, even to New York and other cities, many hundreds of miles away. It was a magnificent entrance — full of light, power and promise — to the twentieth century. And Niagara Falls, known worldwide as the honeymoon capital, could now be called the birthplace of the electrical revolution.

THE RETURN OF DIRECT CURRENT (DC)

In those early years of electricity, direct current had many problems — the main one being that low voltage electricity could not be moved over long distances. Technology had not been able to solve that problem until the development of alternating current. But since those early days, tremendous progress has been made to use direct current as a better transmission system over long distances and at high voltage.

The common practice for the transmission of electricity today is to evaluate both DC and AC for all major projects. The general conclusion has been that DC is less costly and less intrusive, with lower transmission losses in a more restricted transmission corridor, at higher voltage and at distances over 500 kilometres. AC is less costly in areas where there is plenty of room in the transmission corridor, with low voltage and shorter distances.

Of all the scientific breakthroughs, the discovery of electricity and its applications ranks as one of the greatest.

CHAPTER 4
Ontario Hydro: In Debt to Nuclear Madness

The development of a U.S. electrical system, using hydroelectric power to produce alternating current, did not go unnoticed across the border in Canada in the 1890s. But it was ten years later that Ontario began to develop hydroelectric power on the Ontario side of the Niagara River. The Province of Ontario, at that time, did not have the population and business interests to embark on such expensive projects. But there were a few individuals with vision. And there were many areas of dispute about the Niagara River and the falls, as the border between the United States and Canada straddled the waterway.

The amount of water needed to produce electric power was steadily being increased — dramatically reducing the amount of water flowing over the falls. This concerned both countries. Up to 1909 the ownership of the properties along the riverbank was in private hands. The rivalry between all the owners prompted the U.S. government to act first. Although the Burton Act attempted to regulate the commercial exploitation of the waters of the Niagara River, there was still a lot of competition for a place on the riverbank and the use of the water. The U.S. Secretary for War, William Howard Taft, used the Act to terminate all leases on June 29, 1909, on the U.S. side of the river. From then on, no individual or corporation would be allowed to use the waters of the Niagara River as they pleased, simply by owning the riverbank.

In 1909 the Boundary Waters Treaty Act was adopted by the United States and Great Britain — the latter acting on behalf of Canada. The treaty set the framework for water use regulations and for settling disputes on matters relating to riparian rights, irrigation, navigation, diversions and hydroelectric power plants — not only on the Niagara River but also on all boundary waters between the United States and Canada.

Niagara Falls, in those early days, was a hectic place, with honeymooners, engineers and nature lovers all attracted to the majesty of the falls. Here the science and financial experts of the day had come together to show the way for a better future. And on the New York side of the falls, the financial tycoons took the lead while governments looked on.

In May 1906, the Ontario government set up the Hydroelectric Power Commission of the Province of Ontario (HYDRO). Adam Beck, former mayor of London and a member of the provincial parliament, was appointed chairman of the three-person commission. Right from the start, it was a battle between private business interests and the Ontario government for total control of the production and delivery of electric power in Ontario. Municipalities, cities and towns lined up to support public ownership. Beck was a champion of public ownership and total government control. He had watched what went on in Niagara Falls, New York. He did not like what he saw — the competition among private interests all jockeying for a piece of the Niagara River.

After a while, the vast majority of private power companies in Ontario, which had followed the lead of power companies in the U.S., were squeezed out as Ontario Hydro gradually became the electricity monopoly in the province. To cap it off, all the funds needed by Ontario Hydro were guaranteed by the provincial government. No private sector company could compete with Ontario Hydro. All the municipalities eventually became franchisees of Hydro.

It is easy to visualize the economic state of Ontario in those early days. The industrial revolution had taken firm root in North America, and private financiers had shown the way with the harnessing of the waters of Niagara Falls and its AC transmission lines to Buffalo. But advances in the application of science added to the competition between the public and private sectors. For Ontario, it seemed a massive undertaking to provide hydroelectric power. But, as a monopoly, Hydro was marketed as the "people's power company" — built and operated to meet the people's need. But it took the driving force and vision of Adam Beck to bring Ontario cities, towns and municipalities under the umbrella of Hydro. And it was done in such a way that electricity was provided far cheaper than that provided by a patchwork of private companies.

The first Ontario Hydro contract was with a U.S. generating company, ironically called the Ontario Power Company, at Niagara Falls. It was for 100,000 horsepower at 60,000 volts, delivered at three-phase 25-cycle frequency — setting 25-cycle as the standard for its operation. But the 25-cycle proved to be a big mistake for the infant corporation, as it was shown later that it was inefficient and costly for power transmission.

In 1917, the Ontario Power Company was bought by Ontario Hydro for $18.4 million. In that same year, Hydro began to build the Queenstown-Chippewa generating station — later named Sir Adam Beck #1. It was regarded as one of the greatest engineering feats of that time. When the last of the ten generating units was installed in 1925, its total capacity was 480 megawatts. And the total cost was about $76 million. The Sir Adam Beck #2 power station was begun at Niagara Falls in 1954 and completed in 1958. It was on a grander scale and produced 1,370 megawatts.

After World War II, Quebec and many of the Great Lakes states, because of their dependency on each other during times of electrical load problems, decided to standardize the frequency to the more efficient 60-cycle from 25-cycle power. By the time Ontario Hydro had completed the ten-year changeover to the new frequency in 1959, the total cost had spiralled to $352 million — an astronomical amount at that time. When it was completed, it provided a common usable transmission system for Ontario and the neighbouring northeast states in the U.S.

As European immigrants and refugees arrived by the thousands after the war, electrical power supply could not keep pace with the needs of Ontario's factories, industries and homes. In 1947–49 Ontario experienced rotating blackouts and brownouts — an early warning of an inadequate supply of electricity. The pressure on Ontario Hydro continued to mount as the demand for electricity rose.

For the first time, in the early 1950s the building of fossil fuel plants — mostly coal — was begun to help the hydroelectric plants meet the increasing demands for electricity. Over the next 15 years, power plants in Windsor, Lakeview, Toronto, Nanticoke,

Lennox and Westleville were built. These fossil fuel (coal) fired plants cannot be compared to the hydroelectric plants, where the efficiency is as high as 90 percent. The efficiency of the fuel-fired plants is only about 33 percent, and the burning of coal introduced a new problem — lots of air pollution — mostly particulate matter, as well as sulphur dioxide, oxides of nitrogen, mercury and a host of other dirty gases. Pollution controls were minimal, as little, if any, attention was paid to stack gas emissions. These gases mingled with other pollutants in the atmosphere to produce yellow-brown smog over the built-up areas of southern Ontario during the inversions periods of the many hot summer spells. The prevailing winds also brought the same concoction of dirty air from power plants, factories and industries in the U.S.

Some estimates at the time attributed thousands of respiratory problems and many deaths annually to dirty air or smog. And as people began to understand the health impact of breathing dirtier air, the governments were forced to develop standards for flue gas emissions. Attempts were made to catch up with advances in European and Japanese technology so that equipment could be installed to capture much of the offending pollution. But it was always a catch-up role. There was never any serious attempt made to be leaders in the battle for clean air, as cleaning the stack gases would increase the cost of electricity.

Even the few garbage incinerators used by the City of Toronto at the time had no flue gas cleaning equipment. The workers on the floor of the incinerator had to use long steel poles to stoke the burning of the garbage. During the 1960s, air pollution from power plants, incinerators, heavy industries, cars, trucks and buses had a devastating impact on human health. As the dirt and smog from all the obnoxious airborne pollutants smothered cities and towns, anger and environmental opposition began to develop in many built-up areas. As coal was the main culprit in producing air pollution, governments urged people to switch from coal to natural gas in their homes. Emission standards were constantly revised by government agencies to meet the outpouring of concern. Environmentalists were now well organized and their relentless work began to pay dividends in the battle to minimize air pollution.

NUCLEAR POWER

After the atomic bombs were dropped on the Japanese cities of Hiroshima and Nagasaki in 1945, the world looked to more peaceful uses of the atom. Many applications were developed for use in medicine and other scientific areas. By the mid-1960s the peaceful use of the atom was widely promoted, with nuclear reactors seen as the ideal way to produce electricity. It was promoted as the non-polluting answer to the increasing demand for electricity worldwide. Ontario Hydro was determined to take the nuclear road. The first nuclear power reactors were built in Pickering A & B, on Lake Ontario, just east of Toronto, in 1971. It was followed by Bruce A & B on Lake Huron and Darlington, on Lake Ontario.

The Pickering nuclear repair bill, in 2004, to restart four of the eight reactors was given as $2.5 billion and rising. That could provide 2,000 megawatts of hydroelectric power. It is unfortunate that Ontario Hydro had such trust in nuclear power. And no one can be sure that if Pickering restarts, it will not soon die again — like some ancient jalopy, no longer fit for the highway, or an aging jetliner suffering from terminal metal fatigue. Pickering is destined for the nuclear scrap heap. It is only a question of time. The U.S., with 104 working reactors, has already begun decommissioning 19 other reactors.

Ontario Hydro was so enamoured by nuclear power that management of the corporation became totally committed. In the mid-1990s, after the expenditure of a few million dollars to increase the capacity of Adam Beck #2 in Niagara Falls, Ontario Hydro stopped all work, paid off the contractor to walk away and made the full commitment to invest in refurbishing the ailing Pickering reactors. As a monopoly, Ontario Hydro's business structure, construction and operations began to manifest themselves, primarily in enormous over-expenditures on the nuclear plants. By the end of 1999, Hydro had a debt of $38 billion — eventually the responsibility of the provincial taxpayers. It would have been much easier — and in the long run much cheaper — to have developed more hydroelectric power, which is clean and renewable.

DEREGULATION OF ELECTRICITY

The trend to look favourably on competition in the electricity market began in the 1980s, when many countries began to examine the financial benefits to ordinary citizens in the deregulation of utilities such as phone and natural gas companies. Although the deregulation of electricity could not be compared with phone and natural gas, most governments had the simplistic view that if it worked for Ma Bell it would work for electricity. That proved unrealistic.

But in an organized democratic society, public or private systems, or a combination of both, can work. It just requires constant monitoring and supervision through a government regulatory body.

The key difference for electricity production over other services is obvious: electricity has to be used as it is produced. It cannot be stored. Natural gas, on the other hand, is constantly being piped from the gas fields and then stored in vast underground caverns near the areas of greater use. It can then be drawn for local distribution and used as the demand requires. Similarly, in the communications industries, once the equipment and lines are installed, the systems can be used anytime. Any electrical power producer — whether public or private — should have about a 20 percent cushion over the peak demand. The cushion is designed to take into account the planned downtimes for maintenance, as well as unplanned stoppages and accidents.

All this should be factored into the cost of electricity to the users. But Ontario had a provincially mandated fixed price for electricity that did not reflect its true cost. The old system in North America, where state and provincial utilities helped out each other during emergencies and times of heavy demand, had worked very well.

In the United States, where market forces drive the economies of most sectors, the Federal Energy Regulatory Commission — FERC — became the electricity regulator. If any state decided to deregulate electricity, the requirements of FERC would have to be met. The basic requirements were that the transmission lines would become common carriers of electricity for those who traded in electricity and the production of electricity would be open to any company that produced electricity. This required the breakup of power production and delivery companies and the introduction of a government or state market manager — called the Independent System Operator (ISO).

Deregulation got its first major toehold in California, where the state legislature held extensive public hearings and debated all the proposals. In the end the legislature tried to please both the power producers and the users. That was the first big mistake. The bill was poorly drafted and lacked the necessary details and understanding of the obstacles that prevailed in the state at that time. As California's deregulation bill became law in 1966, it was obvious to many in the electricity business that this was a "pigeon waiting to be plucked." The California attempt at deregulation is not a good example to follow. Deregulation was supposed to provide a competitive market in which many power generators would provide plenty of electricity at low prices. But there were serious shortcomings:

- The utilities were forced to sell their power plants or transmission lines.
- There was no practical time frame to help develop the transition to deregulation.
- A few large corporations — mainly Texan — snapped up the generating plants. These companies turned a previously regulated monopoly into an unregulated cartel.

The botched attempt at deregulation set in motion a dysfunctional wholesale market that could be easily manipulated by a generator cartel. And that is exactly what happened. It allowed companies like Enron to become big control traders in electricity. The California legislation froze retail rates until 2002 but allowed wholesale rates to fluctuate as dictated by the spot market. (The same thing happened later in Ontario.) California decided to generously compensate utilities for stranded assets, built before deregulation. Some of these asset costs would be placed on new plants, still to be built. This was a real handicap and a further disincentive for building new plants. It was almost impossible to build a new power plant anywhere in the state. And no new plant had been built in the previous 12 years, as local opposition had been fierce.

The cartel could easily manipulate the production of electricity. When demand for electricity was high, many plants cut off production to fix a generator or service a maintenance problem. All these planned stoppages drove the cost of electricity through the roof. And the taxpayers paid for it. As California generated only 65 percent of its electricity requirements, the abutting states and the Province of British Columbia joined in the feast by supplying the additional electricity needed by California. In the previous decade, California's power demand had increased by 25 percent. By 2000, the demand for electricity had risen dramatically while the generating capacity had fallen below 54,000 megawatts.

California, by January 2001, was a "basket case." Southern California Edison and Pacific Gas and Electric — the two major power producers — paid huge dividends to their shareholders. They also moved assets over to their unregulated subsidiaries so that these assets could not be used as credit to purchase electricity at exorbitant costs. These and other electricity producers were very soon on the brink of bankruptcy and a number of other companies moved in to participate in the financial feast that had been inadvertently offered by an ill-informed and ill-prepared group of state legislators.

As rolling blackouts and brownouts ravaged industry and the economic health of the state, many corporations made plans to move to other states where electricity would be more reliable. And although, at a cost of $12 billion or so, California eventually tried to fix the botched deregulation, it would take many years to get back to a semblance of normality, where residents and business felt secure and protected. On the positive side, the California electricity mess sparked a tremendous increase in energy conservation and energy efficiency as well as the use of alternate energy sources such as solar, wind and biomass.

Many power producers renewed efforts to build more power plants. Some traders of electricity continued to play trading games to keep the cost of electricity high. As the cost of electricity reached abnormal heights, some market observers began to pinpoint the flaws in the system and the corrupt practices of some of the power-producing companies. As soon as that happened sanity began its slow return to the marketplace.

Many states that had planned to deregulate their electricity markets decided to proceed more cautiously and take a little more time to examine their particular circumstances. And the downfall of Enron showed that the rush to deregulate provided many opportunities to some unscrupulous companies. The users of electricity in the California market had been ripped off.

By the end of 2002, the electricity market in the majority of states had tried to adjust to change in the electricity marketplace. Some stability had returned and corrections were taking place. The market, although nervous, seemed to become more stable. In some states there was a surplus of electricity and the future looked promising. Many of the electricity producers, like Duke, AES and Calpine, had to roll back their prices and cancel any plan for new plants. Gone were the days of the energy agony of California, only eighteen months earlier, as cautious calm returned to the electricity market place.

Power producers had to adjust to the surplus in some areas. Duke Energy, as an example, sold its 2003 production for 5.1 cents per kilowatt hour (kWh) and 4.4 cents per kWh for 2004. According to industry reports, at the beginning of 2003 the eleven states in the Western Power Region had a reserve capacity of 30 percent, which could reach 55 percent by 2006. In the North Eastern Region it was 28 percent and could reach 55 percent by 2006.

ONTARIO MOVES TO DEREGULATE

Most Canadian utilities abutting the U.S. saw deregulation as an opportunity to participate in a vast electricity market. Since electricity was much cheaper in Canada, the utilities had visions of making lots of money. All Canadian utilities had to do was meet the requirements of FERC and they had access to the U.S.

grid system. Ontario Hydro wanted access but also wanted to maintain its monopoly. To participate, under FERC rules, Hydro would have to open up the Ontario market to U.S. producers. Hydro took FERC to the Federal District Court in New York, claiming that the FERC rules were unconstitutional. Hydro lost the case — and eventually all provinces abutting the U.S. agreed to FERC rules and began to proceed cautiously.

For Premier Mike Harris, the idea of deregulation fitted his "common sense" agenda. Harris viewed the mounting Hydro debt as cause for concern. It was an example of a public monopoly out of control. He did not want to burden the Ontario taxpayers further as they were already responsible for a provincial debt of $110 billion. And he felt that the time had come when the users of electricity would have to begin to repay the mounting Hydro debt.

Harris and his advisers also saw opportunities to enter the lucrative U.S. market and provide some extra cash to pay for the Hydro debt. He could not help but notice the lucrative market Quebec had developed for its surplus hydroelectric power. Ontario Hydro rates were always lower than in the U.S., but proceeding with caution was the Ontario motto. But the massive Ontario Hydro debt was not the only problem. The condition of the aging nuclear reactors, as well as their management and operation, was of real concern.

The appointment of Bill Farlinger, a Harris confidant, gave the premier an overview of Ontario Hydro. Very soon he was given information that the nuclear component of Ontario Hydro's electricity supply was in deep trouble. Some would say that it was in tatters. The details of an internal report emerged publicly in mid-July 1997. It was prepared by a team of contracted U.S. nuclear experts to help Ontario Hydro. It was a painful admission that showed senior mismanagement problems and incompetence in the nuclear division of the Crown corporation. The honeymoon was over for nuclear power as the first signs of aging or mid-life crisis became public with the closure of seven reactors "for repair." It had suddenly dawned on the people of Ontario that aging nuclear plants would become a menace not only to the present generation but to hundreds of future generations.

On October 29, 1998, Bill 35, the Energy Competition Act, was introduced in the Ontario Legislature. It became law on April 1, 1999, when Harris announced that Ontario Hydro would be broken up and electricity would be deregulated on January 1, 2000.

Bill 35 split Ontario Hydro into five separate corporations:

1. Ontario Power Generation (OPG) — the generator of electricity,
2. Hydro One — the high-voltage (above 50 kilovolts) transmission grid,
3. Independent Electricity Market Operator (IMO) — market co-coordinator,
4. Ontario Electricity Financial Corp — to look after the $38 billion debt, and
5. Electrical Safety Authority — deals with regulations, safety and inspections.

But the California deregulation fiasco, and the resulting skyrocketing costs of electricity, caused chaos. That dominated the news in 2000–1 and sent shock waves through the Ontario government. The plans to deregulate electricity were put on hold after some heated debates in cabinet. The date for deregulation was finally set to be May 1, 2002. As Bill 35 outlined the framework for the breakup of Ontario Hydro, it became clear that Ontario Power Generation and Hydro One would be the two main corporations.

Hydro One, the owner and operator of the 28,900 kilometres high-voltage transmission grid, ranging from 155 to 500 kilovolts, would be regulated. It would be silly to expect that the producers of electricity would be allowed to build their own high-voltage transmission lines, when transmission lines already existed to service Ontario. With Hydro One as owner and operator of the transmission system, all electricity suppliers would have access to the grid under regulated transmission charges set by the Ontario Energy Board.

OPG would generate electricity and be unregulated. It would own about 85 pecent of the power generating plants in the province but would be required to divest itself of much of this generating capacity — to 35 pecent over ten years. The idea was to stimulate competition in power generation by attracting new power generation companies to the Ontario market. In 2000, OPG's peak demand was 24,500 megawatts from its installed capacity of 30,769 megawatts:

- 69 hydroelectric power plants — total capacity of 7,309 megawatts (24 pecent);
- 6 fossil fuel plants, with 23 generators — total capacity of 9,700 megawatts (31 pecent);
- 3 nuclear power plants (20 reactors) — total capacity of 13,760 megawatts (45 pecent).

The Sir Adam Beck #2 at Niagara Falls was the largest of the hydroelectric power plants, with 2,030 megawatts, followed by the St. Lawrence River at 1,005 megawatts. The six fossil fuel–fired generating stations of OPG are:

- Nanticoke, near Sarnia — 3,920 megawatts;
- Lambton, near Kingston — 1,975 megawatts;
- Lennox on Lake Erie, west of Fort Erie — 2,140 megawatts;
- Lakeview, west of Toronto — 1,140 megawatts;
- Thunder Bay on Lake Superior — 210 megawatts;
- Atikokan, west of Thunder Bay — 215 megawatts.

Pickering nuclear power station

In July 1971, the first 500-megawatt reactor of Pickering A came into operation. Over the next two years the other three units came online. In May 1983, the first 500-megawatt reactor of Pickering B came into operation. Over the next three years, the other three reactors were brought online. The total cost for Pickering: $3.8 billion for 4,000 megawatts, or $950,000 per megawatt.

Bruce nuclear power station

In September 1977, the first two 750-megawatt reactor units of Bruce A came online. By 1979 the other two 750-megawatt reactors were completed. In March 1985, the first 840-megawatt reactor of Bruce B was built. Two years later the other three units were in operation. The total cost for Bruce: $5.9 billion for 6,360 megawatts, or $927,670 per megawatt.

Darlington nuclear power station

About 1972, plans were first discussed for a nuclear plant at Darlington. Discussion proceeded for several years. In 1988 construction began. By 1993 all four 850-megawatt reactors, totalling 3,400 megawatts, were producing power. Darlington was originally estimated to cost $2.1 billion but ended up costing $14.4 billion in 1994 — almost seven times the original estimate — a staggering $4.23 million per megawatt.

The real puzzling question in the Ontario nuclear program relates to the cost of the Darlington nuclear station. Why did it cost more than four times as much per megawatt as the Pickering and Bruce stations? There are many attempted answers, but the generally accepted one is that Ontario Hydro was an arrogant monopoly, out of control, with access to the coffers of the province. The truth is probably a combination of many factors as well as poor political direction. The provincial Environmental Act was introduced in 1974 by the Bill Davis Conservative government — two years after the planning of Darlington had begun. Although the EA was not applied to Darlington, it had an indirect influence in slowing down the project.

The Porter Royal Commission on electricity was set up in 1975. That took five years and provided a series of options focusing on energy conservation and efficiency. It also introduced, for the first time, planning for the future electrical needs of the province with emphasis on demand side management rather than the traditional supply side expansion.

David Peterson and the Liberals were elected in June 1986. By that time Units 1 and 2 of Darlington were under construction. Although Peterson had urged the Conservatives to scrap Darlington, when he became premier he eventually decided to complete the station, as $4 billion had already been spent. At that time it was estimated that another $7 billion would be needed to complete it.

In hindsight, the Darlington nuclear power station should not have been built. It was an enormous waste of money. If half the cost — more than $7 billion — had been invested in energy conservation and energy efficiency, the electrical needs of the province would be far lower. But Darlington was planned and built at a time when the slogan "live better electrically" was the anthem of Ontario Hydro and the bureaucrats who promoted supply side management.

At that time, electricity requirements were projected to peak at about 36,000 megawatts by the turn of the century. In reality the demand never reached that, as a prolonged recession hit the economy in 1989 and continued until 1996, when it began to recover and its momentum carried over into the first few years of the new century. The highest peak demand reached was 25,600 megawatts in the summer of 2002. But on the other side of the ledger, the disastrous years of downtime and exorbitant repair costs of the Pickering and Bruce stations in the latter part of the 1990s and the early 2000s severely curtailed the provision of electricity.

Ontario was still clearly the nuclear leader in Canada — still embracing the pitch of the Western powers that nuclear power was the way of the future. By 1993, the 20 reactors could provide almost 60 percent of the province's electrical requirements — if they all were in operation. The three nuclear power plants, Pickering, Bruce and Darlington, were planned and built under the "nuclear culture" of Ontario Hydro. These reactors began with great promise — basking in the public relations promotion of the superior design of the CANDU heavy water reactor. This nuclear culture operated as a monopoly, with access to unlimited public funds. It had little understanding of financing and good business practices in the design and building of nuclear reactors. It proceeded to spend more than $24 billion on these plants by the end of the century.

With support and encouragement from the Canadian government, Ontario became the major customer of Atomic Energy of Canada Limited (AECL). The Pickering and Bruce plants were used internationally to promote the sale of CANDU reactors, which later, as a by-product, contributed to India and Pakistan's nuclear weapons program. Darlington was not used for promotion, as it was impossible to honestly answer all the questions related to cost overruns when promoting the CANDU reactor.

NUCLEAR PLANT WOES

As time went by, things were not working out as originally planned. The Darlington cost and the middle-age problems of Pickering (and later Bruce) were beginning to show on the political radar screen. People began to ask questions about the cost and reliability of nuclear power. It began to dawn on many who looked at the system that there were some real problems. The cost overruns were enormous. And Ontario Hydro, with a blank cheque, just kept shovelling the money into the reactors.

The Pickering station, the oldest of the three nuclear plants — built in 1971, with Pickering A (4 x 500 megawatts) and Pickering B (4 x 500 megawatts) — rated at a total 4,000 megawatts, has not been aging gracefully. As it passed middle age, many defects and problems began to surface, which caused the four reactors of Pickering A to be shut down for repairs in December 1997.

The aging Pickering plant has shown how difficult it is — in actual repair or replacement work. A lot of the work is in unseen areas where costs cannot be measured without detailed visual inspection. And that is extremely difficult and dangerous.

The original estimate in 1997, when the four units of Pickering were shut down for refurbishing, was $800 million. By early 2003 the cost had increased to $2.5 billion, with a new restart date of July 2003 for unit 4. The other three units were promised to be online in 2005. How did all these repairs and time frames go so horribly wrong? That answer is quite simple. There was no "how to" repair manual for aging reactors. Repairing Pickering had painfully shown that.

As Bruce began to age, it also began to exhibit the same problems as the aging Pickering. Two reactors of Bruce A were closed down in 1998 and were scheduled to be repaired and be in operation in 2003. In the meantime Bruce Power had become a division of British Energy Canada Ltd., which operated the reactors under a lease from OPG. It was later sold to a Canadian consortium that included OMERS — the Ontario Municipal Employees' Retirement System.

Many of the 442 nuclear reactors worldwide — most of them now past middle age — needed much more careful attention and expertise management than the conventional fossil plants. There was no track record or account of how to successfully retrofit and repair a nuclear reactor. There was no standard handbook. The only overriding concern and guidance is to be extremely cautious. A simple slip can be disastrous and far-reaching. An accident can be catastrophic, as Chernobyl showed. And Three Mile Island came close to causing a meltdown.

Nuclear energy plants have been treated politically as if they were the same as fossil fuel or hydroelectric plants — a very shallow and dangerous assumption. It should have been obvious that the lifespan of a nuclear plant would not exceed 40 years under ideal conditions. By that time, repairs and retrofitting are not practical and cannot extend the useful life span of the reactor. Trying to fix an old reactor, when it should have been decommissioned, is not the solution. The stakes are too high to risk catastrophe. And age-related problems are not like going in with a few wrenches, blowtorches and some welding gear. It is a totally different repair world from the old fossil fuel power plant.

NUCLEAR WASTE

As of December 31, 2002, Ontario Power Generation had 1,417,714 bundles of highly radioactive spent fuel stored on OPG property. According to John Earl, the spokesperson for OPG, that would "fill four hockey rinks up to the height of the boards." The stored intermediate-level radioactive material amounted to 9,281 cubic metres and low-level radiation material amounted to 47,949 cubic metres. The spent fuel is stored in wet bays or water pools at each nuclear plant for a period of at least 10 years. Each nuclear plant has wet storage space for about 15 to 20 years. After a cooling-off period, the spent fuel is then removed and dry-stored on site. The Pickering nuclear plant had the first storage space, with Bruce opening a dry storage space in 2003; Darlington is projected to open for 2007.

With the introduction of deregulation, OPG became the major electricity generator in Ontario. The work of the Seaborn Panel led to the federal government introducing the Nuclear Fuel Waste Act (NFWA) in November 2002. This led to the Ontario Nuclear Funds Act (ONFA), which came into effect on July 24, 2003. OPG then set up the Used Fuel Segregated Fund and the Decommissioning Segregated Fund. By the end of 2003 these two funds were operating under OPG but at arm's-length from the financial affairs of OPG and with a third-party custodian.

Finally, on January 1, 2004, OPG had laid a foundation for the eventual payment for the disposal of spent fuel and the decommissioning of its nuclear reactors. The amounts and method of deductions of these funds were carried out entirely by OPG and its advisors, without any public input or discussions. OPG's financial liability, based on 2.23 million bundles of used fuel for disposal, is capped at $5.4 billion while the Province of Ontario — that is the Ontario taxpayers — will pick up costs above that figure. OPG made initial contributions totalling $534 million to the Decommissioning Segregated Fund by December 2003 and OEFC made a payment of $1.2 billion on July 24, 2003.

It is not easy to project how much decommissioning costs. In the U.S., the costs of decommissioning reactors to date have been almost as much as the cost of building a reactor. It is generally believed that the cost of decommissioning all of OPG's reactors will be about $13 to $15 billion. That does not include the cost of babysitting the spent fuel for many thousands of lifetimes.

The eight reactors of the Pickering nuclear plant, 25 kilometres east of downtown Toronto, are first in line for decommissioning, as we assess the future of nuclear energy in the first few years of the new millennium. These reactors are stumbling through the strains of midlife and into their declining years. We are ill-prepared to acknowledge the accidents that could befall aging equipment, although many think of it often. This is not being pessimistic. It is being realistic. And being realistic means that decommissioning must begin to take place for the older Pickering reactors without delay.

I doubt if the government of Ontario has a real understanding of the Pickering nuclear plant. It is usually presented as a plant that must be fixed to supply power to meet immediate needs "until we have a clearer plan of what to do." It is a band-aid approach to the most serious energy problem of our time.

But given the casual attitude of the human species to dangers of cataclysmic proportions, I would be surprised if we made the decision to turn our backs on nuclear power. It takes courage to embark on such a journey. It would mean using alternative energy sources, using energy efficiently and conserving our fossil fuels. But that is difficult for most, as it would mean getting more from less and leaving more fossil fuels for future generations.

Most Torontonians choose not to think about nuclear problems. But the simple fact is that since the dawn of the nuclear age, when the first atomic bomb was dropped on Hiroshima, nuclear fallout — radiation poisoning — has proven to be a menacing, deadly nightmare that will not go away. The eastern outskirts of Toronto are very close to Pickering, and an accident on the scale of Chernobyl would be catastrophic. Much would depend on the direction of the wind, but Toronto would not escape.

There is the further risk of a terrorist attack, which may not necessarily involve a working reactor. So much radioactive waste is stored on site that an attack using any form of explosive — a car, truck or airplane bomb — could have serious consequences. One Sierra Club nuclear analyst called Pickering a "terrorist's dream."

Despite the risks, the voices from Toronto City Hall on leading the fight to decommission the Pickering nuclear plant have been silent. Pickering is a ticking, aging and worrisome menace on our doorstep — a legacy for our children and future generations that will prove to be more frightening as it ages. That is why Toronto should lead the battle to decommission it now, rather than pass on the problem to the next generation. That would be showing real leadership.

ONTARIO HYDRO'S DEBT

Dismantling Ontario Hydro as a corporation was not difficult. But scheduling the repayment of debt is always a problem — especially when there is the temptation to add to that debt and saddle future generations with the responsibility of repayment. Some suggested that the easiest way to deal with it would be to add it to the provincial debt and let Ontario taxpayers be responsible for it. But Premier Harris was adamant that a formula had to be worked out so that the users of electricity would begin to pay down the debt in the new marketplace of deregulated electricity.

In April 1999, the debts and liabilities of the dismantled Ontario Hydro amounted to $38 billion. The value of OPG, Hydro One and IMO was estimated to be $17.1 billion. That left a stranded debt of $20.9 billion. Dedicated revenues such as payments in lieu of property taxes, federal and provincial taxes and financing costs were estimated from successor corporations and municipal utilities to bring in $13.1 billion. The stranded residual debt on April 1, 1999, was deemed to be $7.8 billion. This is all very confusing, but with a little accounting gymnastics, it can be properly massaged to show that there is very little difference between a public and a private corporation when it comes to "fixing the books."

But what started out as a bold attempt by Premier Harris to bring some flexibility to the supply of electricity and rein in the mismanagement and reckless spending habits of Ontario Hydro ended up as a terrible headache for the Conservative Party after the departure of Harris early in 2002. The new deregulated system began with few problems, but as the 2002 summer heat increased, the demand for air conditioning dramatically increased. It became evident that the IMO would have to import more electricity than was originally planned. Throughout the summer the cost of imported electricity soared. This would prove to be a worry for the newly chosen provincial premier, Ernie Eves. By the beginning of November 2002, Eves began to panic. He felt that it was a time of political crisis for his party — and opinion polls showed the Liberals were moving ahead of the Conservatives. Somehow he would have to intervene to roll back the cost of electricity to its original cost before deregulation if his government was to be re-elected.

ONTARIO GOVERNMENT STUMBLES

On November 11, Premier Eves held a news conference to announce:

- The "deregulated" cost of electricity would be capped at 4.3 cents per kWh — the same as 1996 — for residential and small business. This rate would be in effect until 2006. Customers would get a rebate for costs above that since deregulation began. Major industries and large business customers were not included.
- All the regulated charges listed in the bill for electricity would be reviewed.
- There would be a new focus, with financial incentives, on the conservation of energy and the supply of clean alternative energy.

When Mike Harris introduced electricity deregulation, he set in motion a change that had far-reaching repercussions. But the complete gutting of the program by Ernie Eves proved to be a disaster. It made no economic sense, led to confusion in the electricity marketplace and added to the woes of taxpayers.

The government's retreat from deregulation was a devastating blow to the new producers of electricity who had been lured into Ontario. Eves had reversed course, and it had all the appearances of a slick piece of political manoeuvring to get his government re-elected. It had reflected the party's fear of election defeat and pandered to the ignorance of the people — certainly not to their intelligence.

The very idea of holding the cost of electricity at 4.3 cents per kWh until 2006 was blatantly political and unrealistic. Eventually the government — that is, the people of Ontario — would have to pick up the tab. The bluff might have worked had it not been for the 2003 blackout, which hit just a week before an anticipated provincial election call. In the first year of deregulation — by May 1, 2003 — the cost of holding the Ontario electricity price at 4.3 cents had amounted to about

$1.5 billion. The taxpayers did not feel it right away, but in the end they would pick up the tab.

One major energy company, Sythe Energy Inc., had made plans, bought land and gone through environmental and planning processes to build two 800-megawatt gas-fired plants — one in Oakville and one in Brampton. They had already spent $20 million and the future looked bleak for a share of the market — a market that began to look more like the old days of Ontario Hydro. Sythe could not deliver power for 4.3 cents per kWh. Their plans were immediately shelved — to be looked at another time, when the political climate was more stable.

The production of electricity can be carried out successfully by public or private sectors. It depends entirely on the role of the government and its regulatory control. Changing over from a complete government monopoly to a free market system in this volatile industry is not easy. On hearing of Eves' new plan for electricity, one old electrical wag likened the intervention to deciding to terminate a pregnancy in the ninth month because the parents now thought they could not afford the baby.

But Eves, as he stumbled through the changes he had announced, realized that the electrical storm he had caused would mean untold chaos to the producers and users of electricity. Now, there were also problems on the regulated side. In Ontario the power transmission lines became the property of Hydro One, which the province owned. The premier began to talk about selling all or a part of Hydro One, but in the end held off for a few months, as opposition from unions began to surface.

Eves later proposed selling off 49 percent of Hydro One for about $2 billion. He planned to use this money to meet the province's revenue projections without running a deficit. There were no takers in the private sector and the premier decided to take it off the table. It seemed that buying the 49 percent had too many strings attached and did not provide any real input in the management of Hydro One. Meanwhile, at the municipal energy services companies, confusion reigned. The province simply had not provided the confidence and leadership necessary for the supply of electricity for the years ahead.

In the spring of 2003, the Ontario Liberals were the first out in the pre-election promises game. They promised that if elected, they would close down the coal-burning plants by 2007. The Conservatives, not to be outdone in the stakes for the environmental badge of courage, announced that they would phase out the coal-burning power plants by 2015 and replace them with clean-burning natural gas. We all know that political promises are easy to make but hard to fulfill. There was no attempt by any party to analyze the availability of natural gas supplies in the years ahead.

The status of Ontario's troublesome nuclear plants was becoming more uncertain, as schedules could not be met and the costs of repairs and retrofitting spiralled out of control. The premier had to have the reactors back in production to meet electrical power requirements — especially with an election campaign on the horizon. But the federal agency responsible for nuclear energy would not give a clean bill of health to any reactor as long as it was not in full compliance with the operation guidelines.

A further energy complication for Canada is the absence of the federal government in developing a blueprint for a national electricity plan; according to the Constitution, natural resources are under the jurisdiction of the provinces. So Ottawa can do little but co-ordinate imports/exports, standardize criteria and assist when called on for financial aid and environmental standards.

WHERE DID ONTARIO GO WRONG?

Ontario, with its mixed electricity production, should have had few problems. But the shutdown of seven of its nuclear reactors for five to six years for repairs — mainly because of age — had been disastrous as Ontario stumbled into the new millennium. Since the formation of "the peoples' power" in 1906, Ontario Hydro could do no wrong. It had become the respected authority on hydroelectricity. But like all monopolies, public or private, the coziness of being above it all and untouchable, with unlimited access to the provincial treasury, became its downfall. It was a unique corporation with little political interference — almost on a par with the Ontario government itself. This glorified role led to few people outside of Hydro understanding the complicated details associated with the provision of electricity.

Ontario Hydro's adoption of nuclear energy and its abandonment of its tried and true hydroelectric knowledge contributed enormously to Hydro's problems.

After the demonstration of the awesome destructive power of the atomic bomb on the Japanese cities of Hiroshima on August 6, 1945, and Nagasaki three days later, the collective leadership of the West began a program to educate the public about the other more benign side of atomic power — "the peaceful atom," as Walt Disney called it. Then the public relations people got busy and changed the name to "nuclear power." That did not have the stench of death associated with the atomic bomb.

Canada, as a supplier of uranium, hopped on the bandwagon, and the federal government developed a nuclear research facility at Chalk River, Ontario. In 1945 the small Zero Energy Experimental Pile (ZEEP) reactor was developed. About a decade later, the federal government, through Atomic Energy of Canada Ltd., developed its own heavy water CANDU reactor as an example of how the "peaceful atom" could be used as a fuel to produce electricity.

At the urging of Ontario Hydro, the provincial government of the day decided to support the use of nuclear power in Ontario. In July 1971 the first 500 megawatts of the four units of Pickering A came online. Ontario had become both the guinea pig and poster boy for Atomic Energy of Canada in its marketing foray into the nuclear power world. It was a unique and intoxicating role for a provincial Crown corporation. By 1981, ten years later, the role of nuclear power was well and truly established in Ontario. It replaced the lead of the hydroelectric system that had been so successful for Ontario Hydro for so many years.

The neighbouring provinces of Quebec and Manitoba were more dependent on hydroelectric plants, which are easy to repair and maintain — and the water is free. Quebec especially, with its capacity of 33,475 megawatts (93 percent of it hydroelectric), has benefited greatly from this abundance of hydroelectricity. In 2002, it exported about 22 percent of its electricity to New York State and the U.S. eastern seaboard at prices as high as 12 cents per kWh. This added about $971 million to Quebec's treasury. Again, in 2003, Hydro-Québec exported its surplus electricity, adding about $596 million to its treasury. Its total dividend to the Quebec government for 2003 was $965 million. Its wholesale rate for electricity in 2003 was 2.79 cents per kWh. And Hydro-Québec sold its electricity to Quebecers at rock bottom prices, which average one-third the price that Ontario users pay.

Quebec, especially, has more power than it can use, although it talks about shortages in the years ahead. It also has an additional 5,428 megawatts from Churchill Falls in Labrador through a 65-year sweetheart deal — 40 years plus 25 years renewal — made with the Newfoundland government and premier Smallwood in 1966. This deal, according to former Newfoundland premier Brian Tobin in a speech delivered in November 1996, was generating $1.4 million per day for Quebec and $45,000 per day for Newfoundland in 1995. And while the cost of energy was increasing worldwide, the cost of electricity from Churchill Falls as per the agreement is decreasing. It will be one-fifth of a cent per kWh when, mercifully for Newfoundland, the agreement runs out.

Quebec was not lured into going nuclear, although, in the 1960s, it built a 250-megawatt CANDU reactor — the Gentilly 1. That was not successful and eventually closed in 1979, after about 300 days of operation. But, at the urging of the federal government, with a promise to pay half the estimated costs of $302 million of a new nuclear plant — the Gentilly 2, with an installed capacity of 675 megawatts, was opened in 1982. It cost $1.36 billion — more than four times the original estimated cost. By this time, Quebec had had enough of nuclear and decided to fight off the pitch of AECL and the federal forces.

With such a cash cow as the Churchill Falls deal, Quebec decided to tap into the hydroelectric potential of its own rivers — especially those on the east side of James Bay, opposite the great Ontario rivers on the western shores.

While Ontario Hydro in the last 30 years has been busy building nuclear reactors — and, later, trying to repair them — Hydro-Québec embarked on a program to build eight hydroelectric plants on La Grande Rivière, which flows into James Bay, for a total installed capacity of 16,000 megawatts. Quebec politicians, especially Premier Robert Bourassa, led Hydro-Québec in developing its hydroelectric potential. This showed vision and understanding of the future needs of the province. The largest hydroelectric plant (5,616 megawatts) on La Grande Rivière is named after Bourassa.

A 1982 report from Ontario Hydro, "Hydraulic Power Resources of the Province of Ontario — Inventory Report" indicated that the utility was producing 7,174 megawatts of hydroelectricity, or 34 percent of a total potential of 21,000 megawatts. It is contained in the 1984 Ministry of Natural Resources report "Water Quantity Resources of Ontario." Since that date there has been little change in tapping into the remaining 66 percent of unused hydroelectric potential, as Ontario Power Generation lists 7,309 megawatts as the amount of electricity presently produced in the province — really no change from the 1982 production figure.

Why cannot Ontario develop the 13,500 megawatts of its untapped hydro resources? It is relatively cheap, clean and dependable. The annual water runoff is greatly affected by climate, as seasonal temperatures vary extensively with latitude.

Ontario's latitude, from about 42° to 55° north (or about 1,450 kilometres), shows the real climate picture. A review of the northern rivers has shown that there are substantial flows after spring breakup and minimum flows in the coldest months of January, February and March. The great rivers of the northeast, draining into Hudson Bay and James Bay — the Severn, Winisk, Ekwan, Attawapiskat, Albany and the Moose — are largely unused, although tributaries to the Moose produce about 1,800 megawatts in the southern area of that watershed.

These rivers alone have a maximum runoff of about 24,380 cubic metres per second (cms) in the spring and summer and a mean runoff of 3,500 cms spread over 12 months. According to Ontario Hydro these rivers have the potential to generate an additional 6,000 megawatts, primarily in their headwaters.

Many generation and transmission problems associated with the extreme northern climate have been successfully addressed by Hydro-Québec and Manitoba Hydro. Northern Ontario rivers require new transmission systems to carry the power to the southern most populated areas of the province. The new transmission line would link Manitoba through a proposed joint venture hydroelectric project on the Nelson River. It would probably be a direct current high-voltage line (DCHV).

More southerly rivers, like the Ottawa, St. Lawrence and Niagara, do not experience such wide seasonal runoff fluctuations. The mean flow of the St. Lawrence, draining the Great Lakes Basin, is 7,180 cms — about 3,000 cms below its maximum flow. They produce about 3,700 megawatts and have the potential to produce an additional 2,600 megawatts if fully developed.

Ontario, with little reliable capacity above 22,000 megawatts — although generators of between 5,000 and 6,000 megawatts more were undergoing repair in 2003 — was caught in a power squeeze. Exports amounted to 2.5 percent, while imports were 4.5 percent. It looked like Ontario's demand/supply problems would not improve in the near future.

As July 2003 rolled around and temperatures soared, daily peak demands exceeded 25,000 megawatts — straddling the edges of brownouts. A brownout occurs when a voltage reduction of up to 5 percent develops across the transmission system in an area. It means that there will not be sufficient electricity available over a particular time period. Ontario flirted with that scenario but escaped the accompanying stigma. A blackout occurs when the transmission system fails entirely, either by overloading or a physical breakdown. And a rolling blackout happens when the electrical supplier has to reduce demand and move the power stoppage from one area to another in intervals of 30 minutes to two hours. The blackout, when it eventually occurred on August 14, 2003, was an accident waiting to happen. Premier Eves may have been politically lucky that it was not confined to Ontario and did not originate in Ontario but in Ohio, where it is reported that some branches of a tree fell on transmission wires.

No matter how determined provincial politicians may be, the road ahead looks bleak and troubling. There are no simple solutions, so the next ten years will be a period of uncertainty and confusion. It will take at least 15 years to develop and put in place a workable supply and demand electricity plan (SDEP) for Ontario. And developing an SDEP will require input from users, energy experts, planners and politicians — all having an interest in the future requirements of the province. Short-term political band-aids will only add to the confusion.

Premier Dalton McGuinty inherited quite a complicated energy mess in the fall of 2003. There was a political urgency to make a few short-term adjustments. In the first few months of 2004, the Liberals abandoned the residential base price of 4.3 cents per kWh set by the Conservatives and introduced a two-price system for residential customers — 4.7 cents per kWh for the first 750 kWh and 5.5 cents per kWh above that. That was further adjusted upwards on April 2005 to 5.0 cents per kWh for the first 750 kWhs and 5.8 cents per kWh above that.

In early May 2005, the government closed the Lakeview coal-fired plant — eliminating 1,100 megawatts. In mid-June the province's peak demand reached a record of 26,160 megawatts. As temperatures soared all summer, the Independent Electricity System Operator (IESO) was kept busy, trying to avoid brownouts and buying very expensive electricity — mostly generated by coal-burning plants in the U.S.

On the advice of Jake Epp and John Manley — two former federal cabinet ministers — the Liberals decided to complete the refurbishing of the second Pickering A 500-megawatt reactor. That decision was expected, as Epp and Manley have been part of the federal scene and supporters of the federal government's attempts to market Canadian CANDU reactors. If their recommendations to the province are any indication, it appears that Ontario will be lured back into the nuclear business. That, to many people, means more trouble. The battle lines are already drawn. And it will be the focus of provincial politics for at least the next ten years.

The Ontario Liberals also decided to put a new face on their plans for the longer term by introducing a new Ontario Power Authority — Bill 100. As the days of summer 2004 slipped by, hearings were held across the province to tap into the mood of the people. Although the Liberals slipped back to the old regulated supply system, they were careful not to completely discourage the private sector, calling for proposals to build 2,500 megawatts of new generating capacity. And to show that they had some interest in encouraging the development of new renewable and non-fossil energy, they called for proposals to provide 300 megawatts of renewable energy. That latter proposal call prompted submissions totalling 4,400 megawatts. Whether that leads anywhere or not, we will have to wait and see.

Like all governments, this one will be rated on its ability to produce a long-range plan for producing electricity for the province for the years ahead. No matter how messy the battle gets, it should be guided by the following criteria:

- Reduce consumption by about 40 percent to a peak demand of 16,000 megawatts. This would move Ontario near the per capita consumption of countries like Britain, Germany, France and Japan.
- Develop a renewable energy tariffs program, as Germany has done. This would allow and encourage electricity users to buy clean renewable energy, while at the same time participating in the development of renewable energy.
- Introduce an education program so that energy users can be reached and helped by energy teachers funded by the province through the local utility.
- Introduce "time of use" electricity rates to encourage users to help reduce the peak demand for electricity.
- Federal and provincial governments should take leadership roles in promoting and supporting energy conservation and alternative energy sources.
- Develop the untapped hydroelectric potential of Ontario — about 13,000 megawatts. It is available, and it is free and non-polluting.
- Phase out the use of all nuclear energy by 2015. By that time, most of the existing reactors will have completed their useful life cycles.
- The overhauling or refurbishing of existing nuclear reactors after 100,000 hours operation should require a full environmental assessment.
- Costs for decommissioning nuclear plants and spent fuel disposal must not be left to future generations but paid for by the present users of electricity.
- Electricity bills should show the spent fuel storage, disposal and reactor decommissioning charges.

- The province must ensure that all fossil fuels meet the same stringent air pollution standards for stack gas emissions.
- Ontario must play a practical and working role in meeting commitments to the Kyoto Agreement.
- Build a new transmission line with Manitoba, across northern Ontario.

NET BILLING

A net-billing program for Ontario electricity users should be developed by the provincial government. It should include the following basic elements:

- The program would entice homeowners and small business to develop non-fossil fuel alternative energy projects up to 50 kilowatts.
- The program, financed through the local utility and lending institutions, would stimulate the development of energy awareness and the education of hundreds of thousands of electricity users.
- The electricity produced by the net biller and delivered to the grid would be credited at the basic energy cost plus two cents per kWh for solar; one cent per kWh for wind; and a half-cent per kWh for small hydroelectric and other alternative energy projects for a guaranteed period of up to ten years.
- After the capital costs have been paid off, or for the 10-year period, whichever comes first, the cost of a unit of electricity to the grid would be the same as the charge of a unit of electricity from the utility to the user.
- A small electricity surcharge would be applied to all customers not participating in the alternative energy program to help cover the cost of that program.

CHAPTER 5
Electricity: Supplying Power to the City

With the formation of Ontario Hydro in 1906, local utilities were invited to join and operate as franchisees. Toronto heeded the call to distribute and manage electricity from its sole superior, Ontario Hydro, which dictated the cost of electricity and the charges to Toronto Hydro customers.

The Toronto Hydro-Electric Commission (before 1998), had a peak demand of 1,450 megawatts and an annual operating budget of just over $700 million. It was headed by a five-member commission — two members of city council, two citizen members appointed by council and one appointed by the province.

Over the years Toronto Hydro had grown tired, lethargic and bloated. Mercer Management Consulting, in a report commissioned by Toronto Hydro in 1990, rated the utility at the lower end of the scale when compared with other utilities of the same size in North America. Amalgamation in 1998 (Bill 103) saved it from further decline, but its size and location dictated that it become the nucleus of the new Toronto Hydro.

Amalgamation of the six municipalities in Metropolitan Toronto into the new City of Toronto in 1998 resulted in the formation of one electrical utility — the new Toronto Hydro. It would have a peak demand load of about 4,000 megawatts, a workforce of 2,400 people, a customer base of 650,000, a revenue flow of about $2 billion, assets worth almost $2 billion and a debt of $100 million. It would follow in the footsteps of its former master, Ontario Hydro, through the deregulation process — a new approach to the electricity business in Ontario.

In April 1999 city council, without going through a public recruitment process for a new board of directors, appointed eight citizen members to the management of the enlarged utility. The new chairman, Clare Copeland, received an annual salary of $75,000 and the other board members received $12,000 plus

$1,000 for each meeting attended. Labelled an "old boys club" by Councillor Michael Walker at the time, the new members had considerable business experience but little experience in the electricity field.

The province, in its deregulation program — the Energy Competition Act, which became law on April 1, 1999 — allowed the 250-plus municipal utilities the opportunity to cut the umbilical cord from Ontario Hydro. The Act also permitted them to set up their own power generation companies or to buy electricity from anywhere, as well as to operate regulated local transmission and servicing companies under the Ontario Business Corporations Act.

In the old system, municipal utilities could not make a profit and paid no taxes. But the new Act changed everything. These newly restructured utilities could now make a profit like any corporation in the private sector. And they would pay federal and provincial taxes as well as property taxes.

The City of Toronto, which owned Toronto Hydro outright, directed it to set up the Toronto Energy Services Company (TESC) — the "wires company" — to enter the competitive energy market to provide not only electricity to its customers but natural gas, as well. The marketing idea suggested that it may lose some of its electricity customers but it could add many natural gas customers. In addition to being a novice in this cutthroat, door-to-door market, TESC had little experience in the competitive marketplace. It had access to a sound financial base, with a blank- cheque mandate to beat the competition. But the door-to-door competition by early 2003 was too much for Toronto Hydro, and it decided to abandon its fight for a share of the natural gas delivery business and concentrate mainly on their core business of delivering electricity. By that time, the electricity business was in reality a regulated system again, so there was no competition from other electricity producers.

As the sole owner of the utility, the City of Toronto could now tap into the vast financial resources of Toronto Hydro. Its book value when Bill 35 came into effect was estimated to be in the neighbourhood of $1.8 billion. It could borrow $1.2 billion (two-thirds of its book value) and have the electricity customers pay all the interest charges. It could then earn an additional $36 million annually — 6 percent interest on the remaining $600 million. Or, with a little creative accounting, it could siphon off many millions of dollars each year. It could take a handsome dividend each year — perhaps a return of six percent on $1.8 billion, or $108 million annually, from Toronto Hydro.

But the city discovered additional pickings when the province opened the door with Bill 35. First it transferred $100 million of unused cash at Toronto Hydro to the City treasury, as well as $30 million of surplus Toronto Hydro property. In Toronto Hydro's first year as a deregulated utility, the City also took shares worth $577 million and a note for a loan of $980 million from Toronto Hydro at 6.8 percent per year. This provided $67 million to the city.

For the first time in the history of the City of Toronto, the municipal government could now legally use the hydro bill as an additional vehicle to divert profit and additional funds to the City coffers to meet the other financial needs of the city.

Even the Hydro workers' union, CUPE Local 1, got into the act. When it saw the windfall that the city would reap, it commissioned an analysis by Douglas Peters, a former chief economist of Toronto Dominion Bank, to have a look at the financial possibilities. The union presented the findings to the City Budget Committee. No doubt the union was also thinking of how some of the spoils would flow its way. At the same time the Hydro commissioners were having their own meetings, behind closed doors, with senior city politicians to examine how more funds, such as transferring the ownership of some city light poles to Toronto Hydro, could flow to the City treasury. Many other utilities across the province were also following the same path to the new honey-pot. It seemed that the Ontario government wanted them to cash in also.

Toronto Hydro had a great opportunity to play a leading role in energy conservation and efficiency. But it failed totally, by ploughing back money collected for electricity use to the City — to be used for services that had little to do with energy efficiency and conservation. It is like opening up a brewery to a group of drunks on a regular basis. Sadly, it will become an annual collection.

Any profit made by Toronto Hydro should have been directed, by law, for the purposes of making Toronto Hydro a real leader in the battle to reduce our electricity consumption. Sacramento Municipal Utility District (SMUD) is an excellent example of how a local utility should work — if an example is needed.

At the municipal level, there are three bills that taxpayers must pay each year to the local municipality — property, water and electricity. The property tax bill pays general taxes to help the City in its day-to-day operations as outlined in the Municipal Act. The water bill pays for the provision of water and the treatment of wastewater. The Toronto Hydro bill now pays for the electricity used plus other city costs that are not related to electricity. Even Metro Toronto, in 1974, had to petition the provincial government for legislation to include the cost of treating wastewater in the charges for water.

It is an affront to taxpayers to see a percentage of the charges collected for the use of electricity being given to the city for other purposes. The restructuring of the electrical market in Ontario by Premier Harris was supposed to provide a more realistic and hopefully lower charge for electricity — not to gouge the unsuspecting electricity customer. With the restructuring of local utilities as part of the deregulation package introduced by the province, the new role of the municipally owned utilities allowed them to make a profit and financially support their masters — the local municipalities.

Toronto Hydro, which should take the lead in energy efficiency and energy conservation, has a dismal record in any of these areas. And the siphoning of funds by the City has shown that little will be accomplished in this area in the near future. It is embarrassing for a city that had so much promise that it does so little.

POWER FOR THE PEOPLE

"Power for the people" was the slogan used in the early days of Ontario Hydro. In the attempt to package the new electricity service it was difficult to use the same old phrase. Deregulation and all the technical buzzwords used by the public relations people could not explain the economics of the new marketplace. Any attempt to do so would lead to the conclusion that electricity costs would vary in the free market.

But one thing was for sure: those who persisted in getting all the facts had to conclude that electricity would cost a lot more in the future. There would be no bargain prices, as electricity users would soon find out. And the restructuring of the marketplace would have to address the repayment of the Ontario Hydro debt in a more open forum.

The cost of decommissioning the nuclear plants would be added at a later date. But that was never mentioned in the restructuring of the electricity market. That would come later when Ontario found the right time to announce it. And that cost would be about the same as it cost to build the nuclear plants — perhaps as high as $15 billion for all of the 20 reactors in the province. That will have to be brought to the public's attention. It cannot be ignored and left off the cost of electricity. It will have to be paid eventually.

When the first residential customer bill arrived from the new Toronto Hydro in the summer of 2002, it was broken down as follows:

Cost Component	Charge	Reason for Charge
Customer	$14/month	Fixed monthly cost for basic service
Distribution	1.4 c/kWh	Construction and maintenance
Transmission	1.0 c/kWh	Transmitting electricity from power plant to city or town border
Debt Retirement	0.7 c/kWh	Cost of repaying debt
System Operation	0.6 c/kWh	Market Regulation and the IMO for the system
Energy Charge	5.0 c/kWh	The cost of generating electricity (the deregulated charge)
TOTAL	8.7 c/kWh	

(Note that the deregulated cost of electricity is about 60 percent of the bill.)

But the cost of electricity (the energy charge) was later changed to a "regulated" 4.3 cents per kWh by Premier Ernie Eves in November 2003 as his party prepared for a provincial election. Eves even guaranteed that rate until 2006.

When Dalton McGuinty and the Liberals won the election in the fall of 2003, the residential rate was regulated at 4.7 cents per kWh for the first 750 kWh and 5.5 cents per kWh above that. These charges were later adjusted upwards in the spring of 2005 to 5.0 cents per kWh for the first 750 kWh and 5.8 cents per kWh above that.

The Liberals still have to make difficult decisions for the electricity supply for the next 25 years. And we still do not know whether it will be regulated or deregulated. It is complicated, confusing and very political, with no indication of how strong and effective the provincial government leadership will be in energy conservation and efficiency programs.

PUBLIC OR PRIVATE

Over the years, there have been many occasions when I was confronted with the question of whether the public or private approach offered the best system. Or put more bluntly, is contracting out a better way to provide a service? No organization — public or private — should have a stranglehold on any sector of the economy. There is a definite need for unions, especially in areas where wages are low and the benefits are few. But once fair wages and benefits are established in a workplace, the usefulness of unions diminishes.

Organized labour has become the same as big business. It *is* big business. Those who really need help find little room in either sector. The pension funds of many unions and their employers have amassed huge amounts of money that are now operated like business conglomerates, with vast holdings in real estate and equity in businesses and profitable corporations. The OMERS pension fund has about $33 billion, and the Ontario Teachers Pension Fund has about $60 billion. The largest pension fund in Canada — the Caisse Populaire in Quebec — has about $130 billion in assets.

Pension funds are so rich and collecting so much money that they are finding it difficult to place it all. They are steadily increasing their involvement in the capitalist side of the business ledger, so the division between big business and big unions is often blurred.

Contracting out is a practical way of providing services in many areas. It is healthy to go to the marketplace periodically to get the best value for taxpayers. Governments should be required to allow private sector companies to compete for work that could be performed by the public or private sectors. In a large urban area there are some essential services where contracting out may not be practical. This is best explained where there is a constant requirement for police, fire, public transit, ambulance and other demand services.

In the electricity industry both public and private corporations can provide services. Both unions and business corporations are constantly preaching that they offer the best system for the taxpayer. The important factor is that the service and the associated charges are provided under government regulations so that taxpayers are well served and not gouged.

The following are a few suggestions that would help the delivery of electricity to the city of Toronto as well as encourage conservation and energy efficiency:

- Toronto Energy Services (Toronto Hydro) should provide some of the electricity needed by the city. The Toronto Integrated Energy Services (TIES) plan of the late 1980s, drawn up by Ontario Hydro and city planners and engineers, recommended that it would be more economic to build a new generating plant near downtown rather than spend $700 million to improve the transmission lines into the city.
- Ontario should introduce legislation to require that all profits from Toronto Hydro and other public utilities in the province be invested in programs for the efficient use of energy — not used as general revenue for the municipality. This would provide an opportunity and an

invitation for the utilities to lead in energy conservation and efficiency, like the Sacramento Municipal Utility District (SMUD) in California.

- The Toronto Atmospheric Fund should work in partnership with Toronto Hydro to develop energy efficiency and conservation programs with the electricity users. It would fit in very well with Toronto's drive to help the Kyoto Agreement. Why not do it?

As I periodically walk across City Hall square to the Hall, I cannot help but notice the eight solar panels over the main entrance. They have been there for over fifteen years. It gives the impression that the city is a leader in promoting solar energy. That is very deceptive. There is no incentive program to promote solar or alternative energy by the city. But leadership from the city is sorely needed.

CHAPTER 6
Energy and Our Dwindling Fossil Fuels

We give little thought to how our fossil fuels developed. We have always taken them for granted. But they were born of our sun, 150 million kilometres away, about 350 million years ago. And in order to understand the development of these fuels we need a general view of our planet in time and space and its place in the universe. First, our concept of time is arbitrary and artificial — an invention of humans trying to understand life and relationships in the universe. The unit of time we call a year is based on one full revolution of the earth around the sun — broken down to the day, hour, minute and second. There is no attempt to project how much time has passed or how much time the future holds. It is thought that time has no beginning and no end.

Using our units of time, it is thought that our universe began about 15 billion years ago in a cataclysmic explosion, a Big Bang that created our sun and the planets — including planet earth. In reality, our sun is a small star among billions of stars in the vastness of space. It is a minor member of a cluster of stars in the Milky Way — a "neighbourhood" composed of countless stars separated by distances so great that it numbs the human mind just to try to visualize it. Our cosmic neighbourhood measures 100,000 light years across. The speed of light is about 300,000 kilometres per second (186,234 miles per second), making one light year a little under 10,000 billion kilometres. Our nearest star neighbour is four light years, or 37,800 billion kilometres, away.

Conditions on planet earth in those early days were much different than they are today. There is no record of those times, but modern scientific tools have allowed us to peek into the many nooks and crannies of the distant past. We know for certain that the oldest rocks are 3.6 billion years old. But we have no idea how old the original core material of the earth might be. Geologists and cosmologists need isotopes with half-lives of billions of years to reach back into the remote past. The isotope of potassium has a half-life of 1.3 billion years. Uranium 238 is also a good measuring instrument. Its half-life is 4.5 billion years. And carbon 14 dating is used to calculate the age of a fossil of the recent past. It loses half of its radioactivity in 5,370 years. In the next 5,370 years the amount of remaining carbon will drop by half again — and so on.

Fossil fuels are part of the turbulent history of planet earth about 300 to 400 million years ago, when the earth's atmosphere was much different than it is today. During those times, the endless life and death cycles of plant and marine life produced the fossil fuels we use today. We know them mostly as groupings of carbon and hydrogen atoms and as coal, oil and gas — the standard solid, liquid and gas forms of the hydrocarbon family.

Before examining the role of fossil fuels in the life of our species, it is helpful to have a sober look at the voracious appetite some countries have developed for those dwindling non-renewable resources. It provides a snapshot of the madness that has taken over our very existence. And it is sad to know that the depletion of these resources, particularly conventional oil and gas, which took so many millions of years to develop, will be depleted within this century.

The modern world is dominated by the wasteful excesses of the most powerful countries of the developed world. In examining that dominance, those who consume the most call the shots and want more. The United States is the leader of the pack in that category. With a population of a little over 5 percent of the world's population, it consumes 25 percent of the world's production of oil and gas. Its addiction to that "fossil fix" is part of the American way of life. Canada, too, as a partner in the North American continent, is an accomplice in contributing to the squandering of oil and gas. Both countries have the highest per capita consumption of energy in the world. But the poorest countries have little or no resources as they search through the dregs and leftovers and scramble for the fallen crumbs from the tables of the most powerful nations.

In a moment of human sanity, we may want to stop and think about what is happening to our planet's resources. Of all the resources of our planet, fossil fuels — the vast deposits of coal and the much smaller formations of oil and gas deposits — are the only resources that are non-renewable. Once they are gone, they are gone forever. But that does not seem to bother our democratic leaders of the developed world. They are acting like they are on another planet with economies plugged into the mad rush to drill and burn — until it is all gone.

The madness of it all is that the developed world is led primarily by people who profess the high moral standards of a monotheistic religion that preaches love, tolerance, justice, sharing and respect for the bounties of nature. Many political activists scream about not selling water, which cannot be destroyed and is always being recycled. Yet the squandering of fossil fuels merits little attention from those who should know better. Sadly ignorance and lack of vision blur any commitments to prudent resources management.

COAL

About 350 million years ago, in the Paleozoic era, when the earth's climate was hot and humid and the atmosphere contained an abundance of carbon dioxide, conditions were ripe for the growth of all kinds of vegetation, trees and plant life. In the endless cycles of life and death, decaying matter built up over millions of years — layer upon layer — mixed with silt and waterborne debris in the swamps, river deltas and marshes of the lush landscape. As the crust of the earth changed, with some lands rising and some sinking, vast deposits of decaying matter subsided and were covered, sealing and adding pressure to the structure of the material over the millions of years.

All this activity over the ages resulted in the formation of coal in its many forms. Coalification, as it is called, varies from the latest or beginning process, which forms peat, then lignite, bituminous and finally anthracite coal. All these varieties are decided by the time, the temperatures and the pressures in the process. Peat — the early stage of coalification — contains more moisture and incomplete decomposition of the organic matter. It has about one-quarter of the calorific or heat value of anthracite, the fully developed hard coal, with the highest carbon content — somewhere between 90 and 95 percent.

The first attempt to quantify the amount of coal on the planet was reported at the Twelfth International Geological Conference, held in Toronto in 1913. It was a very general estimate and was set at a total of 7.397 x 10^{12} recoverable tons. Later estimates in 1979, for the World Bank, suggest about 10.2 x 10^{12} recoverable tons (10.2 trillion tons).

There are widespread deposits of coal throughout the world — by far the most abundant of the planet's fossil fuels. As deposits of most coal run underground in seams from a few centimetres to as thick as 12 to15 metres, the average seam runs about 2.5 to 3.0 metres thick. A seam in Victoria, Australia, was recorded at over 200 metres thick. But a seam of 50 centimetres can be mined. Coal seams may run as deep as 1,500 metres underground. At that depth the pressure and temperatures increase, which add to the dangers of mining. In poorer countries, coal miners, working in dusty, underground confined areas, are constantly in danger of gas explosions. As well, cave-ins can make mining operations very hazardous. But, Western countries have addressed the safety of miners by introducing strict regulations for proper ceiling support of the mined and mining areas, gas monitoring and flooding so that the risks of accidents are minimized.

The coal resources of the planet are estimated to last for another 1,000 years at the present rate of depletion. But that is only a wild guess at best. We do not know if other cleaner energy resources will be found — leaving the coal in the ground for other distant generations. The Geological Survey of Canada reports that coal represents 87 percent of the fossil fuel reserves of Canada, which will last for 800 years. Coal fuels about 100 power plants in the eastern air-shed of North America, which includes four major plants in Ontario. Many of the Great Lakes states use coal to generate more than 50 percent of their electrical power requirements.

For the period around 1850 to 1960, coal was the fuel of choice in most industrialized countries. The air pollution, primarily from the burning of coal, heavy oil and the exhaust gases from vehicles, was so bad in the 1950s and 1960s that many people, suffering from respiratory diseases, died during periods of temperature inversions in London, Los Angeles and in many of the world's larger cities. Governments reacted by banning the use of coal as a domestic fuel and encouraging the use of oil. Later, natural gas was endorsed as a replacement for oil. Coal was encouraged for use only in central power plants and heavy industries such as steel plants, where electrostatic precipitators could remove some of the particulate matter and the stack gases could be scrubbed.

Ontario Hydro built a 1,200-megawatt coal-fired plant on Unwin Avenue in the port area of Toronto in 1955. It was converted to natural gas in the 1970s and finally closed down in 1982. Twenty-three years later it still lies idle on its 72-acre site with its impressive 700-foot stack. Nowadays, its generating equipment is used mainly as a backdrop for movies. It is the only major evidence of coal in our lives, although many of the old buildings in Toronto still have idle coal chutes, from the sidewalks or driveways to the coal furnace rooms in the basement.

Stack gases from coal-fired plants in many countries are still not within acceptable levels. Cleaning up the coal-burning plants requires enormous investments and an understanding of the impact it will have on the price of electricity. But it must be done to maintain a healthy atmosphere. Governments can help by requiring that all fuels meet the same emission standards.

Coal can be gasified to reduce emissions. The Lurgi process uses steam and oxygen on pulverized coal to produce a synthetic natural gas. And there are other processes being developed to reduce stack emissions.

Engineers and scientists in combustion technology have made great advancements in the combustion and cleaning of stack gases from coal to meet emission standards. But carbon dioxide will still be produced no matter which fuel is used. The use of clean combustion of coal will happen only when oil and gas are almost depleted and very expensive. It is unimaginable that governments are waiting until that time arrives.

Coal is the fossil fuel of the future for the simple reason that there is so much of it and conventional oil and gas will be depleted by mid-century, if not sooner. Political moves to ban the use of coal in Ontario are hard to understand when the world demand for coal is increasing and oil and (especially) gas resources are declining. Ontario's decision makes little sense and erodes the credibility of the government. It would be far more meaningful if the government developed legislation to set standards for the emissions of all fossil fuels rather than ban a particular fuel.

The demand for coal — especially metallurgical coal — has been so great that the price of Canadian coal jumped from about $50 to over $100 per tonne by the end of 2004. Publicly traded companies such as Sherritt International, Grand Cache Coal Corp., Pine Valley Mining Corp. and Fording Canadian Coal Trust cannot keep up with demands for coal. The increasing share prices of these companies reflect the confidence in coal as a fuel. That gives a glimpse of the real world.

OIL

The drilling of the first oil well in Pennsylvania by Edwin Drake in 1859 sparked the real beginning of the industrial revolution. Although the first well was only 22 metres deep and produced a small amount of oil, drilling technologies have changed and dominated the economies of all oil-rich countries. The annual consumption of all fossil fuels has grown, at alarming rates, ever since that first oil well was drilled.

Oil formation is thought to have developed many millions of years before coal. It is generally accepted that it formed mainly from marine and other organic material. Temperature and pressure have made oil more subject to migration than formations of coal. In the migration through permeable rock strata, and over time through faulting and folding, it eventually became trapped— very often far away from its place of origin. Coal and oil are rarely found together.

Since the first gusher, tremendous advancements have been made to extract as much oil as possible from a well. The natural pressure that is present when oil is struck is called the primary recovery. It is followed by a controlled pressure system of injecting water — or natural gas, if it is a by-product — into the well to maintain the pressure, which keeps the oil flowing in what is called secondary recovery. A tertiary recovery method, such as steam or underground combustion using injected surface air, is more complicated. This process increases the viscosity of the crude, which helps it flow more freely. If a well gives up 65 to 70 percent of its oil, it is considered a great success. The average recovery of global oil is about 40 to 45 percent. Vertical drilling has been used mostly — but in recent years more precise directional drilling has proved more beneficial. As technology improves, many old wells can be revisited to produce more. Of course, getting "the last drop" from such wells will be more expensive.

Refining oil — from the crude oil pumped from the oilfield — is a complicated and expensive process. Oil wells produce basic oil, from heavy to light crude, and sometimes with a high amount of sulphur.

My first summer employment as an engineering student was in the construction of oil storage tanks at the Isle of Grain Oil Refinery, at the mouth of the River Thames in England. So I had an early introduction to oil refining. When I graduated as an engineer in 1954, I went to work for the Iraq Petroleum Company in the oil fields of Iraq — mostly on the seismic side of the business. There was so much oil there! Our project was to identify the oil locations and tie them into a geodetic survey, as well as to identify the most economical locations to tap the resources.

When the crude oil arrives at the refinery, it is held in storage tanks. It is primarily a raw mixture of hydrocarbons, with small quantities of other non-hydrocarbon elements such as sulphur that are removed before refining. The refining process is simple. It is based entirely on heating the crude oil to about 400°C. As it boils it gives off gases, which rise through tall towers called distillation columns. As the gases become cooler at the various levels they liquefy and are drained off. The heaviest fraction comes off at the base of the process from the boiling crude oil. It is a type of bitumen — used for making road asphalt and tar for roofing materials. The rising gases in the towers produce fuel oil, lubricants, diesel, jet fuel, kerosene and gasoline and petroleum gases at the very top. Some of the fractions also mix well to make various forms of plastics, which are used for many applications in everyday life, such as paint, clothes and pipes.

After World War II, rebuilding began on a grand scale. With the Marshall Plan and the reconstruction of Germany and Japan, the pace of industrial development stretched the available resources — especially petroleum and other raw materials — of the victor nations. Oil was now the postwar fuel of recovery, and it was desperately needed to fuel the exploding manufacturing and transportation industries. By 1950 the production of oil and oil products was completely controlled by a cartel of seven Western-based international companies known as the seven sisters — British Petroleum (BP), Chevron, Exxon, Gulf, Mobil, Shell and Texaco. At that time the oilfields of the Middle East — Saudia Arabia, Iraq, Iran and the Gulf Emirates — were the real producers of oil for the Western world. The Soviet Union and its satellite states produced oil to meet their own needs. Most of the Third World countries, with little oil or natural resources, were always struggling.

In 1962 a group of oil-rich developing countries — mostly Middle Eastern states — set up the Organization of Petroleum Exporting Countries (OPEC). It began to turn the tables on the seven sisters and decided that since it was their oil they would control it. OPEC operates as a cartel and its aim is to control and regulate the supply and price of oil to the developed world. The eleven member countries of OPEC — Saudi Arabia, the United Arab Emirates, Kuwait, Qatar, Iran, Iraq, Libya, Algeria, Indonesia, Nigeria and Venezuela — control about 75 perccent of the planet's conventional oil supplies. OPEC production fluctuates between 20 and 28 millions of barrels per day (mbd) — depending on the price and demand.

As the twentieth century reached its final years, drilling companies were active all over the planet desperately looking for oil — on land and sea — to satisfy the world's ever-increasing appetite for black gold. Oil rigs were operating off the coasts of Nova Scotia and Newfoundland; in the North Sea, between Britain and Norway; off the West coast of Africa; in the Gulf of Mexico; in the Caspian Sea — anywhere that geologists suspected they might find it. At the end of 2004 world oil production surpassed 80 mbd, with the U.S. using about 25 percent of that production.

The U.S. can produce between 7 and 8 mbd from over 500,000 wells — mainly in Texas, Louisiana, offshore Gulf of

Mexico and Alaska. The remaining 12 mbd is imported from Canada, Saudi Arabia, Mexico, Nigeria, Iraq, Venezuela and a host of other countries contributing smaller amounts. According to the International Energy Agency (IEA), the conventional world crude oil reserves in 2003 were listed at 1,038 billion barrels or 141.58 billion tonnes. At the present rate of consumption these resources would last about 36 years.

The Middle Eastern countries have oil resources totalling 685.64 billion barrels or about 68 percent of the known oil resources. The richest are Saudi Arabia, with 261.66 billion barrels; Iraq, with 112.5; United Arab Emirates, with 97.8; Iran, with 89.7; Kuwait, with 96.5 and Qatar, with 15.2 billion barrels. These are all Muslim and mostly Arab countries.

Since the breakup of the Soviet Union in 1991, the oil resources of Siberia and the "stan" republics along the southwestern borders of Russia have been evaluated at about 80 billion barrels. These resources are large and readily available. Oil and gas pipelines from these areas — particularly gas — are already supplying most of Europe. The area in the vicinity of the Caspian Sea has large deposits. Presently a consortium headed by British Petroleum (BP) is building a 1,000-kilometre oil pipeline from Baku in Azerbaijan, through Armenia and Georgia and on to the port of Ceyhan in Turkey, to provide one million barrels of oil per day for export — if insurgents do not blow it up.

Through primitive engineering and terrible maintenance during the Soviet era, the fuel production and pipeline systems in all of the former Soviet states needed to be thoroughly modernized. Simple steps, like having every piece of welded pipe x-rayed so that there are no leaks and "inside the pipe" monitoring systems to pinpoint corrosion or mechanical problems had to be addressed. And pumping stations needed upkeep to keep the fuel flowing.

Canada produces on average about 2.3 mbd and is not a big player in oil exports, although all of the exports go to the United States under the North American Free Trade Agreement (NAFTA). In 2005 oil exports amounted to 1.69 mbd — up from 1.09 mbd in 1995. But because of Canada's dimensions and transport costs, oil is imported through the Atlantic seaports to serve Eastern Canada. In 2001, Canada imported 923,000 barrels per day — up from 683,000 barrels per day in 1996. There are 20 refineries in Canada — owned by the big oil companies — with a maximum processing capacity of about 2 mbd.

North America is well served with oil and gas pipelines. Wherever possible, it is much safer to supply oil and gas by pipeline rather than by tanker ships. This should obviously apply to the oilfields of Alaska so that Alaska oil and gas would reach the lower states by pipelines through Canada. Ecological disasters caused by major oil spills severely damage aquatic and marine life. In many oil spill accidents there is not a complete recovery of the shoreline and abutting aquatic life, and the grey-black remnants of oil can be seen on the rocks for many years.

Since 1967 there have been many major tanker spills. To date, the largest, in 1979, spilled 287,000 tonnes from the *Atlantic Empress* off Tobago in the West Indies. The *Amoco Cadiz* is number four on that list, with a spill of 223,000 tonnes off the coast of Brittany, France, in 1978. The *Tory Canyon* is number seven, with a spill of 119,000 tonnes off the Scilly Isles in the U.K. in 1967. The *Exxon Valdez*, the only major tanker accident in North America, is way down the list at number 35, with a spill of 37,000 tonnes in Prince William Sound, Alaska, in 1989.

The shipping lanes of the world are used constantly by huge double-hulled tankers carrying from 0.5 million barrels to the latest supertankers carrying over two million barrels. Once on the high seas, it is generally thought that the tankers are safe, but accidents do occur. About half of the oil produced — almost 40 million barrels per day — is carried by tankers travelling through narrow, crowded, dangerous bottlenecks to get to the open seas.

The four major oil bottlenecks on the oceans of the world are:

- the straits of Hormuz — between the Persian Gulf and the Arabian Sea — oil from the Middle East and Iran; about 15 mbd;
- the Straits of Malacca — between Malysia and Indonesia, route to the Pacific Ocean — oil from the Middle East and Iran; about 11 mbd;

- Bab-el-Mandab — between Saudi Arabia and Egypt, from the Red Sea to the Gulf of Aden — oil from the middle East; about 3 mbd;
- the Bosphorus — oil from Russia and the "stan" republics, from the Caspian Sea and the Black Sea to the Mediterranean Sea; about 3 mbd.

NATURAL GAS

Underground oil and coal deposits are always accompanied by small amounts of mostly methane gas — about 80 to 95 percent methane. In the early days of oil exploration, when it was noticed that oil wells sometimes produced quantities of natural gas, it was simply flared or burned off. But as natural gas became abundant from some wells, in the early 1950s its potential as a clean-burning fuel was finally recognized. By the mid-1960s gas pipelines had crossed the U.S. and Canada to provide natural gas to cities and towns.

As a young immigrant in Canada, I worked as a project engineer on route layout of the pipeline in Northern Ontario during the spring, summer and fall of 1957. It was at the beginning of the rush to supply natural gas from Alberta to Eastern Canada. At that time most of the engineers were from Texas and Louisiana and had a head start in pipeline construction. For me it was a unique experience — from the blazing desert heat of the Middle East to the cooler wilderness climate of Northern Ontario.

Natural gas can be found on its own or sometimes in association with coal or oil deposits. About 70 percent of all gas discoveries are not associated with oil or coal deposits. Gas is easier to handle as it can be controlled and piped directly to customers if it is dry, or "sweet." If it is wet, or "sour," it has to be scrubbed or processed to remove contaminants. But natural gas is required to have a noticeable odour so that leaks in gas piping distribution systems can be detected. "Associated" gas can become a real problem for an oil-producing well. If the amount of gas is very small, in comparison to the oil production, it may not be practical or economical to collect it or store it, and it is flared as it escapes the system. If there are sufficient quantities of the gas, it can be collected and pumped back into the well for future use. Over the years the flaring of natural gas from oil wells has resulted in the wasting of many trillion cubic feet of natural gas.

The Canadian government began to actively promote the use of natural gas in 1975 and provided generous grants to homeowners to switch to gas. At that time, natural gas was very cheap — much cheaper than oil. By that time oil had almost replaced coal in the furnaces of residential buildings. The use of natural gas seemed a good deal all round — for industry and the homeowner.

On November 1, 1985, the federal government deregulated the supply of natural gas at the well head to allow negotiations between buyers and sellers. But the government regulates the transportation charges of gas supplies from the gas fields of Western Canada. Trans Canada Pipelines Ltd. (TCPL) is responsible for transporting the gas from Alberta and Saskatchewan to Ontario and points in Eastern Canada under regulated prices set by the National Energy Board (NEB). The Ontario Energy Board (OEB) regulates the storage, transmission, distribution and rates of gas in Ontario. As the pipeline system from Western Canada is continually supplying gas to the big markets of southern Ontario, vast underground caverns are required to store the gas, and we, here in the Toronto area, are supplied from these storage caverns.

Gas markets are very volatile and contracts are based on prices set on the New York Mercantile Exchange (NYMEX). In the business section of most newspapers, under the heading "U.S. Futures," the NYMEX lists bids on natural gas contracts. The costs are in U.S. dollars per million BTUs. In December 2004 the cost was around $7 for delivery in February 2005. In August 2005 the cost had risen to almost $10.

As governments began to promote the phasing out of coal-burning plants and switch over to clean-burning natural gas, the known reserves of natural gas had not increased. This led to alarming price increases and accelerated the depletion of known resources. Gas prices soon reached the price of heating oil.

In 1996, I worked on a major industrial natural gas contract. The market was beginning to show signs of the strain as demand was rapidly increasing. By 1997 the price was $2 per 1,000 cubic feet

(Mcf), and by 2002 the price had doubled to an average of $4 per Mcf. Prices at that time were not as wild as they became in 2003. In mid-May 2003 the price quoted for October 2003 delivery was about $6.20 per Mcf (equivalent to about 1 million BTUs). It is generally explained that over the last ten years, hot summers and cold winters in parts of North America have led to wild upward swings in the price of natural gas. But that is only a minor part of the price fluctuation problem.

A more helpful way of using natural gas supplies lies in using the gas only for residential and small industrial purposes. Burning gas in a conventional power plant is a waste of natural gas, when other fuels like coal could be used, with stringent emission standards. Under the NAFTA agreement, natural gas is shared in Canada, the United States and Mexico. The increased demand for natural gas has been a crippling problem for many who rely on a stable natural gas market. Canada uses about 39 percent of its annual gas production, while the remaining 61 percent is exported to the U.S. This amounts to about 17 percent of the U.S. needs. Canada cannot export any more gas because of a tight supply and lack of pipeline capacity.

World reserves of natural gas in 2003 were estimated to be 6,076 trillion cubic feet (Tcf). Russia has resources totalling 1,750 Tcf — mostly in Siberia. The former Soviet Republics, mainly the "stan" republics, have about 250 Tcf. Iran has the second largest proven natural gas reserves with 940 Tcf, with Qatar next with 910 Tcf. The reserves of natural gas in the U.S. as of 2003 were estimated to be 183.4 Tcf — about 3.1 percent of the planet's known resources. Canada's proven reserves were stated to be 60.11 Tcf. Some gas specialists are optimistic and expect that new reserves will be discovered, adding another 80 Tcf, bringing Canada's total to 140 Tcf. That seems to be over-optimistic. But assuming the latter figure is reached, that amounts to about 20 billion cubic feet (Bcf) per day for the next 20 years.

The production of conventional natural gas in Canada in 1996 was 15.4 Bcf per day. By the end of 2001 that production had increased by 13 percent to 17.4 Bcf per day. We know that the demand will increase in the years ahead, but we cannot guarantee that the gas will be available. But more frantic drilling in the Arctic and Western Canada may bring some more gas to the market for a few years more, before the real decline begins and until the wells are dry. The projected natural gas consumption of the planet by 2025 is estimated to be 151 Tcf, if consumption keeps rising at the present and projected rate of 2.2 percent. In this scenario there will be no conventional gas supplies by mid-century.

LIQUID NATURAL GAS (LNG)

At a U.S. government committee meeting in June 2003, Alan Greenspan, the U.S. Federal Reserve Board chairman, predicted a bleak future for U.S. energy requirements unless new gas fields were discovered. He encouraged the U.S. to begin preparations to import vast quantities of liquid natural gas (LNG). The committee heard reports that an additional 15 Bcf per day will be needed by 2012 and only one-third of that would be produced in North America.

To achieve liquefaction natural gas has to be cooled to -162°C. At that temperature the volume shrinks to 1/600, which allows an enormous amount of natural gas to be transported by huge, specially refrigerated tankers. The total liquefaction and re-gasification process can use up to 25 percent of the energy in the fuel. Loading and unloading tankers requires special care. The U.S. has four major ports capable of handling large volumes of LNG — three on the Atlantic coast and one in Louisiana. Plans are already underway to develop three LNG ports on the Pacific Coast, three more on the Atlantic coast and three on the Gulf Coast. In 2003, the U.S. imported 506 Bcf of LNG — mostly from Trinidad. There are presently about 150 LNG tankers in use today. And that number will double in the next twenty years.

Western Europe has ten operating LNG facilities, with a capacity of 2,000 cubic feet — all operating as seaports. Plans are underway to build four new facilities with an additional 2,900 cubic feet capacity by 2010. These terminal ports — all on the Atlantic and Mediterranean coasts — would receive natural gas from Russia, the "stan" republics and the Middle East and ship it as LNG to North America.

LNG facilities have not been welcome additions to many ports, as the public perception has been that LNG is dangerous to handle and is very explosive and therefore should be located away from built-up areas. In truth, LNG, in itself, will not burn and is therefore safer than its gas form.

COAL BED METHANE (CBM)

Coal bed methane (CBM) extraction is a relatively new process of siphoning natural gas from coal deposits by drilling into the coal and extracting trapped methane. There is usually water associated with the deposits and this water can pollute the adjacent land if not handled properly. About 7 percent of U.S. natural gas supplies are produced from CBM in the U.S. and much damage has been caused to farmland because of the dumping of contaminated CBM water. CBM has been successfully tapped in Southern Alberta since 1998 and production has steadily increased without any problems as the extraction is dry and the coal beds are not in water. It is estimated that southern British Columbia has vast deposits of CBM — some suggest that it is at least 20 Tcf, while others predict that it may be as high as 90 Tcf.

Oil and gas drilling — whether for conventional oil and gas or coal bed methane — can cause trouble for local farmers. Friction between farmers and oil and gas producers in Alberta has been very noticeable. Farmers have complained that much of the water that was formerly allocated for irrigation has now been diverted down the producing wells to help regulate the pressure to maintain the fuel extraction. In areas where water is scarce and periods of drought are hurting farmers, oil production has been fingered as a real culprit. Wastewater from CBM operations has caused much damage to many areas of the State of Nevada, where it has polluted streams and farmland. There is no excuse for that pollution. If CBM is approved in British Columbia, care must be taken that the wastewater from the coal beds is returned to the coal beds or properly treated before it is directed to a river or stream or used to irrigate the neighbouring farmlands.

TAR SANDS

The Fort McMurray area on the Athabaska River in Alberta has the largest deposit of heavy oil sands in the world. This is a bitumen sand type deposit, with wide variations of consistency and recoverability, and covers an area of about 34,000 square kilometres. The deposit has a thick, messy, gooey structure. There are other large tar sands deposits in Venezuela and Siberia and smaller ones spread across the world. The world's total oil sand deposits are substantial. Even if only 10 percent could be economically recovered, it would provide oil for many hundreds of years. It is a major challenge for modern technology to find ways to economically recover part of the other 90 percent that is now not recoverable. Methods such as pumping steam and heating sections of a deposit to improve the viscosity of the oil, as well as a combustion process in caverns of a deposit, have been tested with little success.

The Alberta tar sands vary in thickness from 30 to 85 metres, with an average of about 50 metres. In some areas it is a simple open pit mining system and not difficult to handle the material. This is being processed successfully. But most of the tar sands have a thick overburden of between 70 and 500 metres and that means expensive underground mining, rather than removing the massive overburden.

It takes, on average, about 14 tonnes of tar sands to produce one tonne of oil. But it also takes huge amounts of energy — mostly natural gas from the Alberta gas fields. This produces enormous amounts of greenhouse gases. Many engineers look on this as a waste of natural gas and have attempted, with some success, to use synthetic gas from the tar sands base to extract the oil.

According to business reports, the production of oil from tar sands, from deposits with minimum overburden, is economical only when the international price of oil exceeds US$25 per barrel. With that in mind, about 7 to 8 percent of the Alberta deposits are economically recoverable at surface levels. These are substantial amounts. Figures released by the Albert Energy & Utilities Board (EUB) in June 2003 claimed there were 174 billion barrels of established recoverable crude bitumen available. Adding this amount to the paltry 5.5 billion barrels of conventional oil reserves places Canada, with 180.02 billion barrels of oil reserves, second in the world — after Saudi Arabia — in recoverable oil deposits. Alberta will dominate the world oil market in the western hemisphere for years to come.

In the battle between Alberta and the natural gas producers in the area of the tar sands, the EUB, towards the end of 2003, ordered about 1,000 gas wells to close down. The board ruled that the extraction of natural gas from under the tar sands would undermine sections of the deposit. Since gas production was relatively small from the area, the EUB believed that it was not in the province's best interest to jeopardize the stability of the tar sands. The gas companies got some concessions from the board, but the final outcome is by no means certain.

OIL SHALES

Oil shales are often compared to tar sands. But in reality they are hard rocks that contain an organic material called kerogen. When the rocks are heated to about 350°C in a retort or distillation vessel, the kerogen separates into gaseous and liquid hydrocarbons that can then be processed and refined. Oil shale deposits are much like coal and mining is required in much the same manner. Economically they are hardly comparable. Six tonnes of shale must be processed to produce the same amount of energy as one tonne of coal. Mining and processing the shale also causes major environmental problems. It would be more acceptable if a method could be developed to treat the shale in situ for oil and gas extraction. But that is proving elusive.

The U.S. has massive resources of oil shale deposits in over 40,000 square kilometres in the Colorado-Utah-Wyoming area. But very little progress has been made to bring these resources into production. The economics, at the moment, do not make sense. Although in the past small amounts of oil from shale deposits have been used in many places throughout the world, its extraction has proven to be cumbersome and expensive. Oil shales do not have the promise of tar sands. Their development will materialize only when all other fossil fuels have been depleted.

HOW LONG WILL FOSSIL FUELS LAST?

Most experts have given answers to that question. There is a general consensus that resources of conventional oil and gas will last until around 2040. After that the picture becomes blurred, with the most optimistic view being that, with a more aggressive drilling program, much more oil and gas will be found, adding an additional 30 or 40 years to the supply. As dwindling oil and gas deposits become more of a challenge, the scarcity of these resources will drive the price to exorbitant heights. That will cause chaos in our economies by the middle of the twenty-first century as tar sands and other oil shale deposits become the fuel focus for the remainder of the century.

Conventional oil and gas production in Canada peaked in 2002. Drilling has continued at a frantic rate but no major oil or gas deposits have been discovered. There have been many disappointments, which only highlights how difficult the work of geologists is in locating the hidden fuels buried in the bowels of the earth.

According to the IEA, the United States and Canada will need to invest US$3.3 trillion over the next 30 years to modernize, replace and add new energy systems. There is no doubt that new discoveries will be made — perhaps as much as 30 percent or more can be added to the present known resources. Then there are new and emerging technologies for more recovery, which will lead to revisiting old oil and gas wells — and that may produce an additional 20 percent from those wells.

In June 2003, the National Energy Board (NEB), in a 98-page report entitled "Canada's Energy Future, Scenarios for Supply and Demand to 2025," tried to appear optimistic as the traditional supply reservoirs of oil and natural gas began a predictable downward spiral. The NEB focused on extraction improvements, unconventional sources of energy, clean new coal technology and predictions that the Arctic and the Alberta tar sands would become the main sources of energy in the years ahead.

In early 2004, the Canadian Securities Commission introduced new rules to update the practices and mathematical guesstimates for the "certainty" of proven reserves, which previously had been labelled a "high degree of certainty." As one old-timer said, "It is like drawing up new guidelines for measuring fog at night."

To meet these new evaluation guidelines, many oil and gas companies lowered their reserves. The lower estimates had an impact on the value of the affected companies, as the publicly traded stock of many energy companies declined.

Estimating underground fuel reserves has always been very tricky. New rules and regulations will not add or decrease the real amount of fuel that can be extracted. But it is a first step and it may focus a little more light on industries that always looked on the optimistic side of projections. In reality, the rate of the depletion of fossil fuel resources will depend directly on the appetite of nations for oil and gas.

The vast resources of tar sands and some limited recoveries from oil shales around the world could double oil and gas resources. But the full benefit from these resources will not be accepted until the final years of the conventional oil and gas supply arrive and the costs rise substantially. We do know that energy consumption and electricity production have been in a steady climb every year since the first well was tapped.

For the 30-year period from 1971 to 2001, IEA statistics show that the planet's electrical production has gone from 3,800 terawatt hours (TWh) to 9,100 TWh — an almost 2.5 times increase. During the same time period in Canada, electrical production has risen from 230 TWh to 580 TWh — an increase of more than 2.5 times.

MIDDLE EAST TURMOIL

Oil supplies from the Middle East and Iran cannot be guaranteed in the future. The anti-Western seeds of hatred have been well fertilized by the actions of President George W. Bush and the U.S. government and their involvement in the Arab/Israeli conflict. Far from helping bring the two sides together, their actions have done untold damage to peace prospects in the area. And although it has been a thousand years since the Crusaders went to Palestine to oust the Muslims from the Holy Land, many Islamic people look on the plight of the Palestinians and the war in Iraq as a modern-day crusade and an attempt by Westerners to control the oil in their lands. The prospects for the future do not look promising. The next 50 years will bring a lot more tears and misery to the cradle of civilization as the cauldron of conflict continues to consume these desert lands.

It is difficult to imagine the Saudi royal family staying in power much longer without the increased military support of the U.S. If Saudi Arabia had no oil, there would be little U.S. interest. The U.S. would not be its "friend." It would be just another desert waste like Chad or some other Third World country.

I can understand the all-powerful desert sheiks, ruling feudal kingdoms, with bulging offshore bank accounts and massive investments, playing to the oil and gas addiction of developed countries. And I can understand the Western powers propping up puppet governments to keep their oil and gas taps open, as long as the flow is their way. But I cannot accept that this will go on much longer as the ordinary people of the desert states strive to get control of their lives and begin to find out that their oil is being siphoned off to fuel the lifestyles of their rulers and the users of an affluent world they know little about.

Historically, powerful nations, with grandiose ideas of conquering other weaker nations, have always been selfish. Recognizing "might as right" and the intoxication of military victories has led to mistaking blindness for vision. These are very human conditions that accompany our democratic beliefs and our free will to do whatever we want — not burdened by any requirement to do what should be done for the common good. This route will ultimately lead to major failures for the human species in the journey along the road of life.

Attending to local selfish demands reminds me of the comments of satirist Jonathan Swift when the Irish merchants in Dublin in the late 1700s were having a hard time with the established order in the British government. Although these merchants were of English establishment stock and were loyal to the Crown, the British Parliament promoted exporting British goods to Ireland while forbidding the export of most Irish goods to Britain. Ireland had no coal, so it had to be imported from Britain. Swift led a group for fair trade practices. His motto was "Burn everything British — except their coal!"

COAL AND THE FUTURE

When all the oil and gas has been used up, the planet's coal resources will then supply the engines of industry for many hundreds of years — possibly 1,000 years. But these are only guesses, which depend on population increases and the industrialization of developing countries. Imagine what it will be like when countries like China, India, Indonesia and a host of others, using coal, add millions of stacks and chimneys to pump more fumes into an already polluted atmosphere.

Government programs in research and development for the clean use of coal have been absent. Our present course, dictated by short-sighted politicians and many environmental activists with the advice of major oil and gas companies, will have definite long-term disastrous consequences for future generations. But there is no doubt that coal is a fuel of the future. Engineers are continuing to improve technology to use coal in a manner that will make it as clean as natural gas. Meeting tougher environmental standards costs money and increases the cost of energy. It is difficult to market the clean burning of coal as long as natural gas is available — no longer cheap and readily available, but still promoted by the quick-fix political leaders.

Environmental groups, large oil and gas companies and, above all, costs to the consumer, influence politicians. There is little room, therefore, for costlier energy. Even scientists, engineers and a few knowledgeable environmentalists — many with considerable expertise in the technical advancements of coal-burning and stack gas cleaning technology — are reluctant to speak out because of the bandwagon approach to burning gas and closing down coal-burning plants. It would be prudent and good planning if we thought a little about the generations that come after us and the legacy we are preparing for them. Or are we too selfish? Even alternative energy sources, such as solar, wind, biomass, etc., are treated as fads and nuisances by governments.

There are two main influences — one positive and one negative — that will determine the lifespan of recoverable oil and gas deposits. One is the determination of governments to develop energy efficiency and energy conservation programs. If properly developed, conservation and efficiency programs could cut energy consumption in half. But the consumption of oil and gas has been steadily increasing every year, with "conservation" and "energy efficiency" mere political buzzwords.

The second influence, on the negative side, focuses on how much developing countries, wishing to follow the wasteful practices of Canada and the U.S., will accelerate the depletion rate of oil and gas as their economies begin to develop — all leading to the further contamination of the tiny, fragile ribbon of atmosphere that surrounds us.

These two influences will make it almost impossible to even guess how long our conventional oil and gas resources will last. But by mid-century there will be little if any conventional oil and gas left — at least that can be readily recovered. In the real world of "drill and burn," one thing is certain: we have used half of the oil and gas resources of the planet in the last 150 years — since the beginning of the industrial revolution. The remainder will be burned in the next 50 years. After that the picture gets very blurred.

CHAPTER 7
Powering the Planet with Alternative Energy

SOLAR POWER

The constant stream of electromagnetic radiation from the sun — 150 million kilometres away — bathes the earth at an average rate of about 1.4 kilowatts per square meter. This total energy, or total solar flux, represents about 1.7×10^{14} kilowatts, which is tens of thousands of times more than the electrical generating capacity of all the power plants on earth. If only a tiny fraction of this energy was used, it would be enough to service the needs of mankind, without the need for fossil fuel or nuclear power plants.

The temperatures in the core of the sun reach 12,000,000°C through the fusion of hydrogen. This inferno has been raging for billions of years and will last for many billions more. This ultimate energy package provides for all life on earth.

The sun provides us with an environment that gives us the seasons, the rains, the vegetation, the crops, the trees, the ocean currents, the winds, and much more, so that all living things can exist on earth. But the sun's energy also provides us with readily available clean energy through the hydrological cycle in the form of running water to operate hydroelectric power plants, wind energy and solar energy through passive and photovoltaic systems. About 70 percent of all solar energy is absorbed by the atmosphere and the planet's surface. To maintain a reasonable balance of temperature there must be a balanced outflow of energy. This happens as infrared energy, which is bounced back to space. All this enables the temperatures of our planet to remain relatively stable.

When we think of solar energy, the picture is usually of some panels on a roof. But it is much more than that. The sun's energy encompasses the full range of the electromagnetic spectrum — from the extremely short-wave gamma rays at one end to the long radio waves at the other end. The visible light that we see, between ultraviolet and infrared, is only a tiny fraction of the total spectrum. The short wavelength component of the spectrum — from gamma rays to ultraviolet rays — is destructive to the human body and living tissue. About 5 percent of sunlight is ultraviolet. The ozone layer, which caps off our atmosphere, acts as a protective shield. It prevents most of the ultraviolet radiation from reaching the surface of the earth. The small amount that reaches us helps provide suntans, but it can also lead to skin cancer.

A small amount of the sun's energy supports all forms of life on earth. Atmospheric carbon dioxide and water vapour nourish trees, plants and vegetation — the green mantle of the earth. This process, called photosynthesis, leads to the development of molecules of living matter. These are the autotrophy, or self-nourishing, blocks of life, as opposed to heterotrophic, such as bacteria, animals, fish and humans, which depend on other organisms for existence. The right combination of basic elements — lands, water and temperature ranges — decide where and to what extent the many forms of life exist. The search for the key to this unlimited world of solar energy is continuing, but engineers and scientists so far have not been able to fully utilize the sun's electromagnetic radiation to replace our reliance on fossil fuels. Still, small advancements have been made over the past half-century.

PHOTOVOLTAICS

This is the technology that attempts to capture the electromagnetic energy of the sun and turn it into electricity. It is based on the simple fact that when sunlight falls on some elements, electrons are moved in a photoelectric effect. If enough electrons are moved they can be collected and passed through a circuit to make electricity and then be restored to their origin. That is the principle of photovoltaics. Although many materials are photoelectric, some are more usable than others. The most effective and common material is silicon — an element that is most abundant. But pure silicon does not occur in nature. It has to be purified in a complex and expensive process.

The photovoltaic cell consists of a thin layer of pure silicon with a trace of added arsenic or phosphorus to activate electrons in the negative or N-layer. The other thin layer of pure silicon contains a trace of added boron to make up the positive or P-layer. Both the N and P layers are separated by a barrier of pure silicon. When a photon of light is absorbed it separates electrons in the N-plate. This creates a response in the P-plate. The electrons flow through the wire connecting the two plates and create a current. As long as the sun shines on the cells, direct current flows. Using an inverter, this can be converted to alternating current and fed into the local grid or used to replace some of the electricity from the local utility. Photovoltaic solar cells and panels are connected together to provide more electricity. The efficiency of the panels can now reach about 15 percent. If the costs of producing solar panels could be drastically reduced, many of the fossil fuel power plants on earth would disappear.

In the past few years, solar engineers have been attempting to develop a flexible photovoltaic roofing material that would not only be used for roofing but would act a collector of solar energy. The roof would replace the rigid and expensive solar panels. If there is a breakthrough, buildings could become solar buildings and these materials should become a requirement through the Building Code. This would have a tremendous positive impact on the provision of electricity and help extend the lifespan of our non-renewable fossil fuel resources.

PASSIVE SOLAR

Passive solar energy takes full advantage of natural sunlight. The setting and design of a building makes use of the location and natural sunlight to help regulate the interior temperature. The use of recommended building materials for sunrooms, atriums and air circulation can really help. And the use of thicker structural walls and cavity walls, extra insulation, argon-filled triple glazed windows or equivalent, recirculation and reuse of internal air and ventilation — these all add to energy savings and cut down on overall costs of heating and cooling the building. The passive use of solar energy in a building designed to take full advantage of the sun can save as much as 30 percent annually.

FLAT PLATE COLLECTORS

Flat plate collectors are simple flat rectangular box plates. In its simplest form, a collector could be 2 metres long by 1 metre wide, with a depth of 10 to 15 centimetres. A glass or clear plastic cover provides the seal for the enclosure. The inside of the box is painted black to help absorb the heat of the sun. A series of copper pipes complete the interior space. The pipes carry water (or a liquid with a low freezing point in colder climates), which is heated by the sun in the greenhouse effect of the contained area.

The collector sits on the slope of the roof with a southern exposure to take advantage of the sunshine. As the water is heated, it has a natural tendency to rise to the top of the sloped panel, where it is directed to and stored in the hot water tank, which provides hot water for the building. As the hot water moves from the copper pipes in the collector, fresh cold water moves into the collector pipes from the water supply to the building, completing the cycle.

A simple solar hot water system can provide all the hot water necessary for a home in the tropics. That supply of hot water decreases in temperate climates. In Toronto, about 40 percent of the hot water needs of many homes could be supplied by solar heating — costing about $3,500 to $5,000 per unit. Because of our northern climate, the system should be winterized as temperatures go below freezing.

WIND ENERGY

Growing up on the west coast of Ireland — with a window to the broad Atlantic Ocean — offered a unique opportunity to go and grow with the wind. From days and nights of light breezes to raging storms and mounting tides, it was easy to be captivated by the changing moods and power of the wind. With the help of the wind, small sailing boats serviced the coastal communities and fishing boats caught the daily catch. But the industrial age and the introduction of the steam engine changed all that. Then diesel engines, and later small nuclear reactors, propelled the monsters that plough the seas. The freedom of the wind now plays only a minor role in ocean travel. And tall-masted schooners and sleek yachts are used only to display the romance of sail.

The old windmills we see in so many Old Master paintings have a peaceful rustic appeal. A few are still in operation today. They blend into the placid rural setting, the wind slowly moving their large blades, which in turn move the circular heavy stone for the miller to grind the corn and grain. The first water-powered mill in North America, which was used to grind grain, was built on the Allains River in New Brunswick in 1606.

The development of the dynamo in 1831, by Michael Faraday, showed that an iron shaft moving in a magnetic field produced electricity. Falling water and the blowing wind could also turn a shaft, thus acting as a dynamo to produce electricity. This was the beginning of the industrial age — and the age of electricity — opening the door to the future.

Another windmill application — perhaps 1,000 years ago — was used in Persia to pump water for irrigation. About 800 years ago, the Chinese also used the wind for lifting purposes. And many of the early farms across North America used the slim, primitive, stand-alone windmill to act as a pumping mechanism to deliver water to the farmhouse and for the farm animals.

My father, in the mid-1940s, developed the first wind turbine on the County Clare coast. He had purchased a dynamo with a large propeller and mounted it on top of a 30-foot wooden pole, about 50 feet away from the house. It was a noisy contraption. The stronger the wind blew, the faster the blades rotated. This increased the noise. And when the winds reached 70 miles per hour he would tie it down until the winds grew calmer. The wind energy charged "wet" batteries, which provided electricity for the house and pub as well as the only radio for miles around. It was not very efficient by today's standard, but it helped people living along a coast where there was no electricity. My father was always busy tinkering with it. The shelves of batteries had to be recharged constantly and the various parts maintained. Light bulbs were primitive, inefficient, expensive and scarce.

With the help of the wind, my father was able to get news from across the world on the wet battery wireless set he had bought. So, our pub was the meeting place for all the locals for miles around. Local fishermen and farmers would drop by, every night, for a pint and to listen to the news about the war.

There was one night — August 6, 1945 — that I will always remember. I was 12 years old — an inquisitive, barefooted young lad, with little knowledge of the world outside of the Burren and the rugged Clare coast.

I remember it in a fuzzy kind of way, because I saw the sombre expressions on the weather-beaten, ashen faces of the locals gathered around the wireless on the kitchen table, next to the vacant bar. I desperately tried to understand what was going on. I strained to listen to the announcer's words through the crackling static of the radio. I could faintly hear the voice — fading in and out — as he tried to explain the awesome death and destruction inflicted on a city called Hiroshima.

My father tried to explain what was going on. I found his explanation too confusing because he did not really understand it either. He talked about a mighty bomb, dropped by a U.S. bomber, on a Japanese city. It brought death and destruction like was never seen before — wiping out the city and killing many thousands. Then the bomber turned around and flew away as if nothing had happened!

A recent wind study of the 250-metre-high hilltop behind the family pub showed an average wind velocity of 7.2 kilometres per second. My brother had planned to install six 850 kilowatt turbines (total 5.1 megawatts) for the location, but could not get planning permission "because of their unsightliness," in such a sensitive environmental area as the Burren. The turbines would produce 14,694 MWh of electricity annually. With some modifications he may get approval.

Over the past 50 years much progress has been made with wind turbines. The use of computers to design the exact shape, pitch and size of the blades has added greatly to the efficiency of the turbine. By the end of 2002, the cost of producing electricity from wind turbines had decreased below that of conventional power plants using natural gas to about 8 cents per kWh. As natural gas reached $6 per 1,000 cubic feet, it is easy to understand the economics. But Canada's windmill technology lags far behind Denmark, Germany and other European countries where imported oil and gas is expensive. In July 2003, Britain announced an ambitious wind energy program, beginning in 2005, to provide 20 percent of its electricity from wind farms, developed off the coast to take maximum advantage of steady winds.

The key to the success of wind turbines lies in the very simple decision to build where there is sufficient wind. It does a disservice to the promotion of wind energy to build turbines where there is little wind. The government of Canada has developed excellent maps indicating the most advantageous locations in Canada to erect wind turbines. Coastal areas, the Gaspé Peninsula and the foothills in Alberta are a few areas with regular supplies of strong winds. In September 2004, Hydro-Québec and the Quebec government announced plans totalling $2 billion for 1,000 megawatts of wind energy from wind farms in eastern Quebec. That was followed up a month later by an announcement to spend an additional $1 billion on energy conservation by 2010.

Toronto Hydro, in its summer 2004 promotional flyer "Power Shift," displayed a picture of the 750-kilowatt wind turbine at Exhibition Place. According to Toronto Hydro, the $1.8 million turbine was working well and produced about 1.2 million kWh in its first year of operation. While the turbine is located in an attractive prominent area, its performance indicates that the site does not have constant and reliable wind. But it is a symbol, I hope, of better things to come, when the city and Toronto Hydro become real leaders in the field of alternative energy.

But no matter how environmentally friendly wind turbines may be, there are always environmental purists who oppose them because they spoil the landscape and look ugly. Eventually, landscapes where winds are strong will be home to thousands of turbines. About 1 to 2 percent of the sun's electromagnetic radiation generates the planet's winds — providing an enormous amount of usable energy. It is a fair assumption that 10 to 15 percent of the planet's energy needs could be produced by the wind.

DEEP LAKE WATER COOLING (DLWC), OR FREECOOL

In the spring of 1986 I first heard of Deep Lake Water Cooling (DLWC), or Freecool. Bob Tamblyn, an innovative consulting engineer, had suggested that Toronto had a unique opportunity to use the cold deep water in Lake Ontario about two miles offshore. He said that the city of Toronto is the only city in North America with a constant supply of 4°C water right at its doorstep. This vast reservoir of cold water was available where Toronto obtains its drinking water. All that had to be done was lower a water intake to 75 metres below the surface of the lake, and there it was, naturally cold.

It was an obvious winner for Toronto, which needs a constant water supply and uses four water filtration plants. The oldest plant, the Island Filtration Plant, was about to be retired but stayed on as a backup. It was suggested that the Island plant be used for DLWC. If the intake was deeper, the water would be of better quality also. Where was the problem? The cold water could be passed through pipes in the downtown area, where the cold water could be used to cool the buildings, and then returned to the water treatment plan, at about 10°C, for further preparation for the water supply system.

Tamblyn, in a report dated January 24, 1991, estimated that the tunnel intake piping would be quite large and would terminate at a new plant in the vicinity of the John Street pumping station. Smaller pipes, from 12 to 24 inches in diameter, would then service the downtown area. His total estimated costs were about $280 million. The original proposal was to return the deep water to the lake once the "cold" had been used. But if the project could be incorporated into the Metro Toronto water supply system for the downtown area, using the Island Filtration Plant, the costs would be reduced as water supply and DLWC shared the cost.

There was a major political problem in the beginning — two independent local governments, with each one protecting its own turf. Metro Toronto owned and operated the water filtration plants and supplied the water to the municipalities. The City owned or had control over DLWC. With amalgamation in place on January 1, 1998, the jurisdictional problems began to disappear. Bureaucratic roadblocks were eventually removed and a united team with political support began to lay the foundations to develop Deep Lake Water Cooling.

There are environmental assessments (EAs) for everything, and they cost the taxpayers enormous amounts of money. DLWC was no exception. It was a picnic for consultants and professional environmentalists. Environmental assessments were initially introduced in 1974 by the provincial government to review and report on the impact a project could have on the environment. I had interpreted that as an environmental review of projects that could have an obvious negative impact on air, water or land. But very soon it was being used politically to destroy projects that really had little impact on anything. That dawned on me in the late 1970s, when a North York politician on Metro Council wanted an environmental assessment on a new subway station on the Yonge Street Subway line because the proposed location "was not suitable."

The Freecool idea, in reality, is a no-brainer. The quality of the water, because of its depth, is much better than the existing drinking water source. It should therefore have been obligatory to obtain our raw water from the deeper area of the lake, near the city.

With amalgamation, many changes occurred in the peripheral municipal agencies, boards and corporations. The Toronto District Heating Corporation (TDHC) was one such corporation. It was a unique type of organization, operating under special legislation from the province. It provided steam heating for about 80 buildings in the core of the city. It was owned by the City, the province, the University of Toronto and the hospitals on University Avenue. The City had control of the management of the corporation.

When the province announced that electricity would be deregulated, the TDHC board decided it, too, should change. It had to meet the demands of a modern utility. With the deregulation of the electricity supply, TDHC would now be able to produce electricity as a by-product. That would mean the efficient use of fuel, which was long overdue. It would cost hundreds of millions of dollars to make all the changes — particularly the capital investment to produce electricity as well as steam or hot water.

The municipalities and other partners in the corporation were not prepared to make that investment.

Finally, in 1999, Michael Nobrega, the principal of Borealis Energy, approached the City, inquiring if it would be interested in selling all or part of its share of TDHC. Borealis was controlled by OMERS — the $33-billion pension fund of the Ontario municipal employees. After some negotiations OMERS bought 57 percent of the TDHC and the City of Toronto retained the other 43 percent. The name was later changed to Enwave Inc — a corporation under the Provincial Business Corporations Act.

By the beginning of 2003, the activities of Enwave had not focused on the issue needing most attention — the wasteful burning of natural gas to produce only steam. It had been the goal of the TDHC for many years to develop an energy plant that would produce electricity, steam for heating and air conditioning — tri-generation. Ontario at the time liked the idea of tri-generation but claimed that only Ontario Hydro had the right to produce electricity, so the TDHC was discouraged from generating electricity. But the deregulation of electricity by the province on April 1, 1999, changed everything.

With the introduction of deregulation, tri-generation should be a priority. It would also fit into the stated goals of the federal government for energy efficiency to meet the requirements of the Kyoto Agreement. And it would add to the electricity supply for the downtown area, especially in times of heavy demand.

The City could eventually sell its share of Enwave. There is no need to be a part owner in the utility, as all energy matters are under the jurisdiction of the Ontario Energy Board. There are few dividends for the City with this utility — unless the City sees a leadership role in transforming the utility and investing in its modernization. But I doubt that will happen, as the City needs to focus on many other pressing financial problems.

Since the City, and OMERS, own many downtown buildings, it would be an easy switch to deep lake water cooling for many of these buildings. It would show real leadership and make good business and environmental sense. With OMERS now on board, the deep lake water cooling plan began to take shape. By June of 2003 the construction of the piping into the lake to tap into the reservoir of cold water was underway, and OMERS announced that many of its buildings in downtown Toronto would use the cold lake water for cooling.

Eighteen years after it was first proposed, deep lake water cooling was beginning to happen. It began to provide air conditioning to buildings in August 2004. The project had a strange official opening — held at the Steam Whistle Restaurant on August 17. As the many invited politicians, civic and business leaders struggled to adjust in a stifling atmosphere — because of a malfunction in the cooling system — actor Alec Baldwin, who had just flown from New York for the event, heaped praise on the water cooling project.

But Enwave has much work to do. It continues to use natural gas to produce steam only. This has always been an inefficient use of fuel. Electricity should also be produced. It is time to move on that side of the energy equation.

HYDROGEN AND FUEL CELLS

There is enough hydrogen on the planet to provide a totally clean fuel for many millions of years. But there is no free hydrogen. It is locked together with other elements. It is found everywhere — in fossil fuels, as the result of the cycles of life and death of all forms of vegetation, trees, plants and all living matter over hundreds of millions of years. The complex molecules of all fossil fuels are formed around carbon and hydrogen atoms.

But the most abundant source of hydrogen is found in water. A molecule of water consists of two atoms of hydrogen and one atom of oxygen — H_2O. If only the hydrogen atoms could be stripped from the water molecule, in an energy-positive way, the first major hurdle would be overcome. But that is not the case.

The most practical way to strip hydrogen from the water molecule is through electrolysis. An electric current through the water produces hydrogen at the cathode and oxygen at the anode. But, unfortunately, that takes more energy than the recovered hydrogen can produce. Scientists worldwide are desperately searching for a magic key — the Holy Grail in energy research —

to separate hydrogen in a manner that would end up on the positive side of the equation. Reversing the process to make water in a chemical reaction, where two atoms of hydrogen and one atom of oxygen combine to form one molecule of water, is also laborious and energy-intensive.

Water, often called the fountain of life, holds the key to this precious fuel. The basic laws of thermodynamics govern the separation of the oxygen and hydrogen atoms in the water molecule. On top of all that, hydrogen is a difficult, cumbersome, dangerous fuel to handle. It requires massive funding to develop safe containers and distribution systems to fit into a proposed hydrogen economy.

Promoters of hydrogen have talked about producing electricity from renewable energy such as solar, wind, biomass and hydro-electric plants when there is no demand for that electricity from these sources. I cannot imagine such a surplus of electricity. But if there was a surplus of electricity it would be localized and very small. It would produce only a small amount of hydrogen.

The nuclear industry sees a new role for nuclear reactors — producing hydrogen from water. Large advertisements from that industry have recently appeared promoting "air pollution free" energy. It is claimed that reactors could be used to produce electricity, which in turn could be used to extract hydrogen from water. Most promoters of hydrogen recognize that this link-up with nuclear power more than offsets the non-polluting qualities of hydrogen.

But Geoffrey Ballard, who has done pioneering work in fuel cell development and founded Ballard Power Systems of Vancouver, has openly promoted building new "advanced" CANDU reactors across Canada to produce enough hydrogen from water to fuel nearly all of Canada's current automobile fleet. Building more nuclear plants is music to the ears of Atomic Energy of Canada Ltd., which sees the need for about 25,000 megawatts of new electricity generating capacity to produce hydrogen to fuel Canada's cars, trucks and buses. It would mean building 50 reactors of 500 megawatts each at a cost of about $750 million per reactor — not including the costs of decommissioning and the storage and long-term management of spent fuel from the reactor. It is a dream for AECL, but for many it sounds more like the cure being worse than the disease.

Many of the publicly traded fuel cell companies will fade into obscurity as soon as the public knows the whole truth about hydrogen. The media and some scientific magazines have hyped the coming "hydrogen economy" to a gullible public. Sure, there is an unlimited supply of hydrogen locked in water. But it takes more energy to extract that hydrogen than the hydrogen can produce.

Using power plants to produce hydrogen from water would be wasting electricity that could be fed to the power grid for more efficient use. In hydroelectric power plants, the waste energy, during times of low electrical demand, is now used to pump water to a pump storage area — usually a reservoir — to be used later to produce electricity when the demand for electricity is greater.

Another major hurdle for hydrogen is the problem of storing it on board a vehicle. Hydrogen is very light and volatile. It must be compressed and contained under great pressure — about 10,000 pounds per square inch — to provide the same amount of energy as a normal tank of gasoline. And the hydrogen tank will be at least three times the size of a gasoline tank. It will be heavy and extremely durable to withstand the extremely high pressure — probably constructed of titanium, magnesium, carbon fibre or a combination of new materials that are now being tested. There is much unease about vehicles with such dangerous pressure tanks. Even if liquid (cryogenic) hydrogen is used, the storage and maintenance problems are enormous.

The most economical way to produce hydrogen is from fossil fuels — using steam in a catalytic converter system. But the production of hydrogen, no matter what process is used, is expensive and uses energy. Natural gas — mostly methane, CH_4 — is the most economic feedstock for hydrogen extraction at the moment, although coal, gasoline and other hydrocarbon fuels can also be used. The stripping of the hydrogen atom from the fuel molecule produces carbon dioxide — a greenhouse gas — which is vented into the atmosphere.

The fuel cell, in many ways, can be compared to batteries. There is no combustion but the fuel (hydrogen) can be used in an electrochemical process to produce electricity.

Hydrogen has the simplest atomic structure of any element. It is the first element on the periodic table, with one negatively charged electron circling the positively charged proton in the nucleus. It has been used in the budding fuel cell industry with some success for the past 30 years.

Although fuel cells were discovered in the early-1800s, they did not come on the world stage until the beginning of the space age, when General Electric used the proton exchange membrane (PEM) to provide power and drinking water to the crews of the Apollo and Gemini space missions. The development of the fuel cell has shown promise for the use of hydrogen. All hydrocarbon fuels, many with a complex molecular structure, contain various amounts of hydrogen — in methane, ethane, propane, butane, gasoline, diesel, ethanol, etc. And hydrogen is the only atom that makes the fuel cell work.

There are several types of fuel cells. The major differences are related to operating temperature ranges. But the two most popular are the proton exchange membrane and the Solid Oxide Fuel Cell (SOFC). The PEM operates at relatively low temperatures, around 200°F, with high power density, with the assistance of a platinum catalyst. It can vary its output quickly to meet shifts in power demand and can be used for vehicles, home applications and small applications in the place of batteries. Ballard Power Systems uses the PEM system for vehicles, where hydrogen is produced offsite and stored on board the vehicle. This has been an expensive involvement for Ballard and the automobile industry supporters. The road ahead is still uncertain and there have been few successes.

The Solid Oxide Fuel Cell can reach operating temperatures of 1,800°F and can be used in homes, factories, large power applications, small electrical generating stations and stand-by or auxiliary power units.

As the search goes on for a simple, energy-positive way to produce hydrogen from water, the use of fossil fuels such as natural gas is the most practical way to develop the fuel cell — until these resources are depleted. Using fossil fuel, when the hydrogen atom is stripped from the fuel molecule using steam in a catalytic converter, carbon dioxide is released. Although not a health hazard, carbon dioxide is a greenhouse gas and for that reason is not a welcome emission.

Using hydrogen from fossil fuels in fuel cells has one clear advantage: it more than doubles the fuel's efficiency. Coal-fired power plants capture about 33 percent of the energy in the coal and the energy lost in power transmission is about 8 percent. Gasoline and diesel provide about 25 percent of the energy in the internal combustion engine. But the fuel cell can convert about 50 to 65 percent of the energy in natural gas into usable energy. And that is significant.

The SOFC is the most promising fuel cell application at the moment — especially for stationary applications. Many fuel cell companies are using this system to develop a fuel cell stack — about the size of the kitchen fridge — hooked up to the natural gas supply to look after the energy needs of a building or residence. It would provide the electricity, heating and air conditioning for the whole structure. When all the uses of the energy produced are taken into account, the fuel cell could reach efficiencies of over 65 percent.

One company, Fuel Cell Technologies Ltd. of Kingston, Ontario, has become a leader in the SOFC application. The company has developed a five-kilowatt fuel cell system about the size of the kitchen fridge to provide all the energy needs of a building if it has a natural gas connection. But the costs of such a fuel cell system at the moment are quite high. As changes and refinements are made, costs will come down. But the product must first prove its worth and be accepted in the marketplace.

The fuel cell would give real meaning to the idea of living off the grid, with no need for a connection to the electrical utility. Using the fuel cell, the energy bill would be half the standard gas and electric bill. And that is a considerable saving and efficient use of fuel.

In the most common fuel cell process — the proton exchange membrane — the hydrogen is channelled to the anode, where a catalyst causes the atom to split into the positively charged hydrogen ions (protons) and the negatively charged electrons. The PEM allows only the protons to pass through, while the electrons travel along an external circuit, generating an electric current. On the other side of the fuel cell, at the cathode, oxygen is drawn in from the air as the electrons and protons combine with oxygen to form water. The SOFC uses the same basic principle.

But to use water, natural gas, or any fossil fuel as a feed stock for a fuel cell system, the process requires two basic steps. First, the hydrogen atoms are stripped from the molecule of the fuel used — either through the electrolysis of water or through using steam as a catalyst, if fossil fuels are used. Second, the hydrogen atom structure is then separated — the electron is split from the proton — in a process that produces electricity. The rejoining of the proton and the electron produces the hydrogen atom, which reacts with oxygen to produce water.

If hydrogen is to be stored on board a vehicle to replace the traditional engine, the obstacles are enormous. But if hydrogen is extracted from fossil fuel — such as natural gas — and then used directly at a stationary location fuel cell, the benefits are substantial.

Canadian Hydrogen Energy Co. Ltd., of Bowmanville, Ontario, has developed a system to improve the fuel efficiency of large trucks. It uses the waste energy of the engine to produce hydrogen on board. The system includes a four-litre tank of distilled water. The tank has an anode and a cathode. Hydrogen is produced at the cathode when a current is passed through the water when the engine is on. The hydrogen is channelled to the combustion chamber where it enriches the fuel. According to the company a fuel savings of 10 percent is guaranteed.

The key to the future of our planet's energy resources lies in the discovery of an energy-positive way to produce hydrogen from water. And it must meet the basic laws of thermodynamics. If it was inexpensive, simple and practical — like filling the old gas tank with water at the service station, and then being able to drive away — it would be magical. But the idea that we are on the verge of a new era of endless clean energy, where hydrogen is king, has created a public perception that is both misleading and incorrect. It has been great for stock promoters. And many have been able to cash in on the dream of a hydrogen economy. It would be refreshing and in the public interest if all the truth about hydrogen could be told — clear and simple.

All governments must support research in the development of hydrogen and alternative ways of producing energy. We all have a stake in it. It is on a par with research on a cure for cancer, or the search for a perpetual motion machine, or the concept of cold fusion.

Major world cities could play a role in the search for the energy for tomorrow. Toronto could offer a port lands site and participate with governments and industry in alternative energy research. Most of these publicly owned lands have been idle and unused for many years. It would also spark some resurgence in the port lands area.

LEADERSHIP FROM GOVERNMENTS

The federal government can implement a national strategy for energy use, conservation and efficiency. It can take leadership in national programs through grants and tax incentives, as has been shown in the past. The Canadian Constitution is a document with fuzzy responsibilities for the federal government in the energy field. It has jurisdiction in trade with other countries, boundary waters, oceans and fisheries. It provides little national guidance in environmental and energy and resources management. And without federal funding, energy and environmental matters will have no common base.

At one time the federal government provided financial incentives to homeowners to switch from oil to natural gas. It was a huge success. Why not a similar program to stimulate alternative energy and energy conservation? Imagine the impact that would have on energy use. A whole new industry would develop with a focus on alternative energy, conservation and the efficient use of energy. It would create thousands of jobs.

Emission credits have been given a lot of attention lately, particularly since the Kyoto Accord. Although the idea of credits has received a lukewarm reception, as the public hears of power companies paying farmers not to grow crops and other questionable actions, emission credits will have to prove their worth before they are fully accepted in the environmental marketplace. To many, emission credits seem to be a sneaky way to carry on with the old system and do little to reduce greenhouse gases. Emission credits would really get attention and public support if the power companies developed alternative energy projects and promoted the use of other forms of non-polluting energy — especially small hydroelectric projects, solar and wind.

New programs by governments, working with private sector support in a national program to reduce per capita consumption of energy by 40 percent, would provide a powerful tool in restructuring our wasteful economy and it would bring us in line with the per capita consumption of countries like Britain, Germany, France and Japan. If, for example, a home generated 50 percent of domestic energy from renewable resources and through conservation measures and that became the standard for all homes, it would spark a renaissance in the home building industry. Imagine, all Canadian homes producing a significant amount of their energy requirements.

Most young people, who have some knowledge of energy and environmental issues, are beginning to understand that oil and gas resources are finite. Once they are gone, they are gone forever. With an increasing world population, imagine the destructive impact on future generations unless we have the vision to develop a strong proactive energy conservation program. All non-renewable fossil fuel should be used sparingly so that the natural environment will have a fighting chance to absorb and adjust to the increasing products of combustion. A national education program on energy and environment would contribute to better understanding of our planet and its resources.

The Ontario Building Code — and, by extension, a national building code — should set new energy standards for all buildings. New standards for insulation and energy efficiency should be part of the building code, just like structural, health and fire standards. The R2000 residential energy rating is a start. It can be significantly improved. But the energy standards should be designed in such a way as to take full advantage of layout, topography and local building materials. The exterior walls, doors, windows and roof should possess rigid barrier qualities to control the movement of heat and cold.

The federal and provincial governments, in developing programs to meet our Kyoto Agreement targets, should take advantage of that opportunity and review the rate of depletion of all our fossil fuel resources, as well as participate financially in the development of programs for alternative energy such as solar, wind and bio mass. This should lead to a national strategy to use these non-renewable fuels sparingly and focus on alternative energy so that the needs of future generations are part of the equation.

A suggestion for all pension funds is that a minimum of 5 percent of the funds be invested in corporations that develop and promote green energy. This should be shown by the pension fund in the asset mix filing to the government each year. It would be a positive move by governments to motivate corporations and employees to become part of the energy solution of the province and the country.

CHAPTER 8
The Atmospheric Shield: Protecting Life on Earth

As a young lad growing up in the west of Ireland, I spent countless hours down by the sea — observing with awe the strange and wonderful life at the ocean's edge. The rhythmic rise and fall of the tides introduced me to a whole new world thriving in this twilight between earth and water. Whether it was dangling my feet over the edge of a little pool teeming with tiny sparks of life, or poking around the seaweed-covered rocks searching for a rock crab, the fascination of nature at the edge of the sea left an indelible mark on my soul.

As I grew up and learned a little more about my natural environment I began to understand my own relationship with the things around me. My further education in science and nature opened up that door a little more. It was not difficult to view science and nature as a complementary pair. But I discovered later that others have different understandings of this relationship — from the mechanistic idea of the total domination of nature by science to the other extreme of not tampering with the natural world at all.

Environmental science is the use of knowledge to understand, change or control the elements of the planet — for better or worse. Science has given us the most destructive nuclear devices imaginable and also the life-saving technologies to help us live a little longer and enjoy our stay on earth. It has helped us become masters of the universe in a very limited and temporary way — just enough to maintain a constant vigilance.

I have accepted nature with wonder and reverence. For me that acceptance comes with a commitment to safeguard those elements I can control, so that future generations will inherit a planet where the human species can enjoy the wonders of it all — the beauty of a clear blue sky, the fragrance of wild flowers, the sparkle of running water, the rugged face of the mountains, the peace of sheltered valleys and the freedom of the winds to blow and bring a freshness to all living things.

Nature, in our youth, was a grab bag of everything around us that we had to accept but could not control, and in many cases, elements we could not understand. It was the darkness of the nighttime skies; the blanket of millions of stars; the roaring hurricanes off the ocean; the bleak winter landscape, white with snow; the flash of lightning and the rumbling thunder; the eerie ballet of the northern lights and the barren wasteland of the desert.

But nature is much more than all that. It is also very personal. I grew up in the moonscape topography of the Burren, a unique quilt work of rocks and unusual fauna in northwest County Clare. I felt part of the land and the miracle of nature: the salty sea spray on the rugged shore, the stubborn Cliffs of Moher in a constant battle with the pounding breakers of the Atlantic, and the bare and barren Aran Islands guarding the entrance to Galway Bay. I loved it all. I saw nature as the sum total of all things in time, distance and space, bound in an ever-changing equilibrium. Harm nature and it becomes a self-inflicted wound that could prove fatal to our species and our planet.

The Celtic reverence for nature is characteristic of its folklore. Even St. Patrick, the fifth-century missionary to Ireland, sought to harmonize the ways of the Celts with the Christianity he preached. In his younger years he was captured, probably in Roman Britain, and brought to Ireland by a slave trader. His new masters in Antrim sent him out on the hills as a shepherd. Although he spent many days and nights alone looking after the animals, he got to know the simple folk of the countryside. This brought him close to the natural environment. Indeed, the isolation surrounded him and made him feel at one with nature. And he slowly began to think and feel like the Irish Celts.

After 18 years he escaped to Britain. Later, hearing the call, he returned as a Christian missionary. He knew the Celtic relationship with the natural world and he used it as a bridge in his preaching. On one occasion he held up the three-leaf shamrock as an example of the Trinity. The Celts could relate to that and other simple examples taken from nature. And so the Irish began to follow the monotheism of the Christian faith.

Long after St. Patrick had died — about 350 years later, around AD 850 — another Irish monk, John Scotus Eriugena, used the Celtic approach to nature to teach the Britons (in his writings *De Divisione Naturae*) to understand the oneness of God and nature.

For most ordinary people, especially those who thought about life and death, the wonder of nature went a long way to explain the existence of God. And for those who needed to dwell further on these matters, the eschatological path was an easy route to follow. This opened up an age of fervent enlightenment, where monks lived in isolated, wild, and sometimes inaccessible locations. They kept Christianity alive during the Dark Ages as hordes of marauding barbarians plundered the monasteries of Europe.

But man, with a free will and highly developed brain, is always testing the bounds of nature — forever attempting, mostly in a very selfish way, to tame and change our environment. This freedom, intelligence and temptation could lead to our extinction as a species. It is as if we had a built-in self-destruct gene. And although it makes little sense, it seems that we are heading over that cliff — like the lowly lemmings.

It may be true that, in the end, our solar system may flame out like a dying star or simply fade away. But for now, nature has given us life through a relatively constant and regulated thermostat — the sun — which gives us the seasons and nurtures all life on earth. It manages the complex, inanimate physiognomy of the earth. In harmony with the rotation of the planet, it gives us day and night and helps us see the stars in the heavens. And the sun makes it possible for our species to share and enjoy our planet in the natural order of things.

THE GREENING OF LOCAL POLITICS

When I entered local politics, I soon found out that reason could sometimes seem bare and cold. To get elected the candidate had to be mentally alert to the moods and motives of the electorate. Politicians, in a democracy, are elected on what they promise. On the whole, it is a battle of wits for the trust of the voters. Sad to say, total honesty with the electorate is generally viewed as a recipe for defeat at the polls. Constant polling has become the new tool to find out what the voter wants. Once that pulse is known, the issues are tailored to gain the support of the voters. In the modern democratic scenario, there is very little leadership from politicians: "followship" is a more apt and accurate description, and it invariably leads to poor or mostly bad government.

Telling the voters what the voters want to hear is a large part of a winning political formula. People like to hear good news. They want to hear how you will make their lives a little better. Voters do not like to hear bad news from any politician or would-be politician, although negative campaigning (about how bad the other party or opponent is) has been used effectively at times. Any proposals for change must be positive and ensure a better quality of life. The memory of the voter is often short and self-centred. There is no room for looking too far ahead — maybe a few years at the most. Politicians know that. Elections are always full of theatre. Promises, which invariably are so general and nicely sugar-coated, can be dusted off, regurgitated and repackaged for the next campaign.

Politicians, on the whole, appeal to the collective ignorance of the electorate. That simply means, in dealing with the voters: be nice; have a few catchy phrases; support short-term, easy-to-explain policies; do not make any outlandish promises and do not confuse the voters with long-winded explanations. Keeping it simple, and not offending any groups, is a political art that is a major part of a winning formula in a democracy. Election promises, if kept, cost money. Many promises are just giveaways to win the election. Keeping these promises, of course, can lead to make-work projects — many of which have little lasting value. They are expensive and create expanded or new bureaucracies. They usually require more borrowing and therefore an increased debt load as a legacy.

It is difficult for an engineer to be a politician. As an engineer, I could see some things clearly and get straight results using logic. I learned to stretch the truth — even bend it a little or put a different spin on it. At times, I had to simplify details, which would not be acceptable to my colleagues in the engineering profession, but which was necessary to adequately explain the issue in question to the general voters.

When I was first elected, I felt I had a good chance of doing the things I wanted to do and making a difference in the way the city functioned. I had a clear vision of what had to be done. And I was not saddled with old party discipline. I could have a clear shot at influencing my council colleagues at setting a new course on environmental issues, which was never part of the urban political agenda before.

The organized system we live in is governed and controlled by many constraints that determine our quality of life and our relationship with the natural environment. And City Hall is an excellent starting place, if changes are to take place. It was a distinct challenge for me. It was the place to introduce new ideas that would focus attention on how to clean up our environment. I could make a real difference by thinking globally and acting locally, if I could cope with the political minefields of local politics.

People — billions of them — are the real problem. People pollute. Exploding populations are causing the planet many deadly scars and in some areas massive devastation. Overcrowding, hunger, homelessness, disease and unemployment are all too manifest in this rapidly changing face of our small planet. The gap between rich and poor nations is a major part of our human problems. Those who have a lot want more, and those with very little are the major casualties. Greed and selfishness — twin conditions — dictate the living conditions of our troubled planet.

It was difficult to tailor the municipal form of local government to get support to tackle these basic problems. Even to take a few small steps to use our non-renewable resources more sparingly and leave a little more for future generations was not within reach. But it needed local attention, even if only discussion, as a first step. Slowly others began to talk about air pollution, water pollution, waste disposal, recycling, ecosystems and a host of other matters that fitted under the umbrella of environment. The media loved it. It was easy to capture a headline on any of these topics. The more outrageous the comment, the more exposure the media were prepared to give. Environmental groups began to spring up like mushrooms on a green field after a night of soft rain.

The nice thing about being an environmentalist is that there are few qualifications. Anyone can do it. Most environmentalists have little or no understanding of science or its application in the natural world. The good ones develop an art for the ten-second news clip or the staged photo opportunity. A few environmental organizations address the issues with common sense and science. But many become a burden to the cause, with a loss of credibility for the environmental movement in general.

I found myself being sucked into debates where more credence was given to emotions than to logic and science. I had not expected that. But then again it was easy for anyone to become involved and use scare tactics, which in many instances were taken out of context and were downright silly. And it was easy to hijack a community issue using junk science in environmental arguments. The NIMBY (not in my back yard) approach is well known to those who have to deal with such issues. The search for a waste disposal site is probably the best example where emotion, NIMBY and bad science can kill any proposed location. The location may pass all the required technical criteria, but politics will destroy it when NIMBY takes over and the politicians finally kill the project.

Many members of environmental movements are the least informed and the noisiest lovers of street theatre. Some live from government grant to government grant. Some of their antics can be downright absurd. They will do anything to draw attention to the cause they are promoting — anything to get publicity. I do not question their basic sincerity.

AIR POLLUTION

Air pollution in built-up areas can be a real health problem. Yellowish-brown blankets of smog can be seen from time to time if temperature inversions prevent the escape of the smog to the upper atmosphere. Usually, a layer of warm air sits on top of the polluted air and will not let it rise. It can linger for some time and prove deadly for the elderly and those with respiratory problems. Records of inversions from the 1950s and 1960s, primarily from the burning of coal combined with exhaust gases from cars, trucks and buses, caused many thousands of deaths in London, Los Angeles and other world cities.

I remember a day in London in the spring of 1955 when day turned into night. It was a frightening experience. It is a memory etched in my mind. Darkness suddenly descended, blocking out the sky. It did not seem like a cloud, but it was the dark of night. And I was scared. It lasted about one hour and then daylight returned as the blanket of black melted away. London is not a city where temperature inversions are a constant problem. Like Paris, Berlin or Madrid, it is well-ventilated. But the airshed, at times, could not clean itself fast enough because of all the pollution from coal-burning power plants, trucks, buses and industrial plants and factories.

Eventually, London and other First World cities cracked down on the burning of coal. New pollution control regulations were introduced to reduce stack gas emissions. Wet scrubbing and electrostatic precipitators were introduced in power plants. Coal was replaced by natural gas in residential and smaller factory and industrial buildings. These first steps — by weaning off coal — made a significant contribution to the quality of air in the urban environment. But coal was used in large electricity generating stations, where technical advancements in cleaning stack emissions could be installed. These advancements, especially for North America, have been slow in coming and will not fully happen unless governments step in and require them through legislation.

In 1967, Ontario decided that control of air pollution would be taken over by the new Ministry of the Environment. That diminished the role of the Metropolitan Toronto government in matters relating to air pollution, but there was much to do on other environmental issues. The City, through the Board of Health, decided that it should have some role in air pollution control. Many looked on this involvement as duplication without any meaningful role. Duplication always costs money. But retaining some advisory role would have been more effective if it could have been worked out with the province. But that did not happen, once the Ministry of the Environment took over control.

It would now appear, as we ease into the new millennium, that air pollution is worse today than it was in the 1960s and 1970s, if we are to believe news releases of a few well meaning environmental groups. But that is not so. Toronto's air mass has become considerably cleaner over the last 35 years. But we still have days in the summer when temperatures cause the pollutants to linger and health problems for many.

All of the coal-burning facilities without stack gas cleaning equipment have disappeared and been replaced, first by oil and then by natural gas. The 1,200-megawatt Hearn power plant in the Port area closed down in 1982. It had been built in 1955 to burn coal and later switched to natural gas. The Pearl Street District Heating Plant, in the Richmond Street–University Avenue area, converted from oil to natural gas. There are still four coal-burning power plants producing electricity for Ontario Power Generation. They have some pollution control equipment but still pump an enormous amount of pollutants into the Ontario airshed. Still, regulations for stack-gas emissions have become more stringent with the passage of time. Emissions are now considerably cleaner since the installation of more effective gas scrubbing equipment. But there is still much to be done in the further reduction of stack gas emissions.

Incinerators in apartment buildings are no longer allowed and regulations for industrial plant emissions are much stricter. Gone are the days of the 1960s when the air pollution inspector used a visual comparison chart to rate the darkness of smoke from a chimney. Instruments can now measure minute traces of pollutants from any source.

Emission controls for motor vehicles have also improved considerably over the years. The catalytic muffler has made a huge improvement on all vehicle emissions. And there is more research to further reduce emissions through cleaner combustion. But no matter what fuel is used, emissions can be a real problem if the engine is not properly serviced and maintained. Regular maintenance is one of the keys to cleaner combustion.

Stop-and-go traffic produces a lot of pollutants. Some of this is the result of all the unnecessary four-way stop signs and new speed bumps. Acceleration and deceleration causes an enormous waste of fuel — and 10 to 12 times the pollutants of steady driving.

I do not want to give the impression that our air quality meets the pure air standards we constantly try to achieve. Our goal for the emissions from the combustion of all fuel must be as close to zero as possible. The battle for cleaner air is a continuing one.

The development of fuel cells, hybrids and alternative fuels is beginning to nibble at gasoline- and diesel-powered engines. The fuel cell, using hydrogen stripped from fossil fuels, offers a cleaner future, if costs can be reduced for its general use. There, the production of energy is the result of electrochemical reaction.

The day is not far off when the size and fuel efficiencies of all urban vehicles will be tightly controlled. For a city, the urban car, if legislated by city governments, should use no more than four litres per 100 kilometres. The hybrid fuel-electric car will probably be the urban vehicle of the future.

DEPLETION OF THE OZONE LAYER

In the mid-1980s, reports began to appear in the media that observations over the past 25 years had shown that the layer of ozone around the earth was being depleted. The hunt was on, in the scientific community, to find the answers to this phenomenon. The ozone layer occupies an area beginning about 25 kilometres above the earth's surface and is about 32 kilometres deep. If all the ozone was compressed at ground level and spread evenly around the planet, it would be only three millimetres thick. It is a very tiny constituent in the makeup of the atmosphere, but it plays a key role in regulating all life on earth.

Ozone acts as a shield around the earth in the stratosphere. It blocks much of the ultraviolet radiation from the sun. If it was weakened or reduced it would mean that humans, animals and vegetation — every living thing — would receive harmful doses of radiation. Specifically, ozone depletion would result in more cases of skin cancer, especially the most deadly form of melanoma, eye-aging and cataracts and increasing damage to the human immune system. All major crops, such as maize, rice and grain, which are the basic foods for most of the people of this planet, would be drastically reduced because additional ultraviolet radiation would reach the surface of the earth. It is not difficult to conclude that additional health problems, diminishing food supplies and an ever-increasing population would lead to more human misery, death and starvation. The prospect of such a world is nightmarish.

In the natural order of things, the uninterrupted electromagnetic radiation from the sun, which includes energy of different wavelengths, from ultraviolet to infrared, is about 1.4 kilowatts per square metre at the edge of space. About 5 percent of this energy package is harmful ultraviolet radiation. In its eight-minute journey from the sun to the surface of the earth, it hits the earth's line of defense when it reaches the ozone layer. In this cold expanse of space much of the harmful ultraviolet radiation of the sun's energy package is absorbed by the ozone layer. As ozone is not as stable as oxygen and tends to break down, the sun's energy acts as a mechanism to manufacture new ozone (O_3) when some molecules of oxygen (O_2) are split and the two free atoms link up with oxygen to form ozone. This delicate balance of ozone in the stratosphere is critical for the maintenance of life on earth.

British scientists working in the Antarctic in 1982 first noticed the development of a hole in the ozone layer. It was getting larger and more pronounced every year. The international scientific community was notified and began a frantic search to find the reasons for this scary occurrence. Finally, two U.S. scientists, Sheldon Rowland and Mario Molina, announced in early 1985 that they had found the reasons for the depletion of the ozone layer. The culprit was chlorofluorocarbon or CFC, halons, chloroform and associated chemical compounds, which were used mainly as coolants in the family fridge, freezers and air conditioning. Rowland and Molina discovered that when CFCs, halons and other related ozone-depleting compounds (ODCs) migrate to the stratosphere and above the ozone layer, the ultraviolet rays of the sun break down CFCs, halons etc., producing ozone-destroying substances — chlorine from CFCs and bromine from halons — which immediately begin to destroy the ozone. A single molecule of chlorine will destroy as many as 10,000 molecules of ozone, and bromine as much as 100,000.

With this terrible news, countries around the world began to take note. An international conference was convened in Montreal in September 1987 to lay the groundwork to phase out all known ozone-destroying chemicals. It was a beginning, but an uphill battle, as there had not been any worthwhile substitutes developed. Up to that time CFCs, halons and their compounds had been considered totally benign. They were non-toxic, odourless and easy to handle. Their use was widespread. In 1988, Canada produced about 20,000 tonnes of CFCs annually, about 2.5 percent of world production. Ontario used about 10,000 tonnes.

CFCs were used as the coolant in the common refrigerator as well as in all refrigerant and air-conditioning equipment (41 percent); blowing agents in foam product manufacturing (35 percent); cleaning solvents for electrical components (3 percent); spray can propellant (8 percent); and miscellaneous (3 percent). Halons were used mainly for fire extinguishers. Annual production quantities were small, but once released into the atmosphere they are ten times more destructive than CFCs. And since the early 1970s about 800,000 to 900,000 tonnes of ozone-depleting compounds have been dumped into the atmosphere every year. They migrate to the ozone layer where they may stay for a hundred years on a constant ozone-destroying mission.

Challenged by the proceedings and recommendations of the Changing Atmosphere Conference and motivated by all the information I had gathered on the destruction of the ozone layer, I concluded that there was a role for the City of Toronto to play. Toronto was a large city and used a lot of CFCs and other ODCs. Toronto led the way for other cities to follow. I proposed a motion at city council on September 6, 1988, to prohibit and regulate the manufacture, sale, distribution, use and disposal of certain products, material, and equipment containing or manufactured with chlorofluorocarbons and halons. Council supported the motion and instructed the solicitor to prepare the necessary bylaw. On April 6, 1989, council passed bylaw #230-89. It was the first bylaw anywhere to deal with the CFC and halon problem. Other cities and governments took note and developed corresponding legislation.

The Montreal Protocol set the stage for the worldwide phasing out of CFCs, halons and other ozone-depleting substances. They are no longer a major factor in global warming, as the phase-out program has been very successful. Their destructive impact is now a declining factor in the maintenance of the ozone layer.

REACHING ACROSS BOUNDARIES

I had many inquiries from all over the world about our bylaw. On July 21-22, 1989, I was invited by the Centre for Innovative Diplomacy (CID) to explain the Toronto bylaw to phase out ozone-depleting substances at the North American Conference for a Stratospheric Protection Accord held at the Bekman Institute of the National Academies of Science and Engineering in Irvine, California.

I had looked forward to the Irvine meeting, as I knew I would meet Dr. Sheldon Rowland and his ozone depletion research team. I was impressed by the amount and quality of research carried out by Rowland and his staff and the leadership they had provided. At Irvine, I felt completely at home, as many of the municipal politicians attending were like myself, searching for a meaningful role for First World cities to cross geographic boundaries to help the poverty stricken Third World cities and to clean up a mess — most of it of our own making.

SETTING UP ICLEI

The United Nations, following the International Union of Local Authorities (IULA) conference in Oslo, spearheaded a New York meeting to help organize world cities to fight pollution and common environmental problems. It was the first UN attempt to get cities involved in environmental activities. Toronto was well represented as the mayor and a few councillors lobbied other municipal representatives to set up a worldwide cities' organization. Thus, the International Council for Local Environmental Initiatives (ICLEI) came into being.

ICLEI set up its headquarters in Toronto. It was the first real attempt to link world cities and municipalities in a common effort to fight environmental problems and begin the laborious process of healing the planet. Since those early days, ICLEI has been instrumental in bringing together many of the major world cities. Its success lies in the co-operation of all these cities working together to protect the planet's fragile environment. The worldwide effort to implement programs for greenhouse gas reductions is one of ICLEI's top priorities. It is meeting with success in working with world cities and communities, although it has been a hard fight to convince many national governments to live within the new realities of less fuel consumption and more efficient use of energy.

THE BALTIC STATES

After the IULA convention in Oslo, Norway, I visited the Baltic States at the invitation of the cities of Tallinn, Riga and Vilnius to help bridge the gap on how we could help improve their municipal operations — particularly, water, sewage and garbage disposal.

I also visited the Ignalina nuclear power plant, in Lithuania, near the Belarus border, to have a look at its Chernobyl-type reactor. I prepared a report when I returned to Canada and sent it to Mike Wilson, who was our finance minister at that time. It eventually ended up with Ontario Hydro, which later helped with the management of the reactor.

Visiting the Baltics in summer was a wonderful experience. It was early July. Soviet soldiers were not too visible, but there was evidence of the street battles a few months earlier between the soldiers and the local people. Huge boulders had been brought in to block the roads into the old sections of the cities. Bullet holes were not repaired — they were like badges of honour. Flowers and candles marked the locations where young freedom fighters were killed.

When I saw soldiers guarding the statues of Lenin in Riga, Klepida, Tallin and Vilnius, I knew that it was only a matter of time before the Soviet empire would crumble. And it began to happen a few months later, when Estonia, Latvia and Lithuania declared their independence.

Comparing municipal services of all these Baltic cities in the Soviet system to our Western cities was a real eye-opener for me.

Most of the infrastructure for basic municipal services was sorely in need of maintenance, repair or replacement. On my return to Toronto and after the fall of the Soviet system a few months later, I was able to open up new relations with these Baltic States.

CHAPTER 9
From Rio to Kyoto: Getting Our Act Together

The June 1992 Rio de Janeiro Environment (Summit) Conference was labelled a major world event. It was promoted as the place where world environmental issues would hold centre stage. There was much promise for the future. We left Toronto on a fresh May evening, on a Canadian Pacific flight to Rio. The ten-hour flight was full of participants on their way to the Earth Summit Conference. After dinner, as we passed over the coast of Venezuela, the plane headed over the tropical Amazonian forests of Brazil. Occasionally, throughout the night, lightning flashes told us that we were over the vast Equatorial forests. Somewhere down below, loggers were waiting for the new day to begin cutting down trees, burning and opening up vast areas of Brazil for agriculture.

I began to think that it was much like the pioneer days, when settlers cleared and settled much of the land in North America. Now we wanted the Amazon settlers to leave their forests alone. The media was full of stories about deforestation and how these terrible Brazilians were destroying the last great tropical forest. It seemed strange to think of things that way. Land clearance was a fact of life in the history of North America and Europe. Back then, clearing the land for agriculture was part of the equation of life. But now it seems no one else — however impoverished they might be — should be clearing jungles and mangrove swamps to grow food crops.

We arrived in Rio in the early morning and went to the Meridien Hotel on Copacabana beach. The concierge told us that there was no need to go outside, as everything was available in the hotel. He also said that it was not very safe on the streets at night and we should be careful about getting into any cars masquerading as taxis. The doorman would get a taxi when we needed it. We got a taste of the ugly side of Rio when my wife and I went for a stroll, after an early evening meal, along the crowded boardwalk of

Copacabana. Two muggers who demanded my jacket and wallet jumped on me. This surprise attack immediately prompted me to fight back — which is the wrong thing to do. I was lucky to beat them off with the assistance of others, including a local sidewalk vendor, who came to our rescue.

Our attackers did not run or even move when the altercation was over. They just stood around waiting for the next victim. It was quite a hair-raising experience and a real damper on our first day in Rio. Needless to say, we were more careful and tried to blend in for the remainder of our stay in Brazil.

The morning after the mugging attempt, I met Jean Luc, the executive assistant to Mayor Jean Dore of Montreal. He had been in Rio for the last three months, helping with the summit organization. As I explained the happenings of the evening before, he blurted out, "I was mugged three times since I came here." He went on: "You have to blend in and not look like a tourist. I learned that the hard way."

I attended the ECO-URBS conference (May 24 to 28) in Rio's Hotel Nacional, prior to the summit. It focused on the environmental problems of large urban centres. It was not a great event but helpful as a meeting place.

Rio itself is a beautiful city when one looks down from Corcovado — the mountain with the statue of Christ the King. Tree-lined boulevards, curved sandy beaches and breaking surf looked so inviting from this high vantage point. But at ground level the reality of Rio is very different. The face of poverty is everywhere. Countless young children, abandoned on the streets, fend for themselves. Muggers and "helpers" prowl the streets and boardwalks, looking for "rich" tourists or anyone who looks like a good mark. The beaches of Ipanema and Copacabana are often polluted by the sewage from the millions of inhabitants. The drinking water often contains the sewage of a city with no treatment facilities. Notices about cholera and the need to be careful about drinking the water were posted in many prominent locations. So, despite its romantic geographical setting and its delightful climate, Rio bears all the ills of a neglected Third World city.

Rio was the centre for most of the activities for the Earth Summit. But there were other related conferences in the cities of

Curitiba and Sao Paulo, in which I participated. These conferences were designed to be helpful in the decision-making at the Summit itself.

The Curitiba Conference (May 27 to 29) was the place to debate urban issues and then bring the conclusions to Rio. Maurice Strong, a Canadian and chairman of the Summit, attended and helped increase environmental interest and discussions. When I met him there, I tried to find out if there was a structured agenda at Rio. He explained that the summit was designed to influence the heads of government and have them sign declarations on environmental issues. Some would be attending on different days and other major world figures, like U.S. President George Bush, were not fully committed to be there, so the agenda had to be very flexible.

Curitiba is very much like Toronto, an immigrant city and about the same size. The mayor, Jaimie Lerner, was a delightful host. He was very progressive in his approach to urban matters and was reputed to be the mayor of the best-run city in Brazil.

In the afternoon, on June 3, the first day of the summit in the Rio Centre, Montreal Mayor Jean Dore, Jaimie Lerner and a few other mayors were given about two hours to present the Curitiba Declaration, a statement of goals and objectives of a general nature. I doubt that it made much impact on the official delegations. The heads of state were far removed from listening to urban suggestions. For them it was an opportunity to get "green" points at home, have a few photographs taken and say nice things about the environment.

Aldona and I went to Sao Paulo to attend the SPECO 92 Conference (June 5 to 7) with the theme, "The University, Business Sector and Community in Regard to the Environment." We stayed at the Maxud Hotel. I presented a paper on Toronto's environmental work and the progress we were making. Nick Vardin, Toronto's commissioner of public works and the environment, also attended and participated in the proceedings.

After a meeting with the Civil Engineering Department of the University of Sao Paulo, Nick and I were escorted on a helicopter tour of the sewage system and water reservoirs. It was a real eye opener to see all the shanties or *favellas* on the slopes of the reservoirs. The human waste from the *favellas* finds its way into the reservoirs that supply drinking water to the city. I could then understand the reason for cholera signs.

Sao Paulo is an inland city of 18 million people and its sewage flows into a "reversible" river that flows through the city. Flying 1,000 metres above the river, there was no doubt that the smell was from the sewage flowing below. Our engineering colleagues told us that 92 percent of the sewage flows into this river as it tries to make its way to the ocean, about 60 kilometres away. Vardin and I appreciated the fact that we did not have such monumental sewage and water problems in our own city.

Sao Paulo also hosted an International Exposition of Environmental Technology (June 1 to 12). Toronto had a small booth to promote the city and generally to hand out information on how we dealt with water and sewage.

A regular air shuttle was provided between Rio and Sao Paulo to facilitate those attending all the conferences. Another unofficial summit, dubbed the Global Forum, was held in a downtown waterfront park in Rio and attracted about 30,000 people. This rag-tag collection of individuals, groups and organizations provided a real contrast to the Earth Summit at the Rio Centre. It also provided fun and excitement. It resembled a religious convention and exhibition, with many different directions and agendas, each pointing to the road to environmental Nirvana. The Global Forum, at least, got people together and this was an achievement.

But the Rio Summit failed because those heads of states who could make a difference did little. By and large their performances were passionless and lacked any real political motivation to change the present course of events for the future of the planet. Money, poverty, population control, education and the basic necessities for life such as clean water and sewage treatment should have been the benchmark for discussions and actions. The Earth Summit failed in every one of these issues.

Funds for war — little for life. Money is needed in developing countries to meet the basic necessities of life, yet world governments spend about $3 billion per day on armies and weapons of war. Most developed countries recognize this as a proper expenditure, even though there are really no major global conflicts.

Money is spent on plans for war and defense — it is a form of contingency planning and war insurance. This is a very basic failure in the character of the human species — the idea that machines and equipment to kill and maim take priority over the delicate work that must be done to ensure the survival of all living things and the health of our planet. If, in this climate of no major world wars, we could divert 50 percent of the moneys from the global military budgets, it would amount to billions of dollars per year. It could be spent to provide basic necessities and clean up the environmental mess. Imagine, wiping out waterborne diseases, poverty and protecting the natural beauty around us. Imagine, with research and development, how we could become energy-efficient and learn how to tap the power of the sun and use our limited fossil fuels more sparingly. This is only a dream, but it could happen if reason prevailed.

The failure of the Rio Summit to even discuss money spent on arms — never mind the reallocation of those funds to fight pollution and environmental ills — seemed to me to be an appallingly clear indication that we have failed in our stewardship of the planet. To achieve any real or meaningful results, funds would have to be channelled through non-governmental organizations (NGOs) and democratically elected governments.

Unfortunately many grants and loans to developing countries have been wasted. Millions of dollars have found their way into the pockets of crooked politicians, manipulators, middlemen, dictators and generals. Most of these Third World countries have been left with massive debts that they can never hope to repay. It would, therefore, be foolish to give money without some new guidance and rules on how it is to be used.

The World Bank and the International Monetary Fund have larger roles to play to ensure that all loans and grants are given for properly planned and engineered projects that will benefit the people who are in desperate need of help. As well, an international donor review organization, composed of leading world specialists in Third World aid, could be set up to advise on all projects. The efficient use of funds must be one of the main goals when aid is given to any country.

Poverty

Poverty is something that is glaringly obvious in developing countries. It happens mainly where a small percentage of the population makes up a ruling class that controls most of the land, wealth, and positions of power. A general characteristic of this is the absence of a middle class, with the vast majority of people poor and barely eking out a living. Land reform is another key requirement to overcome such poverty. It was easy for me to understand the real reasons why so many people were poor and why a small group of "outsiders" controlled the land. I had learned it all in my youth by studying the sad history of Ireland — and how the Irish farmers became tenants on their own lands.

The population of the planet in the new millennium has passed six billion and is increasing by 1.7 percent annually, with the greatest increases in the poorer countries. It does not take a mathematician or an accountant to figure out that more people means more poverty, more hunger and more misery. Imagine the impact an additional three or four billion people will have on the planet and the additional food, work, energy, etc. that will be needed to provide them with a reasonable standard of living. More people on the planet will bring greater air and water pollution as well as the destruction of most of the open spaces and forests we have taken for granted. The human species will, without doubt, hasten the demise of the planet as we know it. Population control must be promoted and developed, particularly through education.

Education

A good school system decides the economic health and direction of any country. Developing countries need tremendous help in organizing more and better education programs. A full education for all children is the catalyst for change and a better way of life. Education will provide more opportunities for employment and generally enhance the quality of life.

Sewage treatment and water supply

One of the most fundamental requirements for people is an adequate supply of clean water and sewage treatment. If these cannot be provided then waterborne diseases, such as diarrhea, cholera, typhoid, etc., will wreak havoc on vulnerable communities. About 65 percent of people in developing countries do not have access to clean drinking water and about 95 percent do not have proper sewage treatment facilities. The Earth Summit failed to address these very basic environmental issues. No amount of words, political rhetoric or good intentions will help, without the desire to work and develop these much-needed services.

To have a more practical view and search for accomplishments of the Rio Summit, it would be fair to say that all the agreements and conventions were broad-based, with no time frames and no definite commitment for specific action. Although 160 countries participated and most signed agreements, these agreements mean very little because of their limited nature.

The Earth Summit had five main areas of general discussion:

1. **Bio-diversity:** This is an attempt to protect the endangered plants and animals of the planet. Although the agreement was signed by most countries, the United States did not sign. The reason given by insiders was that George Bush (Sr.) felt it might interfere with U.S. economic plans — and besides, 1994 was an election year.

2. **The Rio Declaration:** This is a non-binding statement with many general observations that can be categorized as a "motherhood and apple pie" approach to environment. It spelled out in general terms that pollution is harmful to the environment. It did not go much further beyond saying that everybody should be environmentally responsible.

3. **Agenda 21:** This is a document of some 800 pages that calls for action to protect the environment while encouraging development. There is no time frame and it is so general that it means very little. It would cost about $125 billion a year to implement (under 10 percent of the global annual military budget at the time). The U.S. alone is now budgeting hundreds of billion for defence — and the military occupation of Iraq is incurring vast

additional infrastructure expenditures, supposedly to be paid out of Iraqi oil exports. In contrast, the United Nations suggested that just 0.7 percent of the annual GNP of developed countries should be set aside as aid for developing countries.

4. **Forest principles:** This is a statement on the protection of forests and is a non-binding document. It spells out how important it is — for economic, environmental and cultural reasons — to protect and regenerate forests.

5. **Global warming convention:** This document is a general statement on global warming and the impact of greenhouse gases. It sets out the Framework on Climate Change, which was supposed to lead to the stabilization of greenhouse gases by 2000.

Overall, the Rio Earth Summit could point to the massive amount of news and information generated by the conference. The world media provided tremendous coverage and people became better informed. Only in that context was it a success. When people meet and talk about such issues — looking at how the damaging impact of humans can be controlled — only then can Rio be considered a first step for global action. After listening to many speakers, meeting many like-minded people from around the world and reading many of the presented papers, I saw the road from Rio was paved with good intentions. Now the real work would have to begin to clean up the mess.

The final comment from all those environmentalists attending the summit ended up a few days later as sewage on the beaches of Rio. Perhaps it was not a fitting ending, but it was a glaring reminder of the problems. Aid to the underdeveloped countries peaked in 1992. It has steadily declined every year since. By 1997, according to the Organization for Economic Co-operation and Development (OECD), aid had fallen to $47.6 billion, one-fifth less than 1992, with no sign of a reversal in sight.

THE ROAD TO KYOTO

The road to the Kyoto Protocol, for all those well-intentioned environmentalists who had attended Rio, proved to be anything but smooth. It showed that there was little substance in any of the flashy statements made by the visiting leaders — the elected politicians — who could make it all happen. After Rio, it was an uphill battle for even the smallest environmental gain. One of the biggest disappointments was the total disregard for the reduction of greenhouse gases to combat global warming. It was as if the Rio Summit planned the increase of energy consumption and the production of more greenhouse gases.

Even the City of Toronto, which in 1992 wanted to play a small role as a First World metropolis, fell by the wayside. The Toronto Atmospheric Fund, together with CARE Canada and the Honduran city of San Pedro Sula, had developed a project. It would help preserve a watershed, control erosion, plant trees and help the *campesinos* stay on the land. Three years after Rio, the plan was in shambles — as were most other well-intentioned efforts. The Toronto Atmospheric Fund decided to abandon the project in 1995 and wind up its participation.

But many dedicated people struggled on and got together to salvage some of the good intentions of the conference. The Climate Panel began to work and hold together those countries that had made a commitment at Rio. All six Climate Panel meetings leading up to a Kyoto agreement were highly charged and emotional, with many leading environmentalists and big energy interests locked in bitter conflict. One group believed human activities were responsible for global warming, while the other believed there was little proof of a global warming doomsday scenario. And besides, organized oil and gas companies declared that cutting back on the use of fossil fuels would destroy the economy and hundreds of thousands would be unemployed.

The whole truth about global warming was not easy to find. But there was no doubt that human activities, since the beginning of the industrial revolution in the mid-1800s, had contributed heavily to a more polluted planet. Long-term measurements of carbon dioxide in the atmosphere had shown a steady increase since measurements were first recorded. The carbon dioxide measuring station at Mona Lau, in Hawaii, has been consistent in documenting the annual increases for the past 50 years.

Human history, as we know it, dates back only about 18,000 years to the end of the last ice age — a tiny speck in the four to five billion years of the planet's existence — but the evidence is clear that the earth has become warmer throughout most of that period. There have been mini ice ages and also warmer periods along the way. And it has been pointed out by some climate specialists that from about AD 900, when the Vikings were making their historic voyages to a North American "Vinland" (vine land), right up to AD 1300, the planet's climate was much warmer than it is today.

In much earlier times, about 300 to 400 hundred million years ago, when the atmosphere contained a very high percentage of carbon dioxide, a profusion of trees, plants and vegetation covered the planet. And as hundreds of millions of cycles of life and death produced layer after layer of decayed organic material, the planet's fossil fuel resources were slowly developed, as the carbon from the atmosphere became captive and locked in the fossil fuel deposits.

As we approached end of the century, the debate over global warming continued to dominate all the environmental discussions. An overwhelming number of world scientists supported a reduction in greenhouse gas emissions. But the U.S. — producing about 36 percent of the planet's greenhouse gases — fought against it every step of the way.

Finally, at the sixth Climate Panel meeting in Kyoto in December 1997, it seemed that there was some hope for an agreement on greenhouse gases. The Kyoto Protocol attempted to set legally binding targets for First World countries. The developing countries were not included. The expectation was that greenhouse gases would decrease in the developed countries — mainly in the northern hemisphere. And they would increase for the developing countries — mainly in the southern hemisphere. Overall, the rate of global warming would decrease, but the total annual volumes would increase. The target for Canada was to lower its greenhouse gases by 6 percent below the 1990 level. This would be achieved between 2008 and 2012.

Five years after Kyoto, in September 2002, Canada announced it would sign the protocol before the end of 2002. But Ottawa tried to claim further credits for exporting cleaner energy products to the U.S. market. The European countries would not agree with any tinkering like that. It is still not clear how Canada will achieve these reduction goals and even what those goals are.

According to published figures, Canada produced increased amounts of greenhouse gases every year to 2000 since the 1992 Rio Conference. But emissions decreased by 1.4 percent to 720 megatonnes in 2001.

The 2003 statistics show that Canada produced 740 megatonnes of greenhouse gases that year — a 24 percent increase over the 1990 total of 596 megatonnes. And 6 percent below that is 560 megatonnes. That is our target figure to be achieved between 2008 and 2012. It means a reduction of 32 percent below the 2003 figures. We are going the wrong way! We have to turn around and keep our economy strong at the same time. And it can be done. But it will take strong political leadership and a real commitment to do it right. That is a tall order. But with good will and cooperation, it may come to pass.

The greatest challenge to government efforts to reduce greenhouse gases comes from industry and particularly the energy-producing industries. The first reaction to any suggestion to reduce fuel and energy consumption is that it cannot be done; it would cost millions and it would destroy our economy. The Canadian Manufacturers Association (CMA) estimated it would cost at least $40 billion and 450,000 jobs over 10 years. Alberta led the opposition to the Kyoto Protocol, supporting the CMA's statistics.

Other estimates from those who supported the Kyoto Protocol showed that the benefits would far outweigh the present system of waste and depletion of energy and fossil fuels. Lower emissions meant less pollution and therefore better health. Whole new industries would be created to design and build more efficient materials and machines. And the efficient use of energy would change our whole approach to the way we live. The hybrid engine, making its own electricity with the help of its fuel engine, would replace the gas-guzzling popular automobile. Public transit would become a major means of travel. Building standards would be revised to minimize the use of energy for heating and cooling. Alternative energy would become a large new industry. The old ways of using more oil and gas would be over. And there would be something left for future generations.

Certainly, the fundamentals of our economy, as they relate to finite fossil fuel resources, will have to change. There is no indication that major industries and senior governments have the determination to address the efficient use of fuels and an overall energy conservation plan. The old economic system of waste and squander will be difficult to change. The Canadian commitments to the Kyoto agreement are just promises — like many political promises — that cannot be realized without a workable plan to meet the targets.

The structure of the economy must be adjusted to get more energy from less fuel — not more fuel for less money. And that means re-evaluating the fundamentals of our economy and the way we live.

CHAPTER 10
Global Warming and Greenhouse Gases

Carbon dioxide (CO_2) is only a tiny fraction of the earth's atmosphere, about 0.03 percent, or about 2,550 billion tonnes. It is a clear, odourless and harmless gas in normal quantities. But it constitutes about 50 percent of all greenhouse gases and is used as the measuring factor for global warming. Unfortunately, using CO_2 as a monitoring gas has taken the focus off the other, far more destructive greenhouse gases. They include small amounts of chlorofluorocarbons and various amounts of water vapour; methane (CH_4) — 17 percent; low-level ozone (O_3) — 12 percent; and nitrous oxide (N_2O) — about 6 percent. But the truth is that carbon dioxide, is far more benign than methane, chlorofluorocarbons, ozone and oxides of nitrogen. Methane, for example, on a molecule-for-molecule basis, is 21 times more destructive than carbon dioxide, and nitrous oxide is 310 times more destructive than carbon dioxide.

The last ice age produced a shrinking of the oceans, reducing sea levels by about 420 feet below where they are today. Then the planet began to get warmer and the oceans began to rise with the melting of the enormous ice sheets.

There have been many major variations in climate on our planet over the billions of years of its existence. And the composition of the atmosphere has changed enormously over these billions of years to its present composition, which nurtured the development of life on earth. These changes have occurred without anthropogenic influences, since the human species did not and could not exist in these early times.

Science has shown that human activities, since the mid-1800s, have contributed to global warming. These increases are small but steady. The rate of change, which does not allow sufficient time for gradual adjustment, is most alarming for most climatologists. And the actions of humans will continue to have an increasing impact on our fragile atmosphere as the rate of global warming becomes more noticeable. Humans can also help in reducing the rate of change by practising energy conservation and the efficient use of energy. This would help future generations adjust to and live with the consequences of noticeable climate changes. It would also expedite research in alternative energy development, which would extend the lifespan of our non-renewable fossil fuel resources. And future generations would certainly benefit from such changes to our wasteful ways. These achievements would be real victories.

The oceans are vast storage reservoirs or sinks for carbon dioxide. Trees and vegetation also absorb carbon dioxide from the air and are a major part of the carbon sink. As trees are cut down and not replaced, the carbon cycle is slowly changed as more carbon compounds stay in the atmosphere and contribute to the imbalance in its composition.

Natural disasters like volcanic eruptions and forest fires add huge amounts of gases to the atmosphere every year. And deforestation affects the world's green mantle like no other single intervention by the human species. Settlers have always cleared the land to open it for agriculture and pasture. That was how Canada, the United States and other countries of the developed world have used the land. With an ever-increasing global population, the developing countries are now clearing much of the remaining forests to meet their agricultural and fuel demands. We protest loudly about the destruction of the forests elsewhere in the poorer countries, while we have destroyed our own, long ago.

The atmosphere itself is a complex mix of gases that provide the delicate balance for life on earth. The major components are nitrogen (78 percent), oxygen (21 percent) and argon (0.9 percent), plus minute quantities of other gases, which include the greenhouse gases. Water is always present in the atmosphere and ranges from 1 percent to 4 percent. The magic energy properties of water are displayed in the hydrologic cycle that controls the climate of the planet.

The "greenhouse" label comes from the traditional greenhouse where sunlight penetrates the glass and heats the inside space. This heat is prevented from escaping to the outside by the glass enclosure. The rays of the sun, in a similar manner, penetrate the earth's atmosphere. Some of the solar energy is absorbed by clouds and by the surface of the earth, while the rest is reflected back to space as infrared energy. The amount of infrared bounced back to space is determined by the quantity of greenhouse gases in the atmosphere. These gases trap or absorb some of the escaping heat and help increase the temperature of the earth at ground level and in the thin film of atmosphere around our planet.

The burning of fossil fuels to heat, cool and power our homes, cars, trucks and factories pumps millions of tonnes of carbon dioxide, unburned hydrocarbons, carbon monoxide, oxides of nitrogen and smaller amounts of other toxic gases daily into our atmosphere. Methane is produced from decaying organic matter — landfill sites, dead wood and decaying plant and animal matter. And as the frozen tundras recede, in the global warming scenario, decaying vegetation and newly thawed swamp areas produce an enormous amount of methane, thus accelerating global warming.

Chlorofluorocarbons (CFCs), halons and other man-made ozone-depleting compounds (ODCs) are no longer major greenhouse gases since the successful implementation of the 1987 Montreal Protocol, which caused the worldwide phasing out of these ozone-depleting substances. But the ozone layer will take many decades to restore as the ODCs are still destructive and long-lasting.

Carbon dioxide readings in the atmosphere, recorded since the beginning of the industrial revolution in the 1860s, have showed a steady increase since the records began. There are many monitoring stations for CO_2 around the world. But the most ideally located station is in Mona Lau, Hawaii. The readings from Mona Lau are the most reliable long-term readings available. They have shown a steady increase in atmospheric carbon dioxide.

It is the accepted theory of many climatologists that the increasing levels of greenhouse gases in the atmosphere will warm the planet considerably over the next hundred years, perhaps by as much as 3°C. If this occurs, the polar ice caps will recede further and the oceans around the world will rise about six metres. This will cause untold havoc to coastlines and begin to destroy thousands of cities and towns around the world.

Monster hurricanes and typhoons, spawned by warm ocean waters, will add to the chaos. They will become more frequent and unpredictable. Low-lying coastal cities, if directly hit, will be wiped away. Delta river cities like Dacca and Calcutta will be hit hardest. The city of New Orleans and parts of Holland — below sea level, but protected by dykes and seawalls — will eventually have to be abandoned. Even cities like New York, Charleston, Jacksonville and Miami will not escape rising waters and howling winds.

Just for the sake of argument, let us assume, as some officials working for the fossil fuel industries have suggested, that global warming is a myth and a gimmick to convince the public to reduce the consumption of fossil fuels. If that is the case and the increase in greenhouse gases is not related to the increase in combustion of fossil fuels, then the current understanding of the role of greenhouse gases is wrong. What then will we have gained?

For most rational people, the reaction would be most positive and welcome. We would have contributed enormously by leaving a little more of our non-renewable fossil fuel resources for future generations. That would be a significant and meaningful contribution by a species known for its waste and selfishness and not for its charity and vision.

But the atmosphere cannot continue to absorb these large increasing doses of man-made gases and maintain its quality of life support systems. The conclusion is simple. Measures must be taken to slow down the process and nurture the atmosphere back to a state where life on earth could adjust to a smaller increase of greenhouse gases.

In July 1988, the Canadian government sponsored the Changing Atmosphere Conference in Toronto. The conference focused on the fragile layer of atmosphere around the planet. It was under severe stress and many were worried that it might get so polluted that it could not sustain life. I was delighted with the first small steps being taken by the federal government. I could understand the necessity for convening all those experts in one place to speak about the depletion of the ozone layer, the increasing amount of greenhouse gases and the gradual destruction of the world's forests.

I was sceptical that it would be just another conference staged by the federal government as political "window dressing." I felt that Ottawa was out of touch with what was happening to the natural environment. Environmental issues did not rate very high on the federal agenda. Dirty water, polluted air and piles of garbage were only problems in towns and cities. The government in Ottawa was remote and removed from these problems. I had witnessed 25 years of federal involvement. I just knew this conference would be part of their public relations program and little, if any, real action would happen.

I talked to as many participants as possible and found out that the buildup of greenhouse gases in the atmosphere would dominate the four-day conference and the media coverage. I made it my mission not to let this moment escape. The message from the 500 experts was clear and well-documented. Global warming was here and we had better be prepared to deal with it. We could not afford not to act. And we had to act fast. The 39 recommendations were well-defined and crafted at the final meeting. For me, they were a clarion call for what had to be done. At the conclusion of the conference, Stephen Lewis, an avid supporter of environmental issues, expertly chaired the development of the final position. The adopted recommendations included the following:

- Reduce carbon dioxide (CO_2) emissions by 20 percent below 1988 levels by 2005;
- Reduce deforestation and increase reforestation;
- Establish a World Atmosphere Fund to help finance solutions.

I immediately set about developing a process to implement some of the recommendations at Toronto City Council. I was determined that Toronto would not fail, as it had in the past, but would play its part and lead the way. My vision for Toronto was clear and simple. Toronto would prepare a program to clean up our mess by adopting one of the main recommendations of the conference — reducing CO_2 emissions by 20 percent below the 1988 levels by the year 2005.

A plan for reforestation, especially in Third World countries, would include a major education effort to help keep the people on the land, control erosion and grow the trees and shrubs best suited for that area. Toronto would also lead the way by giving a helping hand to the poorer cities of the Third World. If we were to avoid a future crisis, this reaching out had to be done as soon as possible.

Traditionally, cities like Toronto had only twinned or exchanged expertise with cities of the same stature. It was twinned with Amsterdam and had friendship arrangements with Frankfurt, Lisbon, Warsaw and a few other cities. When it was called on by Ottawa to help in their foreign programs, it became part of a federal team effort. Toronto helped in Lima and Sao Paulo through such a program. But Toronto had never led the way where help was needed.

SPECIAL ADVISORY COMMITTEE ON THE ENVIRONMENT (SACE)

After the conference, my first action was to locate the key Toronto participants and find out if I could put a team together to implement the relevant recommendations. My thinking was to set up a Special Advisory Committee on the Environment (SACE), made up of local environmental experts. They would prepare a plan for Toronto, based on the recommendations of the conference.

I spoke to Dr. Ken Hare, who suggested that I should contact Dr. Harold Schiff, professor of atmospheric chemistry at York University, as a starting point. I arranged a dinner meeting with Dr. Hare and Dr. Schiff. We met at the Sutton Place Hotel, where I outlined my plans to have the City of Toronto follow through with an action plan on the conference recommendations. At first, they were sceptical that a local politician could do a great deal. I got the feeling that they did not expect much action and that this would be just another political act that would go nowhere. But they were willing to listen and give some advice.

Finally both agreed to participate, but would not lead any program. They were too busy and overloaded with work. Besides, they wanted younger people to become involved.

They suggested I talk to Danny Harvey and Phil Jessup. They thought that they could provide the drive to make a city action plan work. Harvey, a professor of geography at the University of Toronto, had taken a keen interest in environmental issues and had authored many papers on global warming. Jessup, planning director of Friends of the Earth, had a well-rounded knowledge of environmental issues and was particularly interested in transportation and fuel efficiency.

I met with Danny Harvey a few days later. He was excited by the possibility of Toronto embarking on such a plan. We then spoke to Phil Jessup and together laid the foundation for the formation of the Special Advisory Committee on the Environment (SACE) to begin an action plan for Toronto.

I was ready with a proposal for a September meeting of city council. It approved our proposal to establish the committee, with a per diem allowance for the ten members. Harvey and Jessup were appointed co-chairmen. I acted as the liaison between city council and SACE.

The committee's primary mandate was to advise city council on ways to reduce Toronto's emissions of greenhouse gases and air pollution, with emphasis on the efficient use of fuels; air conditioning and heating of buildings; pollution from automobiles and other air pollution matters.

After a year's work, in October 1989, SACE produced its first report, "The Changing Atmosphere: A Call to Action." The plan for action by the City of Toronto was ready. It supported and expanded on the many recommendations of the Changing Atmosphere Conference. Its key recommendation was endorsing the 20 percent reduction in CO_2 levels below the 1988 levels by the year 2005, and the steps the city must take to meet that objective. The report was referred to the affected departments, for comment to the first meeting of the City executive committee, in January 1990.

I wrote to the executive committee on November 3, 1989, outlining my general support for the SACE report. I realized that to make any new moves to curb energy waste and become more energy efficient, money had to be available. I, therefore, proposed additional recommendations that dealt mainly with finance and how to pay for the changes recommended in the report:

1. Set up the Toronto Atmospheric Fund with an initial deposit of $23 million or 20 percent of the proceeds of the sale of the Langstaff Jail Farm — which the City had just sold.

2. Request the Province of Ontario to introduce legislation for a 10 percent Carbon Release Surcharge (CRS) tax on all fuels and electricity used in Ontario.
3. Request the federal government to introduce legislation for CRS.
4. Use CRS funds to develop non-polluting energy alternatives and increased energy efficiency in the use of fossil fuels.

After public deputations before the city executive in early January 1990, the report went to city council. The process at City Hall was quite slow. It was January 30th before it received final approval, but approval was unanimous — even my recommendations were passed.

Toronto had become the first city anywhere in the world to adopt the 20 percent CO_2 reduction plan. It put our city in the forefront of energy and environmental matters. Our reputation began to emerge as that of a modern city that worked — leading the way for all other cities to follow. Toronto was becoming the Mecca in matters relating to environmental issues. Other recommendations, mostly organizational and administrative, like setting up the energy efficiency office, were in-house matters and could easily be done. The carbon release surcharge (CRS) tax was another matter entirely. It proved to be very difficult to convince the provincial and federal governments to impose such taxes to achieve the energy efficiency standards we were aiming for and expedite the development of non-polluting energy supplies such as solar, wind and water.

THE TORONTO ATMOSPHERIC FUND (TAF)

When city council supported setting up the Toronto Atmospheric Fund it was the beginning of a long-drawn-out encounter with the provincial government. We needed provincial legislation to make it possible. I worked with Dennis Perlin, the city solicitor, and his staff all the way through. Some days I thought it would never happen. The provincial lawyers were most careful not to give anything to Toronto that might infringe on their territory or allow the city to offer better incentives for industry to locate in the city.

Provincial officials were also very careful that the legislation would not hurt other Ontario municipalities. I found them sceptical of Toronto's intentions throughout the process. Rosario Marchese, a government member of Parliament, introduced the bill for the Toronto Atmospheric Fund. Marchese understood what we wanted and he was very supportive of our efforts. The legislation received first reading on June 30, 1992, and was referred to committee for hearings. At this stage the staff of the Municipal Affairs Ministry and the city solicitor had cleaned up the wording and the details of the bill.

The committee hearing went smoothly and Bill Pr45 received second and third readings and royal assent on December 10, 1992. The act setting up the Toronto Atmospheric Fund and the Toronto Atmospheric Fund Foundation were now in place. The objectives were clearly set out in the legislation:

- To promote global climate stabilization by the reduction of emissions of greenhouse gases and greenhouse gas precursors into the atmosphere through public education, scientific research and technology development;
- To promote public understanding of global warming and its implications for the urban environment;
- To create and preserve carbon sinks;
- To promote energy conservation and efficiency;
- To provide support and funding for projects related to energy efficiency and global climate stabilization in co-operation with non-governmental organizations, governments, industries, corporations, official committees, neighbourhood organizations, universities and public and private schools.

The board of directors consisted of ten members — four from the public, three from council, plus the medical officer of health, the commissioner of finance and the commissioner of public works and the environment.

When city council received permission from the province to set up TAF, I was elected chairman of TAF and the TAF Foundation. After our first organizational meetings we adopted a mission statement and set up the financial role of the TAF with the $23 million from the sale of the Jail Farm.

The mission statement adopted the objectives, as per the legislation, and outlined the philosophy associated with the objectives. It set two broad strategic directions — to reduce CO_2 emissions and to remove CO_2 already in the atmosphere.

One of the key elements of the mission statement was the flexibility of location so that work could be in the Toronto region or at a distance. The statement noted: "In the developing world, initiatives could profitably tie into and encourage NGOs or social agencies, forestry initiatives in the third world. It is the intention of the TAF to support these kinds of initiatives."

Two types of projects would be eligible for funding.

Type 1 projects would receive up to 50 percent funding without returning any money to the fund. These projects could include research, studies, demonstrations, conferences, training and education.

Type 2 projects would receive up to 85 percent of the project cost and would be paid back to the fund within eight years for operating projects and within 15 years for capital projects. The rate of return would be at least equal to the rate of return of a Government of Canada Bond for the same period. A business plan would be provided showing those cost savings will be at least 1.15 times the debt services.

FIRST MAJOR FUNDING

Once the Toronto Atmospheric Fund had been established it was time to begin the real work of saving energy. Our first project was to fund the replacement of the 42,000 incandescent streetlights in the City of Toronto. This was a joint project, with the City funding the project and Toronto Hydro supervising the work. What type of lighting should be used was a battle in council. Eventually metal halide (MH) won out over high pressure (HPS). Council looked at many different types of lighting and took a long time to come to a conclusion. Meanwhile the City lost $1,621,000 in grants from Ontario Hydro because of its tardiness. On January 27, 1993, Ontario Hydro reduced their grants incentive program for street lighting from 24 percent to 15 percent.

I supported HPS lighting. My arguments were drawn from the fact sheets presented by our staff that HPS was $6,710,000 cheaper than metal halide. Annually, HPS was more energy efficient and needed less maintenance than MH — to the tune of $2,350,000. HPS had a solid track record in street lighting, but it looked too yellow for many people, who thought that it was a poorer quality of light. Metal halide's big attraction was the very bright white blue light it produced, whereas HPS had a soft yellowish tinge. Council decided on metal halide after a long debate. Electrical Contractors Black and Macdonald won the contract at a price of $14.8 million.

One of the projects I wanted TAF to become involved in was to reach out to some Third World city and give a helping hand for a basic service. This would be in keeping with the spirit of the just concluded Rio Conference. And our terms of reference in setting up the fund allowed us to do that. I contacted CARE Canada and ended up meeting Tom Hammond, the officer of CARE assigned to Central America. We decided to look at some of the neediest cities in that part of the world and then choose one for our first project.

The idea was simple enough. TAF would provide some money and guidance, the NGO would manage the project and invest some money and the local municipality would have a small investment and be fully involved in the planning and development of the project. I visualized a project with a little of everything: protecting a watershed, controlling erosion, planting trees, educating and working with farmers on crop development and keeping them on the land.

I persuaded Danny Harvey to join with me in a fact-finding visit arranged by CARE. We visited CARE projects in Costa Rica, Guatemala and Honduras. After our return we met with Tom Hammond and decided that the ideal project should be with the city of San Pedro Sula, in Honduras. Hammond carefully prepared the plan for a working partnership between the Toronto Atmospheric Fund, CARE and the San Pedro Sula water department. The project was ideal — it had everything to meet all our criteria. The mountains to the north of San Pedro Sula included the catchment area for the water supply for the city. The cutting down of the hillside trees by local *campesinos* led to extensive erosion. This hampered the water supply and was destroying the land.

Tree nurseries were needed to supply indigenous saplings. The *campesinos* had to be given basic agricultural education and shown how to plant and harvest the best-suited crops for the land.

Tom Hammond made a presentation to the Toronto Atmospheric Fund Board on June 18, 1993, for the first year of the three-year project. The board approved the project and allocated $200,000 for the first year. Matching funds would be provided by San Pedro Sula and CARE. The TAF board also recommended "that funding for the second and third years be considered by the Grants and Loan Committee." It was assumed that there would be no problems and funding would be available after a successful first year. The total commitment of TAF would be $600,000. With the framework now in place, it was time to begin the real work.

REACTION TO THE HONDURAS PROJECT

About a year after the project began, and everything was going well, I read a front page story by David Lewis Stein in the *Star* on June 25, 1994, lambasting TAF for the expenditure in San Pedro Sula. Stein made a big issue of who would own the trees in San Pedro Sula. He totally misunderstood such a project, following the Rio Summit. I was surprised because I expected more from the *Star*. When local politicians read the article, especially six months before an election, they were immediately hostile to the project, saying that it was a waste of money that could have been better spent at home. The *Star* article was followed by an article in the *Globe and Mail* on August 16 by writer John Barber. He had picked up the Stein spin on the story — proclaiming that the trees should have been planted in Ontario, rather than in some foreign country.

By this time the remnants of the Rio Summit of June 1992 were in tatters. It was as if it had never happened. The rich countries had abandoned any meaningful commitments they had made. The gap between the rich and poor was widening and getting worse. It was devastating for those who had concern for the future environmental heath of the world. The way was now clear to destroy the San Pedro Sula project. Toronto would not be the leader or catalyst to lead the way to help the poorer cities of the world. Our meager attempts to take leadership and begin to repair the planet were shipwrecked on the shores of our selfish abundance. Paradoxically, the attacks were from those who constantly preach the brotherhood of man and the need to reach out to help our wounded planet.

When the subject of second-year funding came before the TAF board, I soon found out that it would be impossible for the project to continue as planned. Councillor Peter Tabuns now declared a conflict of interest as he stated his wife had some relation with CARE. The TAF board, after some discussion, decided to postpone the matter until after the November 1994 municipal election. I was not re-elected to council in that election and had no opportunity to influence the San Pedro Sula project after that.

After the election, with Councillor Dan Leckie as chairman, TAF wound down the project and gave a "go away" donation of $50,000 to CARE Canada. For me it was a sad end to a most worthy cause.

Cameron Smith, an environmental writer whose column appears in the *Toronto Saturday Star*, later decided to visit the Honduras project in early 1996. After visiting the San Pedro Sula site, he wrote an account of the project, calling it "the most impressive undertaking of its kind that I have ever seen." He stated that the project was so successful for the local area that other centres in Honduras were planning to copy it.

I have had little contact with TAF since I left municipal politics. My contacts are mostly gone or doing other things. But I do attempt to keep abreast of what is happening to the fund and how the money is used.

With the introduction of electricity deregulation in Ontario, it was timely to re-evaluate the role of TAF, as it was becoming a bit of a slush fund for those who had access to City Hall. As an example, TAF gave $1,000 to the first ten purchasers of natural gas taxis — literally convincing the taxi propane users to switch to natural gas! Does the gas company need to be subsidized? Why not fund other alternative fuel vehicles where financing is really needed.

TAF deserved a complete review on its tenth anniversary. But that did not happen. TAF would be much more effective if it teamed up with Toronto Hydro and provided a service to customers like the Sacramento Municipal Utility District (SMUD).

BETTER BUILDINGS PARTNERSHIP (BBP)

The City set up the Energy Efficiency Office (EEO) to co-ordinate all activities and assist the private sector to use energy more efficiently. Many projects have been completed successfully. But the first ones were related to City-owned facilities and buildings. There could be no excuses, as the work was there to be completed without any reference to outside decision makers. The City had to show leadership and convince the private sector that what was good for the environment was good for the economy as a whole.

As the street re-lamping got underway, Richard Morris of the EEO, with the help of funding from the Toronto Atmospheric Fund, decided that the private sector should also be promoting the retrofitting of a large number of their buildings in Toronto. There were many large downtown buildings that were not energy efficient. And they were costing their owners a bundle. The time was ripe to get them involved. Morris and his group knew that. With a little push and a few examples, it makes sense to save money and energy.

Meetings with building owners and the Building Owners and Managers Association (BOMA) convinced them that there was money to be made by using energy more efficiently and at the same time reducing the amount of greenhouse gas emissions. It all made sense and it benefited the environment. It was a win-win for all. Building owners began to realize that energy efficiency retrofits could make their buildings more comfortable and more competitive and would save energy and money. The costs would be recouped through the energy savings over a reasonable time period.

Since the beginning of the BBP program in 1994, tremendous progress has been made — and it is just the beginning. By the beginning of 2003, participants had already invested more than

$60 million. Eventually the BBP program could have a full-scale economic impact of $3 billion.

With the involvement of over 150 buildings, by the beginning of 2003 the BBP had already reduced energy consumption by more than 100 x 10^6 kWh. And it had achieved a CO_2 reduction of 70,000 tonnes. By 2005 the BBP expected to reduce CO_2 emissions by more than three million tonnes. The Toronto Dominion Centre at 77 King Street West, with five million square feet built in 1969, reduced CO_2 emissions by 35,000 tonnes, with savings of $5 million annually. First Canadian Place at 100 King Street West, with 2.7 million square feet, built in 1974, reduced CO_2 emissions by 27,000 tonnes, with savings of about $3 million annually. Even City Hall at 100 Queen Street West, with 560,000 square feet built in 1964, reduced CO_2 emissions by 6,600 tonnes at a savings of $570,000 annually.

The BBP has been an example of city leadership, without much fanfare. It shows that with a little imagination, co-ordination and direction, much can be accomplished in the overall battle for energy conservation.

With the federal government's commitment to the Kyoto agreement, which came into effect in February 2005, the work, leadership and example of the BBP should be a major help to the federal government to meet its GHG targets before 2012.

CHAPTER 11
Water: The Story of Life on Earth

The story of water is the story of life. The sun, gravity and water — the trinity of life, all life — have made it possible for our species, the highest form of life, to exist with other forms of life on planet earth. Without water, this planet would be a bare, barren and lifeless dust bowl. Whether it is the Archimedes screw, the Eastern *shaduf,* the Roman aqueducts, the water wheels of long ago or the early canals of primitive man, the human endeavour to provide and harness water, where and when it is needed, has been a struggle through the ages.

While the role of the sun and gravity can be explained through science, water is a baffling element that "plays" with the basic laws of physics. It is because of its magic properties and its ability to rigidly obey some laws and totally ignore or bend other laws that it baffles most people who try to understand the most simple, complex and contradictory qualities of this liquid key to life.

The water molecule consists of two atoms of hydrogen and one atom of oxygen — H_2O. Although this molecule sounds simple, given that hydrogen and oxygen are two of the most common elements, their joining together forms an incredible bond that ensures that the "marriage" lasts — even as liquid, vapour or solid.

But it is the tough, aggressive and scrappy qualities of the hydrogen atom that dominate the molecule. Water molecules are held together through strange and paradoxical properties that are unlike any other compounds. As a liquid, the molecules merge in a placid and easy manner — easily sliding over each other — giving water its liquid characteristic. As a vapour (steam) the molecules become detached and irritated, taking up much more space as the temperature increases. And as a solid (ice) the molecules are rigidly bonded together to form hollow rings, giving ice its bulk and allowing it to float.

Seventy-four percent of the earth's surface is covered with water. According to many estimates, planet earth has 1.4 billion cubic kilometres of water. Most of that water, about 97.6 percent, is in the salty seas and oceans. The other 2.4 percent is stored in ice caps, underground rock formations, aquifers, lakes, rivers, vegetation and the atmosphere. About 0.25 percent of this fresh water is readily available for human use.

Water is the common, universal solvent in the daily lives of humans. Most compounds, held together by electrical or ionic bond, easily dissolve in water. But a few elements — the most common, oil — will not bond or mix with water.

Pure water does not exist naturally — it always contains impurities — traces of other elements and substances. Sea water, for example, contains between 3 and 4 percent of sodium chloride (salt), which makes it salty. And as the vapour in the atmosphere falls to earth as rain, it picks up many impurities and trace elements.

One of the most significant and contradictory properties of water occurs when its temperature falls. Almost all substances contract when temperatures decrease. At temperatures above 4°C, water obeys that rule. But at 4°C water begins a complete reversal — it begins to expand and get lighter. At 0°C it turns into ice and gains about 9 percent in volume. In other words it is heavier as a liquid than as a solid. It is this unique property that provides enormous benefits for the existence of life on earth as we know it. If ice were heavier than water, it would freeze from the bottom up. Very soon life would disappear from earth as the oceans, rivers and lakes would become solid ice, which would radically change the workings of nature as we know them.

Through the sun-powered hydrologic cycle, which provides for its endless circulation and distribution, water obeys the fundamental laws of physics — what goes up as vapour must come down as water. As the sun heats the surface of the earth it vapourizes water, which expands and rises into the atmosphere where the winds, temperature and gravity complete the cycle. It is estimated that thousands of cubic kilometres of water are distributed through the atmosphere at any one time. This constantly moving and ever-changing amount of water favours some fortunate areas where life abounds and avoids others where deserts prevail. This regulates the earth's climate and has a direct influence on all life on earth as the planet's winds set in motion predictable and at times marauding masses of enormous amounts of energy.

The energy properties of water are enormous. It is used to produce over 95 percent of the world's electricity — either through falling water, hot water or steam. In hydroelectric plants the head (height) and volume of water decide the amount of electricity produced. The industrial revolution, in the eighteen century, was ignited by the development of the steam piston by Swedish engineer Carl de Laval. He showed that when water is converted into steam, it expands as much as 1,600 times, providing another application of water to produce energy. The modern refinement of the steam turbine, using superheated steam, is the workhorse of electric power production whether fossil or nuclear fuel is used.

But in its role as the instrument of life, water seems to ignore the basic rules of gravity in what is called capillary action. This can be shown when water rises in a circular tube. The smaller the circumference of the tube the higher the water will rise. This happens when the hydrogen atoms of the water molecule strive to attach to the oxygen or nitrogen atoms of the material of a circular tube wall. To make that contact the molecule is dragged up by the aggressive hydrogen atoms in the molecule, giving water the ability to defy gravity and creep uphill. This enables water to nourish living matter, like trees and plants. Even the blood of living creatures, including humans, is aided by capillary action.

The human body is about 70 percent water. It is a complicated machine that requires constant attention and maintenance. It cannot survive without water. It takes about three to four litres per day to keep all the organs working properly. Breathing carries air to the lungs where the oxygen nourishes the blood. Arteries carry the blood to all parts of the body through the pumping mechanism of the heart. Sweat glands help maintain body temperature. Glands protect and lubricate the eyes. And the kidneys are used as the body's treatment plant to maintain, nourish and clean the blood flow.

The life-giving qualities of water are known to all. But water can also bring death and massive destruction. On December 26, 2004, an earthquake registering 9 on the Richter scale occurred in the Indian Ocean, off the northern tip of the island of Sumatra.

It spawned a massive tsunami, which hit that area, wiping out Banda Aceh — a city of 300,000 people and the capital of Aceh Province. Travelling at 500 kilometres per hour, it hit the coasts of India, Thailand, Sri Lanka and the exposed coasts of Indonesia, other Indian Ocean islands and the coast of Africa about seven hours later. Over 200,000 people were killed and millions more were left homeless.

In its placid forms, water can also bring death to humans, as deadly bacteria and viruses survive and multiply there. History has recorded many plagues where communities and populations were wiped out by waterborne diseases.

The contamination of the drinking water of the town of Walkerton, Ontario, in May 2000 led to the death of seven people from E. coli bacteria. But, although it caused a lot of soul searching, with every political party pointing the finger at the others, the sad fact is that the most basic water and wastewater services do not merit much attention — until a disaster happens.

The provision of an abundant supply of clean water should not be a problem for any community in Canada. We have plenty of water and the technology to guarantee its wholesomeness. Perhaps it is not a politically glamorous issue, since we take its supply and purity for granted. Besides, proper water supply systems and sewage treatment plants cost a lot of money to build and operate. But these are necessities that, collectively, we cannot do without.

TORONTO'S WATER HISTORY

The first major well in Toronto was dug by a private contractor in what is now the St. Lawrence Market area — a short distance from the old Toronto Jail, in the vicinity of the old Consumers Gas building, on Toronto Street. Private companies tried to supply water in the early years, but with little financial success.

In 1843, the Toronto Light and Water Company, following an Act of Parliament in 1841, began to distribute water to households through wooden pipes, laid within the street allowance. At that time Toronto had more than 150 kilometres of roads and only 30 kilometres of water pipe.

The water was piped from Blockhouse Bay, where larger wooden pipes were submerged and extended into the lake. Very often, after a major storm the wooden pipes would be uprooted and left floating on the top of the water. Major repairs were required. It was an amateurish attempt to supply water. At that time most water was contaminated as the technology for water treatment and supply was far from perfected.

Over the next 15 years, the company changed hands, but by 1858, only 900 of the 7,500 homes in the city had piped water. The water system had little capacity — just 50 hydrants with minimal pressure — and it was little use against the fires that razed many of the older wooden buildings. Ironically, the original Parliament Buildings had been burned down by American invaders in the War of 1812 — in retaliation for which Canadians torched the White House in Washington (it was painted white to hide the scorch marks).

Clearly, all cities desperately needed an efficient means of piping water, but the Ontario Parliament did not give Toronto power over its waterworks until 1872. The city then began to lay the foundation for a major water supply system.

As research in hygiene increased, and Pasteur discovered bacteria, it became evident that water contamination was the cause of many diseases. The need to develop a constant supply of clean water became a requirement for every community. Toronto built the Island Water Filtration Plant in 1910, with cast iron pipes to the intake, a half-mile offshore. The John Street pumping station was built to distribute the water in cast iron pipes under city streets, marking the beginning of a modern water supply system for the city. Many downtown streets use these same cast iron pipes to supply today's water needs.

The provision of an adequate supply of clean water also had to keep pace with the increasing population. By the mid-1990s, three water filtration plants, with a total capacity of about 2,497,000 cubic metres per day (cmd), or 550 millions of gallons per day (mgd), were in operation — the RC Harris Plant, the Easterly Plant and the RL Clarke Plant. In 2003 the Island Plant had been brought back into service as part of the Deep Lake Water Cooling system. Toronto also provides water to parts of York Region and has water reservoirs located in that region, mainly to provide adequate storage and pressure for the water distribution system.

United Nations statistics show that 50 million people die annually from drinking contaminated water. These deaths occur mainly in Third World countries, where there is little if any understanding of how deadly dirty water can be. Another 3 billion people — half the world's population — do not have direct access to clean water. The problem is that water supply systems, especially for small communities, need a lot of capital investment. Without proper guidelines, technical equipment and fully trained staff, they are always vulnerable to accidents that can be fatal.

The provincial inquiry into the Walkerton disaster was far-ranging. Justice O'Connor laid down a new framework for the provision of an adequate supply of drinking water and the treatment of wastewater. As the politicians and civic unions pointed fingers at each other — each trying to cast more blame — it was evident that the collective responsibility lay with everyone involved in the water supply business. The unions did their utmost to turn the tragedy around to show it as an example of what would happen if private contractors or non-government staff were responsible for the water supply. In the Walkerton tragedy, the public system failed. But the simple facts of Walkerton have little to do with public or private service delivery.

It did, however, reflect on the inability of the Ontario government to enforce their guidelines to ensure that clean water is available to all communities. Essential services should be available, whether from public or private interests. Walkerton was a local utility, operated by the municipality under the jurisdiction of the provincial legislature. The town of Walkerton was directly to blame for the tragedy. But the province must share some of the blame for not been vigilant and active in monitoring the services provided by the local water utility.

The Walkerton Inquiry made many recommendations that should be used to develop further guidelines for water supply, but the basic requirement to ensure safe drinking water at all times should be self-evident:

- The sampling of water — both raw and after treatment — must be carried out at regular intervals;
- Water must be collected and tested by duly recognized laboratories;
- Treated water should be free of bacterial or fecal coliform;
- Wells should be located where farm drainage cannot contaminate the water;
- Surface water, such as rivers and streams, must be properly protected from runoff from farms and sludge-type fertilizer;
- The chemical content of treated water must be within the maximum acceptable concentrations (MACs);
- All treated water samples showing a coliform count or excess MACs must be reported immediately to the Ministry of Health (MOH), the local municipality and the Ministry of the Environment (MOE) and the supply of such water must be withdrawn immediately;
- Ontario must review the role of sewage sludge on farmland and particularly the problems caused by farm runoff, which can contaminate surface water, wells and local water supplies;
- Residents must be advised immediately of any contamination;
- Ontario should set up a Clean Water Fund to deal with emergencies. It could be funded by a surcharge of half a cent per cubic metre from all utilities.

Most of the above are already regulated criteria. The problem is monitoring and enforcement. Municipalities, after the Walkerton tragedy, are now creating procedures and directing qualified staff to regulate and control water sampling and quality control.

Municipalities process new developments in different ways, but the final objective is the same — to have zero coliform and bacteria in the treated water. All water for bacteria testing is sent to a provincial lab for testing. However, some municipalities allow private sector companies to take water samples. This opens the door to potential misuse. But large municipalities have their own qualified staff take the samples and then analyze the samples.

The design of new systems and the improvement of existing water mains must be reviewed and approved by the MOE. Drilled wells for individual homes do not need MOE approval. But any water system that draws 50,000 or more litres per day and/or provides water for five or more residences must follow MOE design guidelines and have MOE approval prior to construction. In addition, all systems that require MOE approval must also follow MOE guidelines for testing. For example, there are different levels of decontamination for the different volumes of water drawn by systems. Systems that draw 50,000 litres per day, or service five residences or more, must have a chlorination system and provide contact between the water and the chlorination system for a certain amount of time to ensure proper decontamination. In addition, the water must be sampled on a predetermined schedule by staff that is qualified by the MOE.

COST OF WATER AND SEWAGE TREATMENT

Up to 1982, the federal government, through Central Mortgage and Housing Corporation (CMHC), provided two-thirds of the financial assistance, at low interest rates, towards the construction of trunk sewers, pumping stations and sewage treatment plants. A large portion of the loan was also forgiven. This was an attempt by Ottawa to expedite improved treatment of sewage in towns and cities across Canada. In the late 1970s the federal government let it be known that it was getting out of the financing of sewage projects. It was a blow to municipalities as they scrambled to find other sources of funds. Queen's Park was still active in providing financial assistance through various programs to expedite the building of new sanitary sewers and separating combined sewers, but the economic squeeze was evident as provincial funds diminished.

Rumblings were rampant that a pay-as-you-go or user-pay system was on the way. Metro councillors discussed at length the concept of a user-pay philosophy for the cost of water pollution control facilities. Metro finally, in 1974, introduced a proposal. The idea was simple enough, in that a surcharge would be added to the cost of water sold to the six constituent municipalities of Metro. This charge would help in the piping and cleaning of the contaminated water at the sewage treatment system. The surcharge would increase annually until it eventually paid all the costs of wastewater treatment. On March 26, 1974, Metro Toronto asked Queen's Park to enact legislation to permit the municipality, by July 1, 1974, to add a surcharge to the wholesale cost of water. On June 24, 1974, the enabling legislation received third reading and Royal Assent.

To avoid the impact of applying full costs immediately for pollution control projects, it was determined that the percentage applied to the cost of water each year would be gradually increased, from 10 percent in 1974, until the amount of the surcharge would pay for the water pollution control system. The 1975 surcharge was set at 15 percent and continued to increase from there on until the total cost of water pollution control was covered.

The Metro Works Committee report on May 6, 1975, states, "We consider that the principle of offsetting costs of water pollution control by a surcharge on water rates has been well established and that in the final analysis when the total cost of water pollution control is recovered by that means, the user of the water pollution control service will be paying proportionately for such use."

At that time, the City of Toronto also collected development charges for sewers for all new developments over 3,000 square feet. This fund, known as the sewer impost fund, helped defray some of the sewer replacement costs. Since the old city had an aging combined sewer system, the needs were totally different from those of the newer surrounding municipalities, where most of the new sanitary and storm sewers and water mains were built under a "Plan of Subdivision." Developers included the cost of servicing in the sale of the lots. As the newer, mainly dormitory communities of Scarborough, North York and Etobicoke began to develop, the Ontario Water Resources Commission required separate sewers. The wastewater went directly to the sewage treatment plant and the storm water was carried in separate storm sewers to the nearest watercourse or stream.

In 1967, the City of Toronto embarked on an ambitious 25-year sewer separation program, at a projected cost of $125 million. The program was completed on schedule in the early 1990s with funding from various sources. Since the City of Toronto did not have access to lot levies or other residential developer charges, the costs were debentured and charged to the general tax base. The provincial government granted subsidies based on a complicated formula tied to the diameters of the sewers and directly to road drainage. The Metro Toronto Corporation also provided a subsidy for all sewer separation projects, since the sewage treatment plants would have less effluent to treat.

It was easy for municipalities like Mississauga, Markham and Vaughan to gloat every year about no increase in taxes. They were simply adding to their coffers from the enormous lot levies — moneys that were, in reality, coming from the buyers of new homes, factories and industrial buildings in their municipality.

In some residential areas, when sewers replaced septic tanks, the costs were debentured for the specific project and collected through the Local Improvement Act from those properties benefiting directly, and not from general tax revenue.

The financing for the development and operation of water and sewer services has been securely laid by Metro and the City of Toronto over the years. The total revenue collected through the water surcharge system from 1966 to 1988 was $107,065,000. From 1989 to 1995 it was $94,800,000. This amounts to $201,865,000 collected over the past 30 years from water surcharges. The City of Toronto adopted its surcharge of 22.7 percent in 1966 under authority of the Municipal Act. The city's surcharge on water from 1967 to 1975 was set at 18 percent.

When Metro began with a water surcharge in 1974, it brought the cost of water to the municipalities up to 6.05 cents per cubic metre. Some local municipalities then added an additional surcharge to cover part of their costs for sewers and sewer maintenance. All these surcharges were increased annually. By 1996 the Metro surcharge was 24.85 percent, bringing the cost to 38.58 cents per cu. metre. The costs of the development, maintenance and operation of sewer systems are now permanently tied to the cost of water. The cost of water to a household in Toronto was $1.05 per cu. metre by the year 2000. By 2005 the cost of water had risen to $1.26 per cu. metre. That is just 0.126 of a cent per litre! By comparison, imported bottled water, which is popular in city restaurants and cafés, costs about $2.25 to $3.50 per litre.

A WATER POLICY FOR CANADA

Over the years I have noticed much political turmoil on how to handle our water resources. Politicians have not been able to agree on a practical water policy. With 32 million people — about 0.5 percent of the world's population — Canada is endowed with about 20 percent of its fresh water, although only about one-third of that is readily accessible. So much water! That makes us rich beyond the wildest dreams of those who have to eke out a daily existence in developing countries. Yet we have not been able to understand the stewardship of this precious gift.

With more than 6 billion people on earth, the migration of many looking for a better life and the widening gap between the rich and the poor are adding to the tensions of an unsettled world. Most do not have access to the basic necessities of life, which we take for granted, or know what a daily drink of clean water tastes like. But history has shown that the actions of humans can be cruel and selfish. The survival of the fittest has always been at the forefront in the development of nations. Those who have a lot will strive to amass more, while those with little or nothing will constantly fight to survive. We Canadians are hoarders and wasters, like our neighbours to the south.

We have to treat water as a resource to be wisely shared for the benefit of all living things. Fortunately, nature decides the distribution of water and how it moves on our planet, without the artificial boundaries of sovereignty. Altering the natural boundaries, for the most part, is difficult, but not impossible.

Many people find it illogical that we sell our non-renewable oil and gas resources, which took hundreds of millions of years to develop and will be squandered by the end of this century, and say no to selling water — a renewable resource that can never run out. That contradiction is part of a very troubling understanding of resource management. It needs a thorough review and should be explained to the general populace — if there is a rational explanation. It is probably driven by a small group of self-proclaimed water experts preaching to an elec-torate that knows little about the rest of the world and the abundance of our water resources.

Yes, we should have a practical national policy on water. The responsibility for resources rests with the provinces. Water is a resource and as such its distribution and management is a provincial responsibility, within our borders. But the federal government has jurisdiction over water as it related to fisheries, navigation, export and the waters along the Canada–U.S. border.

Bulk shipments of water — especially from the Great Lakes — make little economic sense, as the water is not fit for drinking without treatment and the Seaway charges are expensive. It would be much more practical for anyone looking for a water supply to build a desalination plant. Many large coastal cities now rely on such plants.

Canada is such a vast country that water use and water needs change with the landscape. The attempt by the province of Newfoundland and Labrador to sell bulk water from Lake Gisbourne caused an uproar in a few segments of the broader Canadian community. It demonstrated how impractical it is to have one inflexible policy in Canada and the need to support the provinces in managing their resources within their boundaries. Bottled and bulk shipments of water should be permitted with provincial approval.

INTER-BASIN TRANSFER

Taking water from one basin to another was a practical way to guarantee the existence of a community in ancient times. But it did not happen without much investment and hard work. Water has always determined whether a community flourished or died. The Romans, Incas, Persians and a host of other civilizations were experts at building aqueducts and water supply systems to provide water by gravity. There are many examples of massive stone aqueducts from Roman times and there are expert examples of underground water systems in many Middle Eastern countries still in use today.

The diversion of water from one sovereign nation to another is a different story, as any attempts to transfer water in large quantities through diversions would cause political turmoil. But there have been proposals, given the projected water shortages for irrigation, especially in arid regions of the United States and Western Canada.

These proposals have never passed the proposal stage because of the enormous costs and the jurisdictional hurdles. The International Joint Commission (IJC), under the Boundary Water Treaty Act of 1909, has allowed small diversions over the years.

The Great Lakes watershed is 1,070,000 square kilometres. Since Lake Ontario is located at the end of the chain, it receives all the upstream water, spilling over Niagara Falls and on to the St. Lawrence River — carrying a mean annual flow of about 7,800 cu. metres (or 7.8 million litres) per second, as it flows through Cornwall to the sea.

As Lake Michigan is entirely within the territory of the U.S., the Chicago River diversion — to carry the water wastes of the city down the Mississippi River — was a unilateral decision of the U.S. Chicago wanted 10,000 cubic feet per second (cfs) — about 280 cubic metres per second (cms) — and had reached that amount over the years until the U.S. Supreme Court stepped in and set the limit at 3,200 cfs — (90.56 cms) — in 1967. Canada had no say in that decision.

The Longlac and Ogoki diversion from the James Bay basin into Lake Superior was approved by the IJC, since Lake Superior is common to both countries. On the other hand, once the St. Lawrence River passes Cornwall, it picks up the Ottawa River and the other smaller Quebec rivers. It carries about 14 million litres per second as it flows through Quebec to reach the sea. That leaves Quebec (and Canada) with sole jurisdiction over the waters of the St. Lawrence River.

Yes, water is precious. We could sell, barter and trade it, if the market is available and our domestic needs are protected. It is like lumber, grains and other crops, a wonderful natural resource that is forever being recycled and renewed. Water will always be the simple magic key — the liquid manna for life on earth.

On October 12, 1999, we celebrated the arrival of the six-billionth person on earth, according to UN estimates. From the shantytowns of Africa to the *favellas* of Brazil, the migration of poor people looking for a slice of a better life increasingly dominates the news. And increasing populations and the widening gap between the rich and the poor add to the turmoil of water supplies. Most of these unfortunate people do not have access to the basic necessity of life — clean water.

The United Nations, through its Convention to Combat Desertification, is monitoring the declining supply of water for Third World countries. As the populations of these countries continue to increase, the impact of too many people has led to the depletion of wood fuel supplies; soil erosion from the cutting down of trees; little knowledge of conservation; slash-and-burn agricultural methods and increasing desertification. Areas in Africa and China — especially areas near to the advancing deserts — are the most vulnerable.

As we reached the new millennium, the desert areas of the planet were increasing by 3,500 square kilometres per year. That was up from 1,560 square kilometres in the 1970s.

Even at the local level, some municipalities with abundant water oppose any exports to adjacent municipalities. The municipality of Collingwood, drawing water from Georgian Bay, sends water south to municipalities such as New Tecumseth and Allison. It objected to the pipeline proceeding further south to meet the water needs of other municipalities. There are also pipelines running north from Toronto to service areas in York Region and Durham. But there are always political and environmental obstacles to overcome. And concerns are raised by local politicians that moving water from one region and sending it to another will create an environmental imbalance for the exporting area.

But since water is constantly recycled through the hydrologic cycle, the decisions on water distribution depend entirely on planning and the ability of politicians to understand the role of water. A global perspective on the use of water is best seen in the Middle East — the cauldron of present-day Arab/Israeli conflicts — where water is mainly drawn from streams but mostly from underground aquifers. As development occurs downstream and thus at the deepest point of the aquifer (downhill, so to speak), water is consumed faster than the aquifer is being replenished. This has caused many wells upstream in the aquifer to dry up. And in turn this has unfortunate consequences in regions where technology and even-handed planning has little influence and political power decides everything. As such, many communities have disappeared when water is used as an instrument of conflict.

MANAGING TORONTO'S WATER SUPPLY

Generally, Toronto's water supply is well-managed and well-maintained. The four water treatment plants use a basic filtration system. The submerged intakes provide a reasonable supply of raw water, which must be further treated and cleaned before it is distributed into the water mains of the city. On reaching the filtration plant, travelling screens are used to capture stray material from the lake through the intake tunnel. Water is then pumped into the process where pre-chlorination, coagulation, flocculation and sedimentation occur prior to filtration by rapid sand filtering. Post-chlorination and fluoridation then take place before the water is pumped to the storage reservoirs.

The city's laboratories analyze about 300,000 samples each year, just to make sure that the supply meets all the guidelines for physical, chemical and bacteria content. People who drink bottled water do so because of their reluctance to accept minute and different amounts of chemicals in the standard Toronto water. They usually prefer water with no fluoride, chlorine or other minute quantities of toxic materials. And besides, it is the "in thing" to drink bottled water.

There have been many epidemiological studies carried out over the years on the impact of long-term ingestion of trace toxic substances. Queen's Park, Ottawa and the World Health Organization have all adopted guidelines for drinking water and set maximum acceptable concentration for chemicals and impurities in water. The water I prefer would not contain any substances considered by many water specialists to be injurious to health over a long period.

My recommendations for an improved quality of water for Toronto include the following:

> **Fluoride:** The cumulative impact of fluoride over a number of years is now considered to be harmful to bone structures and joints. Many recent studies throughout the world have noted the health impact of water with high fluoride content. Toronto adds fluoride to its water — at the rate of 1.0 milligrams per litre or 1 part per

185

million. The ideal tap water for Toronto should not contain fluoride. The $1 million spent every year to add fluoride would be better spent handing out free fluoridated toothpaste to schoolchildren and teaching them better oral hygiene.

Chlorine: There is no doubt that the use of chlorine as a disinfectant in water filtration plants has been most beneficial in destroying bacteria. In smaller doses, it has been effective in the distribution system, where it prevents the growth of bacteria. Chlorine does not kill viruses. And it also forms chlorinated organic compounds in water, which are carcinogenic. They are known as trihalomethanes (THM). The prime water disinfectant should be ozone. It has been the disinfectant of choice in most countries outside of North America. Ozone kills viruses as well as bacteria. But ozone has no residual qualities like chlorine — it disappears very quickly. Small doses of chlorine should be used in the distribution pipes and reservoirs, when required.

Aluminum: Aluminum should be removed from drinking water, as there is some concern about a possible link to Alzheimer's disease. Ontario Drinking Water (ODW) guidelines are 0.1 milligrams per litre. Many water researchers would feel more at ease if the aluminum guidelines were further reduced.

Hardness: Increase the hardness of the water by adding calcium carbonate and magnesium. There is much medical evidence that hard water is much more beneficial and leads to less heart disease (Royal Free Hospital, London and Water Research Centre study in the 1970s, published in the British Medical Journal in 1980). The finished water product may be carbonated or non-carbonated.

Bottled water: In 1998, Toronto made an agreement with Molson's Breweries to bottle a Toronto beer, using Toronto water, of course. But after a few years it faded away. I wish Toronto had gone a little further and looked at the potential of developing a saleable Toronto water product to compete in the marketplace with imported bottled water. It is needed far more than beer. Toronto should enter a partnership with a bottling company and market a designer water to compete with the highly priced imported bottled water found at all Toronto restaurants. The product would be a winner. At least we would know exactly what it contains. It would be far superior to any of the high-priced imports we have become addicted to.

CHAPTER 12
Sewage: Contamination Seeps In like a Plague

When water is contaminated by sewage or other foreign substances that make it unfit for human use, it is called wastewater. Two of the basic ingredients for the viability of any community are a good water supply and the proper sewage treatment of wastewater. The people of Walkerton found that out in May 2000 at great cost when a serious outbreak of waterborne E. coli bacteria hit the Ontario town. It made some 2,000 sick and seven people died. For many it was the straw that broke the camel's back — the political end-game in a lengthy history of water pollution and disease that had plagued villages, towns, communities, towns and cities alike down through the ages.

Drinking water, sewage and disease have been tied together in a dance of death since the beginning of the human race. Whole communities have been wiped out by waterborne diseases. The plagues we read about in history were invariably spread or worsened by dirty or contaminated water.

EARLY HISTORY

Poor hygiene and epidemics appear to have been linked. Just over 150 years ago cholera, typhoid, diarrhea and many other scourges of the time were thought to be incubated by dirty water and generally unsanitary conditions. Scientists of the day were loud in their call for better sewage treatment and the need to use clean water.

In 1775 Alexander Cummings patented the first S trap for a toilet. A simple application, it prevented the return of odours from the sewage holding tank of the toilet. Joseph Bramah improved it a few years later by installing a valve in the centre of the bowl. The royal houses of Europe, in the 1800s, began to look for some invention that would do away with the bed pan, as well as outhouses and smelly street ditches. Inventors from many cities took up the challenge. Although the water closet (WC), with a flushing mechanism, as we know it today, was developed by Sir John Harrington for Elizabeth I in about 1597, it was not until the late 1800s that it became popular. The nobility were the first to embrace these conveniences, as Queen Victoria encouraged this new sanitation.

In 1851, George Jennings displayed his monkey closet at the Crystal Palace Exhibition in London. It was the forerunner of the wash-out toilet and became a huge success. Jennings is best known as the father of public washrooms. Following his great success at the exhibition, towns and cities across Britain began to install public toilets. S. Stephens Hellyer was another great promoter of better sanitary facilities. He improved the Bramah valve design of 100 years earlier with his own invention of the Optimus. The Optimus was so popular among the nobility that all of the European gentry wanted them installed in their homes. Queen Victoria had them installed in Buckingham Palace, Windsor Castle and the House of Commons, to mention a few locations. About 1875, Daniel Bostel of Brighton developed his Excelsior wash-out. This was followed in 1881 by the National — a wooden enclosed wash-out designed by Joshua Twyford. By this time competition was fierce as toilets were so popular.

Enter Thomas Crapper, about 1884. He was the most flamboyant and successful sanitary inventor of his age. His business pitch was "Crapper's valveless waste preventer — certain flush with easy pull." As a salesman, he was superb — and the best toilet promoter of the 1800s. His models had such names as Niagara, Cascade and Deluge. His major invention was a mechanical shut-off for clean water when the toilet tank was full. Crapper installed the drains and sanitary system in Sandringham Palace between 1886 and 1908. He is regarded as one of the pioneers in sanitary engineering. The word "crap" is understood by most English-speaking people. It was introduced to the language by returning American GIs from World War I who could not escape the name Crapper emblazoned on most English toilets.

Urbanization or the growth of towns and cities was encouraged by the arrival of the industrial age in the mid-1800s. More people and poor sanitary conditions meant more diseases and epidemics.

A way had to be found to clean up the smelly wastes from the human body. Cities had to invent and create public facilities for the public good. Most large cities arrived at those conclusions around the same time. Paris, Berlin, London and hosts of other cities hired engineers and builders to construct sewers to take the dirty effluent away. But it still meant that the effluent was dumped into the nearest river or body of water.

The latter years of the nineteenth century saw the development of the septic tank. It was a simple invention, built of concrete in a covered box-like shape with a divider across the middle and located about 50 feet from the dwelling. The house drains flowed into it. The solids settled to the bottom where anaerobic action took place. The liquid drained off, through to the receiving tile beds, where it percolated through a sandy soil. The septic tank provided the first early attempt to treat domestic sewage and replace the outdoor privy. It became popular and the new way to treat sewage in the early years of the twentieth century. It was the beginning of the development of the modern sewage treatment plant, using nature to neutralize human wastes.

In 1899 the first major biological treatment plant was built in Paris. That opened up the twentieth century with an effective system to address the basic needs of exploding populations in urban areas. The French, through their research in hygiene, followed by the Germans, British and Americans, continued to lead the way, and the sewage treatment plant concept became the goal of every city in the Western world.

By the end of the nineteenth century, most of the developed world had adopted the activated sludge process for the treatment of sewage. The building of sewage treatment plants took a little more time, primarily because of the costs and the political unease about building costly underground collection systems and smelly treatment plants, which has little political appeal. Unfortunately many world cities, as we begin the third millennium, still have not taken the steps necessary for the full treatment of sewage.

Toronto, unlike the great European cities, was in 1831 a town of just under 4,000. It was a struggling little hamlet, surrounded by bush and wilderness on the shores of the deep and cold Lake Ontario. Like all other outposts and settlements, the trickle of immigrants slowly took root and the town began to grow. In those early days, disease and malnutrition plagued the population. The town leaders had no knowledge of how to deal with sewage and did not know that dirty water was a carrier of disease. The provision of clean water was sporadic. As sewage flowed into the lake, it contaminated the lake water close to shore — sometimes called "bathtub rim" contamination — the same water used for drinking. And good hygiene was not evident in many of the homes of this fledgling community.

It was easy to contract the various waterborne diseases that were prevalent in places where people lived close together. Bacteria and viruses were unknown. The vast majority of people lived in what we would now call squalid conditions. People began to suspect that there was a relationship between polluted water and disease. In 1831 all buildings had outside privies. In some cases wooden drains carried the sewage to the street where side ditches collected the flow, which found its way directly to the nearest watercourse. Drinking water was usually taken from the Humber and Don rivers and other streams, as well as Lake Ontario. The more affluent homeowners dug wells on their property. Here at least the aquifer had acted as a filter for their drinking water supply.

Drinking water was easily contaminated by sewage. Few people suspected that cholera and typhoid — which became serious problems with the arrival of coffin ships from the Irish Famine in the late 1840s and 1850s — were related to sewage seeping into their drinking water. Although medical doctors and engineers suspected that waterborne diseases were related to the consumption of polluted water, it would be many years — and million of lives lost — before towns and cities around the world began to build proper wastewater systems and water treatment facilities for their inhabitants.

Like all towns and cities everywhere, early Toronto had the same sanitation problems. Waterborne diseases were a scourge. As urbanization and population increases brought more people in close contact, the disposal and treatment of body wastes eventually became a preoccupation with politicians. This resulted in the development of the public health system and the recognition of the need for proper sewage treatment.

Although many of the ancient civilizations had developed systems to provide clean water from distant hills and carry away sewage outside the walls of the building or town, it was not until the latter part of the nineteenth century that any real progress was made.

All new houses built around Toronto after 1920 were required to have septic tanks. The lots had to be large and the soil had to be sandy and porous. The standards set by the provincial authorities were rigid and supervised by health departments. The building and maintenance of septic tanks became big business in the early days of the developing municipalities surrounding Toronto. Septic tanks are widely used today in rural areas where there are no community treatment plants. They are an ideal replacement for the outdoor privy.

The City of Toronto, with its outdoor backyard privies and patchy understanding of sewage, began to focus on building sewers in the 1880s. By 1900 the city had over 300 kilometres of sewers. Homes and other buildings were connected to these sewers. All of the sewers were brick construction and many replaced the old wooden drainage systems. Some old brick sewers are still in use today. Unfortunately the sewers ran directly into streams and gullies and then into the lake, where they contaminated the drinking water. This caused many outbreaks of typhoid and other diseases. The city council was inundated with complaints from citizens about the pollution of the lake and its health-related problems. Reports were commissioned by a troubled council to solve the problem.

SEWAGE TREATMENT

Sewage treatment followed much the same pattern as developing the water supply system. Once disease and dirty water were proven to be related, the Toronto councillors began to take matters more seriously. Finally, after much debate, a sewage treatment plant was approved and built in the Ashbridges Bay area in 1913. The city also approved $2.4 million for the construction of trunk sewers and high and low-level interceptor sewers, connected to the Ashbridges Bay treatment plant, to service most of Toronto and planned future developments.

A small sewage treatment plant of 6 million imperial gallons per day (mgd) capacity was built in 1929 adjacent to the Don River in the north Toronto area to service that section of Toronto. The early sewage treatment plants were basic primary plants with a simple secondary treatment. That meant that the primary system consisted of settlement where the solids sank to the bottom and were removed. The secondary system consisted of the aeration of the liquid with a good supply of air to begin the biological action. The solids and sludge were hauled away to the dump and the liquid was discharged into the nearest watercourse or lake.

Later on, as technology improved, the sludge was further treated for 8 to 15 days in large sludge digesters where anaerobic action took place. Methane was produced during the process and fed to the fuel system to help run the plant. After the digesters, the sludge was dewatered using presses. It was then hauled away to landfill sites for disposal.

As the municipalities around Toronto began to grow, smaller sewage treatment plants were built to meet local needs. Most of these plants were less than 1 million gallons per day and were located next to a stream. By the mid-1950s, Toronto and the adjacent townships were adequately served with sewage treatment plants. But the plants could not handle the huge volumes of sewage combined with rain water after a heavy rainstorm. Consequently much of the overflow carried raw sewage, which polluted rivers and streams and ended up on Toronto beaches where people went for recreation during the warmer months. Engineers and planners — with the support and guidance of the Ontario Water Resources Commission — developed new plans to relieve the treatment plants from such heavy flows after every downpour.

From about 1954 onwards, sewers would be separated. The newer communities of Scarborough, North York and Etobicoke, developed since the mid-1950s, had separated sewer systems. The formation of Metropolitan Toronto, from 16 municipalities in 1954, required the new council to take over the provision of water and the treatment of sewage for the whole Metro area. It inherited the sewage treatment plant at Ashbridges Bay and the North Toronto plant in the City of Toronto, plus 12 smaller plants — all handling less than 1 million gallons per day, serving the outer areas of Metro Toronto. This led to the present-day treatment plants, which are looked on as among the finest anywhere.

Storm sewers now carry rainwater — runoff from roofs, roads, sidewalks and other surface areas to the nearest watercourse, river or ditch and then to Lake Ontario. But sanitary sewers carry only liquid wastes that could be biologically treated at the treatment plants. This provided for greater control at the treatment plant. For economic reasons, these two pipes may occupy one trench.

But the City of Toronto, York and East York, being older communities, struggled for 40 years to find sufficient funds to separate their sewers. The City of Toronto embarked on a 25-year sewer separation program in 1969. It was completed in 1992, with the exception of a few combined sewers that were too expensive and too complicated to separate. But York and East York, because of their smaller financial base, were not able to complete their sewer separation programs. As part of Metro's long-range plans for sewage treatment, the Ontario Water Resources Commission (OWRC) directed that upstream plants should be phased out and that sewage be treated in large plants on the lakefront. Metro proceeded to build the Humber plant, and later on the Highland Creek plant, to comply with the rules of the OWRC.

By 1994, Metro operated four sewage treatment plants (STPs) to treat up to 1,490,000 cmd (330 mgd). The main STP at Asbridges Bay, the largest, could treat 817,000 cmd (180 mgd); the Humber STP, 400,000 cmd (90 mgd); the Highland Creek STP, 200,000 cmd (45 mgd); and the small North Toronto STP, 33,000 cmd (6 mgd). The treatment plants meet all the environmental requirements of the Province of Ontario, with primary and secondary treatment as well as additional tertiary treatment for the removal of nutrients such as phosphorus. The final effluent is chlorinated and released into the lake.

DESIGNING STORM SEWERS

The design of the storm sewer is not as precise as the design of the sanitary sewer, as rainwater and runoff can vary widely in different geographical areas and at different times. The basic design is based on the amount of water of a rainstorm of two- to five-year intensity. The intensity varies for different areas and the system is designed to carry volumes of water over the tributary area during the two- or five-year storm intensity.

City of Toronto storm sewers were designed for a two-year storm event because many of the city's sewers were combined sewers. All new developments were later designed for a five-year storm event. The city also developed criteria to handle certain parts of storm water infrastructure to relieve the type of flooding that occurred in 1986 and 2000. The city had about 100 major combined sewer overflows (CSOs) at the end of 2000 and its new wet weather flow master began to address these CSO problems.

The different ground cover of the tributary area also affects the design of the system, because different surfaces have different absorption abilities. So this will also determine the size of piping used. For example, asphalt, concrete and roofs have no absorption ability and water will just run off. However a field or grassy area will slowly absorb the falling rain and will not allow the water to stand unless the ground is already saturated with too much rain. All these surface conditions have to be taken into consideration when designing a storm sewer. It is not precise because of the unpredictable nature of rainfall, but it can handle the runoff from rainstorms that occur every few years. These rainfall intensities are on record and provide the historical data for the design.

Built-up areas, with a lot of roofs, roads and paved surfaces, increase the volume and velocity of runoff. Such areas are responsible for the dangerous flash flooding of streams and rivers after prolonged heavy rain. These floods raise the water tables and surcharge sewers. Therefore, engineers must design outlets to control the release of water from the new developments at the same rate the water was being conveyed before development. This is done by sizing the outlet pipe to restrict the flows. However, this will generate a backup of water, which then needs to be controlled. This is done by creating surface storage ponds or other areas on roofs or parking lots to handle the storage of storm water for a short length of time — until the piping system can handle it.

Finally, storm sewer systems must also release water that is relatively clean. This is to mitigate the environmental contamination of the open watercourses. The major contaminant is sediment, which is released uncontrolled into the watercourse. If the storm water is contaminated it will kill fish and other aquatic life.

Municipalities, the Ministry of the Environment (MOE) and the Toronto and Region Conservation Authority (TRCA) all have storm water quality guidelines for different conditions. These approval agencies are particularly important when development occurs in environmentally sensitive areas. In Toronto, all rivers and streams are designated as sensitive areas. And there are many areas throughout Toronto that are regulated under the TRCA.

All new residential, commercial and industrial developments must construct storm water management facilities to provide runoff quality and quantity control. When land is not available to install these facilities, or the area of development is relatively small, underground tanks are used. These tanks are designed and built to the requirements and specifications of the MOE and the TRCA. The TRCA has review and approval authority for municipalities that surround Toronto — in the Toronto watershed. Many of the rivers and streams that flow through Toronto to Lake Ontario have their tributary areas outside of the boundaries of the city, and so control of these tributary lands is important to Toronto.

Hurricane Hazel, in 1954, caused many deaths and enormous destruction — but it also helped the understanding of flood control, especially in heavily built-up areas. And the Conservation Authority set the building levels, called flood planes, below which no buildings can be built.

All sanitary and storm sewer pipes should be below the frost line — providing a minimum of coverage for the piping. The minimum coverage in the Toronto area is two metres. And all basements must be above the level of the sewers on the street. If not, sewage and rainwater would back up into the basement.

DESIGNING SANITARY SEWERS

Sanitary sewers, usually made of concrete in the past, are now all polyvinyl chloride (PVC) except for large diameter trunk lines, which are still made of concrete. These sewers are designed to carry the liquid wastes of a residential community and the amount of effluent from commercial and industrial buildings in the area. The size and therefore capacity of existing sewers decide the limits of a development. This is a key factor in planning — whether in an old or new development. The first question that must be asked relates to the capacity of the existing sewer system to handle the proposed development. The other question, equally important, relates to whether or not the sewage treatment plant has the capacity to treat the expected new volume of sewage. New sewers can be built or a treatment plant can be enlarged to treat more sewage. It may be a simple question of economics, if the development is big enough to justify the major changes to the existing sewage treatment plant.

For new areas, where development is planned for 10 to 20 years or more of growth, the sanitary sewer system is designed and built to accommodate future growth. Planning also includes the design of sewage treatment plants to accommodate predetermined future volumes as development comes online. The larger downstream sewers are built first to the sewage treatment plant. These first pipes are larger pipes and more expensive — since the end pipes are designed to accept the sewage from future development. Future development must share in the costs of the oversized pipes and the treatment system.

Municipalities often control this by setting up a fee system for development charges to pay for this infrastructure. These fees are also used to maintain and upgrade the existing systems. The size of the system places a cap on the number of people who can live or work in the area.

Designing a sanitary sewer system for a community has become a standard procedure for engineers. First, the number of people it serves decides the capacity or size of the sewer. The standard design figure is 400 litres per person per day. Sanitary sewers — usually made of PVC or concrete — are designed to service a maximum number of people in a specific area. This is one of the essential criteria used as a planning tool for development. And since sewer systems are costly, it is a constant concern to ensure that the sewer pipes are laid in such a way that gravity flow leads to the treatment plant. If that cannot be done, a force main, using pumping equipment, has to be included in the system to pump the sewage to a higher level, where gravity flow can take over again. The minimum grade of the sewer line should not be less than 0.7 percent, although it can be as low as 0.4 percent for large pipes.

If the grade is low, the solids in the sewage may not move in such a flat grade and partial treatment takes place in the piping. This will cause odours in the vicinity of manholes and become uncomfortable for pedestrians. Low-flow toilets in the six- to ten-litre range, on a street with flat sewer grades, may also add to the odour problem. The grade of the sewer line also decides the volume of liquid the pipe will carry. The steeper the grade, the more volume it will take — up to a point. A system usually begins with a ten-inch diameter pipe at the top of the system, and the pipe diameter increases as more volume is added.

But sewers can also be installed too steep, and there is a calculated maximum slope allowed for sewers, where the increase in steepness no longer increases the capacity of the sewer. The design of sanitary systems, including pumping stations, and sewage treatment plants must conform to city standards and meet the approval of the MOE.

DETENTION TANKS

In the early 1980s, the closing of the many Toronto beaches to summer bathing was common and became an irritant to those who liked to be in or near the water. Although the sewer separation program was on target, a small number of sewers could not be separated. After heavy rain, the overflow was still finding its way into the lake. City engineers were asked to provide solutions.

In May 1987, consulting engineers James F. McLaren and Gore and Storie were hired to examine the possibility of building detention tanks for the Eastern Beaches. These tanks could capture the big flush from the few remaining combined sewers after a downpour instead of emptying pollutants into the lake. After the rain, the water in the holding tank would be pumped to the sanitary sewer and channelled to the Ashbridges Bay sewage treatment plant.

After extensive local consultation, city council approved the building of a 2,250-cubic-metre detention tank. The contractor, S. McNally and Sons, began construction in September 1989 and completed the contract in June 1990. Total cost was $4,091,391. The Ontario Ministry of the Environment paid 50 percent of the cost, with funds from the Toronto Area Water Quality Improvement Program.

The system worked very well. The Eastern Beaches became pollution-free during the summer months — unless a massive storm brought so much rain that the sewer system and holding tanks were not capable of handling it.

The city decided that the same approach should be taken to clean up the Western Beaches. But that would be a bigger, more difficult and more expensive detention system. It also had the added problem of an enclosed narrow stretch of calm water between the breakwall and shoreline, which has proved a good incubation area for water contamination. Eight major combined sewer outlets dumped into the lake between Strachan Avenue and Parkside Drive. They overflowed 20 to 50 times every year — dumping about 2.9 million cubic metres of contaminated water into the lake. The Western Beaches are the most polluted in the city, and are posted as unsafe for swimming by the Toronto Board of Health for most of the summer months.

By 1991 city engineers began preliminary designs for the detention tanks. The costs were estimated at about $80 to $90 million. That was a prohibitive amount, without outside help, for Toronto taxpayers. While the politicians and engineers agonized over the cost, it became clear that a sizable amount of financing could come from the newly announced Federal Infrastructure Program. If Toronto could get a corresponding response with some innovative ways to save money from the builders of the system, the City could fund the remainder.

It was then decided to call for a "design-build" project. It had been used successfully in the private sector as a way of getting the best end product for the lowest cost. Simply stated, rather than calling for tenders in the traditional manner, the City would call for proposals under specific guidelines to design and build a detention system to meet all the objectives of the engineers. The first attempt to call for a design-build proposal resulted in the lowest bid of $74 million. This was 30 percent above the estimate of City engineers.

The City could not afford to proceed with this design. The excess cost was based on 95,000 cubic metres of storage capacity in a 5.5-metre diameter tunnel, four kilometres long, from Strachan Avenue to Parkside Drive. It would have 12 shafts, a wet well/dry well separated pumping station and an ultraviolet disinfection system. The City decided to review the design guidelines and give more latitude to the contractors and their consultants. This time the lowest bid was $59.5 million from C & M McNally-Frontier Inc. In this design the tunnel was three metres in diameter and four kilometres long. It had three main shafts, each approximately 45 metres deep and 27 metres in diameter. In this new proposal the storage capacity would be 85,000 cubic metres. The Western Beaches Tunnel was completed in June 2002.

WASTEWATER FROM INDUSTRY

Metro Toronto had developed a good working relationship with industries that produced a lot of wastewater of an organic nature with a high biochemical oxygen demand (BOD) and suspended solids. It developed a bylaw to take and treat this over-strength effluent, which can be biologically treated at a cost that is favourable to the industry. In this way Toronto ensured that full treatment takes place. This is a great benefit to about 100 companies that process food products, abattoirs, etc. It saves building expensive in-house treatment facilities and it also adds about $20 million to the city's coffers. It is good wastewater management, as the municipality has a firm hand on the treatment of liquid wastes that might not otherwise be properly treated.

But the new Toronto City Council decided in 1999 that it might be better if some industries developed their own in-plant treatment facilities. According to the politicians, this action would free up treatment capacities at the city's sewage treatment plants. In reality the extra capacity was negligible and the issue had more to do with politics than sound wastewater treatment practices.

Since federal funding for sewage treatment terminated in 1982, the development of sewage treatment plants, in many municipalities across Canada, is not a priority. Raw sewage, in many areas, continues to be dumped into the oceans, rivers and streams of this rich land.

CHAPTER 13
Knee Deep in Sludge: The Cost of Pelletizing

When a massive blaze gutted a seven-storey sewage sludge pelletizing plant at the Ashbridge's Bay Sewage Treatment Plant in Toronto's east end on the night of August 22, 2003, it created a multi-million dollar headache for city politicians. The plant was built by the Canadian arm of US Filter Inc. It had many start-up problems and was undergoing tests the two years before it burned down. According to city officials, after the many delays — mostly equipment testing — the plant was 60 days from being handed over to city management, supposedly to launch a program of fertilizing Ontario lands with pellets of sludge, rather than the more water-laden cake sludge from the presses of the treatment plant.

Whatever secrets or market assessments the burned-out plant computer system might have contained, the "sludge-as-fertilizer" plan had always been controversial. Farmers across the province had reported anecdotally on mysterious illnesses that may have been related to the use of contaminated sludge. The sludge was supposed to be treated to remove dangerous chemicals and heavy metals.

To add some drama to the plant burning itself, it was ironic that at the very hour the flames roared through the structure, the friends and staff of the City Works Department were honouring Bob Pickett, the city engineer in charge of the pellet plant, at his retirement reception in Toronto's Boulevard Club. As Works staff rushed out of the club when informed about the fire, a colleague of Pickett muttered, "Bob did not deserve such a send off." Pickett was a respected engineer through the years. But the strains of amalgamation and the new City Works management, coupled with the pressure of a few well-placed local activists, had given him additional headaches and sludge "digestion" problems in the last few years prior to his retirement.

When Toronto's wastewater flows into the sewage plant for biological treatment, there are two by-products — water and solids. The solids, after aeration and settlement, are siphoned off to digester tanks, where they are held for the 15-day anaerobic treatment (without oxygen). The gases from the digester tanks provide energy for the running of the plant. After digestion the sludge goes through presses to release as much water as possible from the sludge. The solids content may be as high as 30 percent. The rest is water. Over the past six years, the Ashbridges Bay Treatment Plant (ABTP) produced a sludge cake averaging about 28 percent solids, with the other 72 percent being water.

The measurement "dry tonne" was intended as more precise for payment purposes, as the water content of the sludge, when it left the presses, could vary between 70 percent and 75 percent. This percentage was constantly monitored. A dry tonne has zero water. The sludge that leaves the plant for disposal is wet and is more than three times the dry tonne weight.

Generally, a community of 1,000 produces about 50 wet tonnes of sludge every year — depending on the efficiency of the presses. Toronto produces about 210,000 tonnes of this cake (wet) sludge per year in its treatment plants. This includes human wastes as well as effluent from many manufacturing plants whose waste products can be biologically treated. These include waste from slaughterhouses, abattoirs, dairies, food processing, canning factories, etc.

In the early 1970s, the Metro Toronto government developed a bylaw that required that effluents from the process in these plants be treated either in the plant by the industry itself or at the municipal sewage treatment plant. If treatment is provided by the municipality the cost of treatment is based on the volume of the effluent and its biochemical oxygen demand (BOD).

Up to the end of the 1970s, the sewage sludge was hauled to the nearest dump and mixed with the garbage. After many attempts by the Metro Works Committee, the Ministry of the Environment agreed to look at alternate means of disposal. Finally, it was decided that the sludge should be incinerated. Six incinerator units were built at the Ashbridges Bay Treatment Plant.

By the mid-1980s, local citizen activists and politicians began to lobby for alternate ways to dispose of the sludge. Air pollution was cited as a major problem from sludge incineration — especially in the east end, near the plant and in the port lands area. In 1994, after many meetings between staff from the Metro Works Department, politicians and local activists, they decided to call for proposals, which they hoped would lead to what was called "the beneficial use of biosolids." This really meant that the sludge would be marketed as a fertilizer. From then on, the word "biosolids" would replace the more vulgar word "sludge."

Just before amalgamation — in the mid-1990s — two pilot projects, each of five years duration, were approved as suitable for non-incineration methods of sludge disposal. It was hoped that these pilot projects would lead to the eventual phase-out of incinerators.

THE HAUL & SPREAD PROJECT

Terratec Environmental Ltd. was selected for the first project. The company would haul and spread about 36,000 wet tonnes per year (10,000 dry tonnes) on farmers' fields outside Toronto. The sludge would be taken directly from the digesters for land application. The Terratec land application contract went quite well. Many farmers were willing to accept the sludge as a good soil conditioner. As farmers had already been using barnyard manure for generations, this new type of human manure was free and would probably work well.

Agricultural officials worried about the consistency of human waste sludge. Humans eat a wide variety of foods, whereas the food stock for animals was very basic and totally controlled. Human sludge, on the other hand, and the wastes from processing factories contained heavy metals, which would be taken up by root crops and could then enter the food chain.

The Toronto sludge quantities were large and there had been previous concerns about the high levels of heavy metals. The Province, in discussions with Metro Works officials in the early 1970s, had suggested that incineration would be preferable to land spreading. Ontario also turned down an attempt by Metro in 1977 to use the sludge as a fertilizer for agricultural land and in reforestation areas, because of the heavy metals.

Records for Toronto sludge showed that the heavy metal content had been above the accepted level for land application.

But in later years the heavy metal content had fallen to acceptable levels, as stricter regulations were applied to the wastes from private companies using the municipal sewage treatment plant.

Metro Toronto, at the time, was hauling most of the sludge to landfills and some was being incinerated in small old polluting incinerators. Metro, after much discussion, decided to build new incinerators to handle all of the sludge it produced. New incinerators were built at the Ashbridges Bay plant by 1982 at a cost of about $32 million. A few years later, some of the sludge from the Humber Treatment Plant was directed to the Ashbridges Bay plant via the Mid-Town Interceptor Sewer.

By the early 1990s, all of the sludge from the Humber STP was directed to the Ashbridges plant, which now processes about 88 to 90 percent of all the sludge produced in Toronto. That added up to about 175,000 wet tonnes, or about 50,000 bone dry tonnes annually. Highland Creek STP produces another 35,000 wet tonnes of cake sludge annually, which is incinerated at the plant.

Metro Toronto also developed "sludge and leaf" compost from the leaves gathered every fall. The final product was provided at a few locations, free of charge, to anyone who wanted to use it. It was a good product and suitable as a fertilizer. But it was never marketed aggressively.

COVERING MINE TAILINGS WITH SLUDGE

Harbour Remediation & Transfer (HR&T), a company set up for soil remediation and associated with a company in the earth trucking business, was selected for the other project. That project called for the preparation of about 10,000 dry tonnes of sludge (36,000 wet tonnes) per year to be hauled to Falconbridge Mines in Sudbury and to be spread on mine tailings.

The HR&T process called for heating the sludge to about 70°C and adding lime. The heat would destroy the pathogens in the sludge and the lime would increase the pH to 12. The high pH was needed to neutralize the acidity of the mine tailings. It would be applied or spread one metre thick. Railway cars would be used to haul the material to Sudbury, where it would then go by truck for application on the mine tailings.

One of the requirements of Metro Toronto, in the HR&T contract, stipulated that the sludge must be processed away from the Ashbridges Bay Treatment Plant. This later proved to be a terrible mistake. HR&T leased a City-owned plant at 97 Commissioners Street — about a kilometre west of the sewage treatment plant. Darling Rendering Ltd. had previously used the buildings and property for its operations. The plant was modified for the processing of the sludge and the railway siding was upgraded to receive flatbed cars.

Metro Works claimed there was insufficient space at the treatment plant for the processing of the sludge. But the real reason was soon evident — if the HR&T plant was built on the site and operated by HR&T, there would be a conflict with CUPE, the local union. That may lead down the road to privatization — the bogeyman of civic workers.

Metro Works never thought that shipping the sludge to a building one kilometre west also meant that it was shipping a new smell into an area that already had enough identifiable industrial smells of its own. As well, Metro Works did not have a detailed understanding of the characteristics of the sludge odour. The thinking seemed to be that if it was acceptable at the treatment plant, it would be acceptable in the same industrial area outside the plant. The project was headed for trouble unless the exported odour could be controlled. HR&T accepted the direction of Metro Works, who believed that all the necessary studies had been completed before the call for proposals.

HR&T began the start-up operations in September 1996 and achieved full-scale production by November. In the meantime, HR&T, the Ministry of the Environment and local politicians began to receive calls about the smell. After discussions, it was decided that processing should stop until the odour problems were solved. But HR&T did not expect the political turmoil that the new smell would cause. It could be controlled at the new HR&T processing plant at 97 Commissioners Street, but it would cost a few million dollars more — money that HR&T did not have and that Metro Toronto was reluctant to spend.

Smell is one of the five senses. But it is one of the most difficult to characterize and identify. It cannot be scientifically measured with any instruments. It depends entirely on the individual's nose. And the nose can become accustomed to a smell, sometimes to the extent that it is no longer a problem.

But the new smell at Commissioners Street was definitely noticeable to most business people in the area, especially when the wind carried it. It could be identified up to 400 metres from the plant. If the project was to work, the smell had to be treated and contained in the plant.

During 1997, the search for a solution to control the smell dominated activities and little sludge was processed. Many suggestions were looked at and consultants were asked for proposals for an odour control plan. But the cost was deemed to be too high by some and the uncertainty of achieving complete odour control was doubtful, particularly since the movement to shut the plant had received local and political support. HR&T stopped operations again in October 1997 to prepare and implement an odour control plan.

By then, Metro realized that sufficient information was not available when bids were invited for the project. It was thought that not enough characterization of the sludge was carried out. Metro staff was prepared to recommend that the municipality finance the project and support the HR&T plan, which included a detailed characterization of odours and rigorous pilot testing of odour control technologies, as an integral part of any upgrades.

The key components of the financial package for HR&T were:

- $2,000,000 for consulting services, odour characterization, engineering design, and procurement of odour control technology;
- $400,000 for odour control equipment already installed;
- $1,200,000 for operating the new odour control equipment;
- $1,200,000 for business interruption.

HR&T had developed a business plan to double the processing to produce 20,000 dry tonnes per year for the next two years to meet the five-year project target. The business plan was presented to the bank and approved. It looked like everything would work out.

NEW DIRECTIONS AFTER AMALGAMATION

During the early months of amalgamation, in the spring of 1998, Terratec carried on with the haul and spread contract while the new management team of the Works Department pondered what to do with the HR&T contract. The odour now from the HR&T project had assumed new characteristics — it had become a political smell!

But amalgamation, with a new city council, brought new management staff and new ideas. This new management was not so receptive. The past problems of the project did not occur on their watch. It seemed that they had no wish to prolong this inherited smelly mess. In January 1998, the new Works and Utilities Committee requested a report on the feasibility of accelerating the shutdown of incineration at the Main Treatment Plant. On July 10, 1998, city council established the Biosolids Multi-Stakeholder Committee (BMSC) and an Independent Review Committee (IRC) retained consultants and requested proposals to allow for the shutdown of sewage sludge incineration within a three-year period.

The City also decided not to spend any more money on the odour control and to back out of the commitments made earlier by Metro Works to HR&T on the overall financial package for odour control. In June 1998, city council, on the advice of new Works Department staff, decided to unilaterally cancel the contract with HR&T and work out a termination settlement. In an effort to maximize the settlement, HR&T hired lawyer Jeff Lyons, the top lobbyist at City Hall, to represent the firm. Lyons could not get the financial settlement that HR&T wanted and advised that a colleague at Cassels Brock (Lawyers) be retained to carry on further negotiations. Lyons felt he had done as much as he could.

The cancelled HR&T project now became a sideshow while the City went on a spending spree to prove that the sludge could be sold and beneficially used instead of incinerated. On July 28, 1998, council, in an ambitious mood, moved the target date for closing down the incinerators at the Ashbridges Bay Treatment Plant to the end of December 2002. On February 8, 1999, Works staff presented the details of the 1999–2003 water and wastewater capital budget and identified the costs of achieving the 100 percent biosolids beneficial use program and required design-build program.

The 1999–2003 capital works program for the closing down of the incinerators and the beneficial use of biosolids totalled $76.6 million net after GST rebate, with $15,710,000 in 1999, $53,030,000 in 2000, and $7,855,000 in 2001.

The 1999-2003 capital works budget, prepared by staff, is as follows:

- A $22,235,959 contract with U.S.F Canada Inc. for the design, construction and implementation of a biosolids pelletizing facility (as a result of an RFP on Sept 8,1998). The facility was to be built at the Ashbridges Bay plant, on the foundations of the demolished two units of the incinerator.
- $30,000,000 for a new loading facility with a capacity to store up to 2,000 cubic metres of sludge at the plant.
- $15,000,000 to install additional boilers and make modifications to the heating system to allow the plant to continue operating after the demolition of the incinerators. Incineration of the sludge produced steam to heat the plant's buildings in winter and the digestion process all year round. With the shutdown of the incinerators the plant would not be able to produce enough heat during the winter months.
- $10,000,000 for a new odour control facility. The high temperatures of the incinerators are very effective in destroying the odours produced in the plant. With the demolition of the incinerators, new odour control facilities would have to be built.

By the end of 2002, the City had spent about $89 million to replace the incinerators, construct the pelletizing plant and change over to a beneficial use of biosolids program. But the biosolids program, by that time, was in tatters.

What happened? In order to understand the slippery movements of the sludge use between 1996 and 2002, it is necessary to look at two distinct programs for the "beneficial use of biosolids." One is the "haul and spread" system and the other is the "pelletizing" system.

HAUL AND SPREAD

When Terratec Environmental Ltd. was awarded a contract by Metro Toronto in 1996, it was a fairly simple process, with reasonable and straightforward guidelines. All Terratec had to do was sign up willing farmers who would allow Terratec to haul and spread the sludge on their land, under minimum guidelines. It was not such a big deal, as smaller municipalities had been doing it for decades. Quantities were not large and farmers had always used animal manure to fertilize their fields. The province had no objections to the smaller rural municipalities disposing of sludge in this manner. But Toronto quantities were large and there had been concern about the heavy metals content in the past.

By the mid 1980s, Toronto environmental activists had decided that incineration was not an appropriate way to dispose of waste. Council was constantly lobbied to oppose incineration. Many attempts were made to close down the existing incinerators. Eventually, two non-incineration projects were developed for a five-year test period. Terratec Environmental Ltd. won the "haul and spread" contract and HR&T won the "mines tailings cover" contract — using heat and lime stabilization.

When Terratec's haul and spread contract began, there was little worry about the impact of the sludge on farmland. It amounted to about 36,000 wet tonnes of cake, weighed after being through the presses. But when controversy began with the odour problems from the HR&T project, Terratec soon became the focus of attention and its project was portrayed as an example of how sludge should be managed. With the cancellation of the HR&T contract, Terratec was called on to help out and take more sludge.

As the HR&T project made the headlines in Toronto, rural residents and farmers began to ask questions about the sludge. Gradually, it became more difficult for Terratec to obtain approval from farmers. Municipalities outside Toronto began to ask questions also. And very soon rural folk began to get the smell of Toronto sludge: if the sludge smelled in Toronto, it smelled in rural Ontario also.

As the Terratec five-year contract was to expire at the end of August 2001, the City asked for an extension of the contract. City Works officials claimed that due to increased staff workload, negotiations with Terratec had been delayed. They wanted the extension to develop a new four-year contract with Terratec. On July 30, 2002, council approved the extension of the Terratec contract to October 31, 2002, to allow time for staff to finalize negotiations with Terratec for a new four-year deal to apply 25,000 dry tonnes to farmland annually. That had originally been directed by council in March 1998 — almost four years earlier. City Works officials claimed that the contract should not be tendered, as Terratec was the only contractor with experience that could successfully do the work. Council decided to accept the new Terratec contract for four years.

Even as Terratec was being lauded as the only contractor capable of handling Toronto biosolids for land application, the Ministry of the Environment, on September 16, 2002, laid charges against the company, accusing it of violating its certificate of approval for dumping sludge on a field in Cambridge between November 28 and December 4, 2001. The ministry said the sludge could flow down the field and into an adjacent stream.

The new contract with Terratec stipulated that if the sludge was applied to the land, the price was $121.67 per dry tonne, and if it was hauled to the Michigan landfill site it was $112.29 per dry tonne, plus $20 per dry tonne for tipping fees. The contract was really an open-ended contract to haul the sludge to Michigan.

With all the new regulations following the passing of the Nutrient Act in May 2002, it was bound to be expensive and difficult to spread Toronto's sludge on Ontario farmland. It was also very difficult to obtain local permission for a sludge storage facility in the municipalities around Toronto. It seemed inevitable that most of the sludge would be trucked to Michigan with the rest of Toronto's garbage, at least for the foreseeable future.

The Ministry of the Environment was bound to be vigilant to ensure that all the new requirements were followed. The fee for a certificate of approval doubled and site permits became more difficult to obtain. The permit could take up to 12 months. Rural municipalities also were developing bylaws to obstruct and slow down the land application of sludge. Field storage or stockpiling was prohibited. A conveyor belt had to be used from the storage facility to the application vehicle. And the reporting, managing and inspection requirements became much more stringent.

From 1996 to 2000, Toronto sludge was stored during periods when land application was not possible, such as wet weather and the wintertime. The sludge was held in Halton Region at a storage facility owned by the Region but operated by Terratec. As a result of the odour concerns, Halton Region terminated Terratec's contract and prohibited storage of Toronto's sludge, as of the end of 2000.

There is no doubt that the land application of sludge, farm-yard manure or liquid manure has come under a great deal of public scrutiny since the Walkerton water supply tragedy in May 2000. The Justice O'Connor Walkerton Inquiry ensured that more stringent regulations were introduced. That meant that the land application of sludge, whether of human or animal origin, would be less acceptable in the rural municipalities of Ontario.

PELLETIZING

Pelletizing means the packaging or bagging of processed sludge in pellet size for land application. The idea was to develop a market to sell Toronto sludge as a fertilizer and soil conditioner, which Milwaukee has successfully done for the last 60 years. The pelletizing proposal was seen by many as the ideal way of removing smelly waste from the neighbourhood, while at the same time helping farmers in rural Ontario.

US Filter Canada Inc., having been selected to design and construct the pelletizing plant, expected to operate the plant and market the biosolids. The City and US Filter entered into negotiations for a 15-year contract to market, transport, distribute and sell the pellets. City council approved the deal in March 1999. The construction of the pelletizing plant was completed in the spring of 2001, and commissioning and testing began on May 18, 2001, and continued to June 17, 2001. It seemed that the testing of the facility went without any hitches and US Filter sold the small quantities of pellets produced to farmers.

But there was one small storage problem. During the test period, pellets were "inappropriately stored" as they were exposed to the elements at a farm prior to land application. The pellets got wet and began to decompose and smolder. The fire department was called to deal with problem. No property or building damage resulted.

City Works officials worked hard to develop an agreement with US Filter in March 2001. They were prepared to proceed to council when US Filter notified staff, prior to the April 24 council meeting, that it could not sign the agreement, as there were now several concerns. The company was extremely concerned by the actions of city council, since US Filter had little control over the management and operation of the plant. There were other menacing storm clouds on the horizon for the City Works Department as marketing negotiations got bogged down with US Filter. Marketing a product under deteriorating conditions did not make much sense to US Filter. The old days of spreading sludge on farmers' fields in Ontario were over.

It did not help that city council had finally decided not to award the operations contract for the pelletizing plant to US Filter. In other words, city workers would operate it — not US Filter. This limited the company's role, and it was not prepared to absorb any more marketing risks.

The most devastating blow to the marketing of the pellets came when the City decided that US Filter could not sell the pellets for home use for three to five years in the city. Councillor Jack Layton spelled out his health concerns in a letter to council. That sent a clear message not only to US Filter but also to those outside Toronto that the sludge was good enough for them, but not for Toronto!

Anti-sludge activists, hearing about the sludge plans of Toronto, decided to oppose using Ontario farmland as a dumping ground for Toronto's sludge. Ontario had introduced the Ontario Nutrient Act in June 2002 with regulations to be in place by summer 2003. Regulations would be tightened, making it more difficult to market the sludge pellets as suitable manure for farmers' fields.

Works Department staff worked on the US Filter pellet marketing agreement for the next year. The staff reported to the Works Committee on March 26, 2002, that they had completed negotiations and would be recommending entering into an agreement with US Filter. It seemed the city had softened its position. But, as the summer wore on, it seemed that opposition to Toronto sludge was increasing in rural Ontario. Many municipalities were developing bylaws to discourage Toronto sludge being dumped in their areas.

By the end of 2002, the agreement with US Filter was still elusive. It had not been presented to the Works Committee. The Biosolids Advisory Committee (BAG) and some city politicians fought hard to impose strict controls on the marketing of the pelletized product. These actions prompted US Filter to rethink its proposal — and it finally backed away from the marketing.

After attempts to address the Works Committee on the sludge problems in the fall of 2002, I finally had an opportunity on April 30, 2003. Carlos Silva, a local business man, came with me and presented a few blocks or bricks that had been made of 48 percent sludge and 52 percent cement mix. It was an example of what could be part of a solution for sludge. The proposal was referred to the staff of the Works Department for examination with a direction to report back to the committee within six months. That report never came.

I made a presentation to the committee on what I thought had happened to the sludge to cause problems. I mentioned that the whole subject of the sludge should be referred to an inquiry to get all the facts of the mess out into the open. The commissioner was angry at my suggestion. The project had been mired in an obfuscation process for the past four years. It was painful and difficult to get information from the Works Department.

Finally, after I had made my presentation to the Works Committee on April 30, 2003, I was informed that the Works

Department had just tabled two reports as late additions before the committee dealing with the sludge. The first report dealt with a new proposed contract with US Filter for the pelletizing, and the other dealt with a proposed contract with Terratec for haul and spread.

The Works Commissioner sought authority "to enter into an agreement with USF Canada Inc. on a contract for a five year term to transport, store and market up to 32,500 dry tonnes of biosolid pellets from Ashbridges Bay Treatment Plant at an initial cost of $13.35, inclusive of GST/PST, per dry tonne, on terms and conditions previously reported."

The Works Commissioner also sought permission to "enter into an agreement, commencing March 15, 2003, with Terratec Environmental Ltd., a subsidiary of American Water Services Canada Corp., to land apply biosolids from the Ashbridges Bay Treatment Plant (ABTB) at a cost of $121.36, inclusive of PST/GST, for each dry tonne of biosolids land applied, and during periods when land application is not possible to transport the biosolids to landfill, at a cost of $117.37, inclusive of PST/GST, per dry tonne, based on transportation to the Republic landfill in Michigan, for up to 50,000 dry tones annually for a period of four years on such terms and conditions as previously reported."

I found the report to be very confusing. It was what is generally called a "paint-over-the-cracks" report. But it sounded great to the members of the Works Committee, who were looking for some good news from their costly experts. But on examination, it was a masterpiece of obfuscation.

US Filter Canada had been commissioned to build the pellitizing plant with an annual capacity of 25,000 dry tonnes on average and the ability to handle peak volumes of up to 32,500 dry tonnes per year. The original report from the commissioner to the Works Committee on February 8, 1999, was requesting permission to commence negotiations with US Filter "for the transportation, marketing and distribution of up to a maximum of 28,000 dry tonnes per year of biosolid pellets with an expected minimum of 25,000 dry tonnes per year of biosolids at a cost of $13.35 per dry tonne, such agreement to be for a period of 15 years."

Note that the new contract, after messing around for four years, is 32,500 dry tones for five years — not 32,500 tonnes per year. That's 20 percent use of the pelletizing plant if spread out over five years. There is no minimum amount set for processing. The designation of up to 32,500 tonnes means that is a ceiling but there is no floor. Technically, according to the proposed contract, US Filter Canada needed to process only a few tonnes to pellets to meet the contract requirements, as there is no minimum amount to be processed.

In the proposed contract, the City would continue to own the sludge until it was sold or hauled away. The $100,000 liability was also loose and gave an out to US Filter to pack it in anytime it reached expenditures of $100,000. According to City officials, the Ashbridges Bay Treatment Plant produces an estimated 53,000 dry tonnes of solids per year. The US Filter 32,500 dry tonnes over five years is 6,500 tonnes per year or 12.5 percent of the sludge produced. What would happen to the other 87.5 percent of the sludge? Would it be spread in rural Ontario, or would it be hauled to the landfill site in Michigan? Enter Terratec!

HAULING TO MICHIGAN

The new four-year contract with Terratec Environmental Ltd. called for the haul and spread of up to 50,000 dry tonnes (182,000 wet tonnes) of biosolids annually on Ontario farmland. If that did not work, it would all go to Michigan. If Toronto hauled its sludge to Michigan with all the other garbage produced in Toronto — at least until Michigan decided it could not handle any more — it would add many more millions to the annual operating budget. And what would become of the pelletizing plant at the Ashbridges Bay Treatment Plant? That problem was conveniently solved when the new pellet plant burned down on that warm evening of August 23, 2003 — opening up the road to Michigan!

What had started out as a simple project to replace incineration mushroomed into a monumental fiasco of obfuscation, incompetence and bungling. The fire at the plant in August 2003 wrote a kind of ironic end to the mess — except it wasn't over. Since the introduction of amalgamation the sludge mess had been an expensive, poorly managed foul-up that cost Toronto taxpayers dearly. The staff and management of the Ashbridges Bay Treatment Plant (ABTP), on a day-to-day basis, did their best to work under conflicting pressures. But the failure had been at top management, who presided over the blowing away of $89 million.

The first twelve months of the new amalgamated city council provided a management vacuum and an opportunity for local "experts" and politicians to micro-manage the coup to destroy the incinerators. The pellet plant was built without a marketing plan and with thwarted direction from top management. In trying to follow what happened over the past four years, the paper trail to council was cluttered with bits of information that did not address the overall, real, ongoing problems of sludge management. The two contracts — one to Terratec for haul and spread and the other to US Filter for pelletizing — were mere window-dressing to hide the shipment of sludge to Michigan.

The Terratec "haul to Michigan" contract guarantees the company a profit and a final resting place for Toronto sludge — at least for now. But the US Filter contract was a born loser for the city and for US Filter as well. US Filter did not have to pelletize a minimum amount. If a market could not be developed for the pellets, the sludge plant would lie idle as Terratec could haul away 50,000 dry tonnes (182,000 wet tonnes) every year, for at least four years.

Unfortunately, the Walkerton tragedy changed everything for Toronto. Works administration staff should have recognized that and sought guidance from council. They could not hide behind BAG, BMSC, the consultants and a few influential local activists.

After five attempts, since August 2003, to get information on what happened with the sludge at the Ashbridges Bay sewage plant during the first two terms of amalgamation (1998 to 2003), and the capital costs for these years, city council finally, on July 20, 2004, directed the Works Commissioner to provide the information. I received the information a few days later. The information, which should be public and available to any taxpayer, shows that Toronto sludge is now hauled to Michigan, with Toronto garbage. It is part of the red ribbon of shame that snakes its way daily along Highway 401 to the U.S. border.

And the new price tag, according to Works Department staff, for the sludge as fertilizer to the end of 2003 is $95 million!

That does not include the Michigan haulage and disposal costs. On top of that, there is the uncertainty of how long Michigan will continue to allow Toronto wastes to be dumped in its landfills.

Year	Mine Cover	Pellets US Filter	Land Apply Terratec	Incineration At Plant	Landfill Michigan	Total Sludge
1998	271.4		18,006.2	34,063.9		52,143.8
1999			20,741.0	28,593.2		49,334.2
2000			23,541.2	22,959.1		46,500.3
2001		1,955.8	17,310.0	28,021.0		47,286.8
2002		4,416.2	5,115.2	18,175.0	18,704.8	46,411.2
2003		3,263.0	2,287.3		45,547.2	51,097.5

The above figures in dry tonnes were provided by the City. Incineration ceased in December 2002. The City hauled 45,547.2 dry tonnes to Michigan in 2003. That translated into 164,430 wet tonnes going to Michigan in 2003 — using the (cake) dry factor of 27.7 percent.

As spring 2004 faded into summer, garden supply outlets across Toronto offered manure products for gardens and lawns. One company, Hortibec-Modugno, of St. Laurent, Quebec, had cow or sheep manure in 15-kilo bags at $1.99 per bag (about $130 per tonne) at all garden outlets. According to the information on the bag, it contained a minimum of 25 percent organic material; nitrogen (N), 0.6 percent; soluble potash (K_2O), 0.4 percent; phosphoric acid (P_2O_5), 0.4 percent and a maximum of 70 percent moisture. Loblaws Inc., Montreal, offered a cow manure product, similar to the Hortibec-Modugno product, but the moisture was listed at a maximum of 60 percent, and nitrogen, soluble potash, phosphoric acid all listed at a minimum 0.5 percent each. All the products are black, odourless material with the caricature of a sheep or cow on the bag. They proved popular with local gardeners. But I found it hard to imagine gardeners rushing to buy 15-kilo bags of 100 percent human manure in pellet form. It would need a lot of promotion to compete with the cow and sheep stuff.

City council needs an arm's-length investigation — a total re-evaluation of the sludge mess and the reasons it happened. It needs an MFP type of inquiry. That sadly would probably cost $10 million and would only prove how incompetence rules our city.

There are no benefits in hauling Toronto's sludge to Michigan — only misery, sorrow, and a terrible image for a city that should know better.

On October 15, 2003, a 38-year-old truck driver from Kitchener was drowned in the Michigan landfill when he was sucked into 10-feet-deep pit for Toronto sludge, as he tried to open the truck's tail gate. At around 72 percent water, sludge should not be considered solid waste and should be subject to special regulations if dumped on landfill.

And on the morning of March 23, 2005, a tractor-trailer load of Toronto sludge skidded down the main street of Flat Rock, Michigan, and dumped about 31 tonnes of sludge over an entire block — stinking up the town. Michigan hazard materials crews, dressed in protective gear, spent the day cleaning up the smelly mess.

No amount of public relations will erase the environmental damage done by hauling Toronto's sludge to Michigan. It is a monumental disgrace. We should be ashamed.

The following suggestions on sludge handling are practical:

- The waste of $95 million for any city is a tragedy. At least the MFP affair resulted in acquiring some computers.
  The sludge mess resulted in the sludge joining the daily ribbon of shame to Michigan. It deserves an independent review so that taxpayers might know how and why it all happened.
- Re-examine the rail haul of sludge from the Ashbridges Bay Treatment Plant to cover mine tailings in the mining areas of Ontario.
- Incineration, with modern cleaning equipment, works very well. It is much better than sending the sludge to Michigan. Incinerators could be used very effectively to heat the plant and control its odours. Incineration of sludge works very well in the Highland Creek Sewage Treatment Plant.

CHAPTER 14
Waste: Making a Mess of Managing Garbage

Most cities are built on the buried wastes of their past. The study of ancient habitations has been helped by the close examination of their old midden heaps — the garbage dumps. I was in Dublin in 1986 when workers, digging the foundations for a new civic building, stumbled upon the old wall that had surrounded the original city over 1,000 years ago. At that time the garbage was dumped outside the walls. Imagine the excitement of the archeologists when they discovered the old midden heap. I was given a tour of the roped-off site. It was astonishing. It contained old leather footwear, bone combs, cooking utensils, a variety of shells, jewelry and ornaments. The find caused much excitement and added to the knowledge of the old city, which was founded by Viking raiders who created a port and a settlement there.

Toronto, too, has garbage in its past. All of the area south of Front Street has been filled in with waste and rubble from the early days. The port lands and Ashbridges Bay areas were built mostly with refuse from the growing community. Since the early days of York, later Toronto, about 130 garbage dumps have been identified in and around the expanding metropolitan boundaries. They were all within easy distance and were nothing more than holes and ravines filled with waste, rubbish and leftovers. There were no rules or regulations for the earlier dumps — just fill them and level them off.

In those early days, the variety of waste was limited, not like the waste from the throwaway society of today. Toronto dumps were filled mostly with household wastes, rubble, ash and cinders. As factory and industrial wastes were small, the throwaway waste from these areas did not present a real problem.

It was only after World War II, in 1946, that politicians and municipalities began to think of developing plans for the organized disposal of garbage. At that time, there was no mention of reduction, reuse or recycling — the now familiar three Rs. The industrial age had arrived with a vengeance. The word "garbage" was considered too crude, so a more acceptable word, "waste," crept into the language.

In 1967, Metro Toronto was given responsibility for the disposal of waste, with the introduction of the Goldenberg Report. Collection was left to the six local municipalities. Consulting engineers McLaren/Black and Veach produced a report in 1966 for the disposal of waste for the next 20 years. The report called for the phasing out of the old incinerators and the existing small dumps. It called for a new incinerator and two other large waste disposal sites, properly managed under the new provincial environment guidelines. The goal was that 75 percent of the garbage would go to "landfill" — a new word for "dump" — and 25 percent to incineration.

Metro had inherited a hodgepodge of dumps and seven old incinerators and most of them were in appalling state. It would take a lot of time and money to bring the management of waste up to some reasonable standard. The dumps were just places where municipalities, companies and individuals disposed of all sorts of liquid and solid waste.

Dumps were unsightly and a source of nuisance to those who were unfortunate enough to live near one. There were few, if any, regulations for the control and operation of the sites. When a dump was full, it was levelled off and topped with a little topsoil and grassed over, often becoming a local park. But the incinerators were big air polluters — a health hazard for anyone who lived or worked near them. Only one, at Chesswood Drive, made an attempt to reduce emissions. The rest had no emission controls. And some had to be manually stoked by labourers using long rakes. These unfortunate workers probably developed respiratory problems because of such a polluted environment. Little thought was given to air quality at that time. It would take a few more years to understand the impact of the old incinerators.

Records from 1967 show that Metro disposed of 1.4 million tons at the dumps and 760,000 tons were incinerated, for a total of 2.16 million tons. With the McLaren report as a guide, Metro proceeded with a plan to close all of the small dumps and phase out the worst incinerators. There was no recycling program. A proposed new incinerator, in the vicinity of Horner and Kipling avenues in Etobicoke, ran into stiff local opposition. The residents fought it every step of the way for the next few years. Finally, Metro withdrew the proposal. The incinerator was dead.

Whether to use landfill or incineration for local municipalities depended entirely on trucking distances. That made economic sense, as local property taxes paid for the cost of collection and haulage. Later on, Metro built transfer stations, which were strategically located to provide more efficient access for the local collection trucks. Metro then used tractor-trailers to haul the compacted waste from the transfer station to the landfill sites.

Two large landfill sites were developed, one originally started by Etobicoke at Thackery Road in the vicinity of Steeles and Kipling avenues to handle the west and northwest areas and one at Beare Road in Scarborough to serve the east end areas. Incinerators continued to serve the old City of Toronto and parts of North York and York, but were gradually closed down until only Commissioners Street, Chesswood Drive and Ingram Drive remained open. Later on, these incinerators were also phased out as Metro began to rely totally on landfill.

As a member of the Metro Works Committee, I had a unique opportunity to participate in changing the way waste was handled. I had a constant battle with those who did not want much change, and I had to deal with the political realities of the day. I could carry the crusade only so far. Even when I became chairman of the committee, I did not inherit any additional clout. I began to see that it was part of the political establishment's plan to burden me with work and keep me busy with routine committee matters. At least that was what I thought.

I got to know my limits. So I had to have a working relationship with Commissioner Ross Clarke and his staff as well as my colleagues on council. Most of the time, I had to be thankful for little things — small steps. I did not win many big battles, but I succeeded in laying the groundwork for a lot of change. As in other environmental issues like air, water and sewage, how to handle garbage was a constant and growing municipal challenge. It was not a glamorous topic, but I was fighting to get it on the radar screen. There was so much to do! Our bloated and throw-away lifestyle produced about four pounds of garbage per person per day. This placed us on top of the planet's garbage heap with our American neighbours.

Poor countries throw away very little. Almost everything has to be recycled and reused. Garbage disposal was not a priority. What reached the dumps was of little value. Even so, in Third World countries thousands of people actually made their living by picking through the dumps. In Cairo, Mexico City, Manila, Bogota and other teeming cities, people live in makeshift shacks in the dumps. To these unfortunate people, our dumps would be like finding a treasure. I used to feel ashamed of our blatant arrogance and misuse of our resources every time I visited one of Toronto's landfill sites. We had so much to throw out!

Eventually, I was able to stimulate interest in attempting to reduce the amount of garbage we produced. There was a growing interest in the three Rs — reduce, recycle and reuse. I chaired a Metro subcommittee on recycling in early 1972. After months of meetings, deputations and 84 submitted briefs, the subcommittee submitted a report with 39 recommendations. Metro Council adopted many of the recommendations and the three Rs program was finally on its way.

The provincial Ministry of the Environment set out to have a look at waste disposal and set up the Solid Waste Task Force in 1973. I was appointed to it and I sat through numerous meetings, which became the battleground for the packaging industry, canners and bottlers — all trying to protect their industry. When the report was finally released in 1974 it contained many recommendations. With the support of the industries involved, it set out a provincial approach for the three Rs.

Metro introduced a separation-of-waste and a recycling program with the appearance of the Blue Box in 1980. It was a major step to get citizens directly involved. A separate curbside recycling collection was introduced every week — one week for glass, plastic and metals and the other week for the collection of newspapers and cardboard. Although the revenue from recycling was not as originally expected, the program levelled off in 1997. It diverted 250,000 tonnes from landfill annually. The paper and cardboard market remained very volatile, with wild fluctuations in prices. The value of glass, plastics and metals was constantly low. Overall, it was a limited success, with 18 percent of waste recycled. But it was by no means a financial success.

RECYCLING OLD NEWSPAPERS

The 1972 Metro subcommittee on recycling was the first attempt to recycle and reduce waste. The *Toronto Star* made a commitment to use newsprint with recycled fibre when technology justified the financial investment for a de-inking plant. Eighteen years later, in 1990, that commitment had not been realized, although de-inking plants were being used to supply newsprint with recycled fibre. Only the *Toronto Sun* and the *Financial Post*, in Toronto, were using newsprint from Ontario and Quebec Paper Ltd. that contained 55 percent recycled fibre.

I estimated that about 40 square miles of forest were used every year to provide 270,000 tonnes of newsprint for Toronto's newspapers, with the *Star* using 140,000 tonnes. Old newspapers can be recycled only about four times. Each recycling process shortens the length of the wood fibre and eventually the paper becomes too brittle and cannot be used for newsprint. Nevertheless recycling offers quite a saving of our virgin forests.

Over the years we have not been kind to forests. Clear-cutting has scarred the forest areas, leaving ugly wounds and images of destruction. Our approach to the development, maintenance and use of the forests has been wasteful and ill-planned. Very often, the natural environment was tragically polluted by the effluent of mills located in remote areas of the sparsely populated northlands. The constant odour of hydrogen sulfide (like rotten eggs) creates a nauseous feeling in most of Canada's pulp and paper towns, which are in sparsely populated areas. The dumping of plant effluent containing dioxins, furans, neuro-toxic mercury and chlorinated organic compounds etc., into the nearest river or holding area is a vexing and tragic problem. Unfortunately it is an "out of sight, out of mind" scenario for most Canadians, few of whom ever visit a pulp and paper mill.

In the fall of 1990, I introduced a motion to council to require that newspapers in Toronto contain 50 percent recycled fibre by July 1, 1991. That sparked deputations before the City Services Committee from the Pulp and Paper Association, the mill towns, unions and others who wanted to defeat the motion. After many meetings and many debates the proposal was finally defeated. Council members were swayed by the arguments of the well-organized opposition — the cost to build de-inking plants, the loss of jobs in tree-cutting, setting up collection systems for old newspapers and sludge disposal from de-inking plants. At that time the pulp and paper industry in Canada was worth about $20 billion per year. It employed about 173,000 in 110 mills across the country. Another 100,000 were employed in the solid wood products sector.

About 800 million mature trees were cut down annually to feed this gigantic market for 25 million tonnes of pulp and lumber products. About 10 million tonnes of this was newsprint, which was produced by pulp and paper mills located near virgin forests and scattered along the northern section of most Canadian provinces. The United States was, and still is, Canada's single largest customer for newsprint — consuming 88 percent of Canadian production, or 8.8 million tonnes per year. Canadian newspapers use the rest — 1.2 million tonnes. The massive advertising sections of major newspapers — the *New York Sunday Times* and the Saturday edition of the *Toronto Star* — are examples of the excessive use of forest products.

COMPOST

Metro Toronto always had a composting program. The leaves collected from the roads, sidewalks and boulevards were hauled to the landfill site. Some of these leaves were mixed with sewage sludge and naturally composted. This compost was advertised from time to time and was available free at a few Metro sites. But it was difficult to get rid of the material, even when it was free. Compost works very well in a poor economy where topsoil and fertilizer are expensive and difficult to buy. Most poor countries have a very practical natural compost system, but Toronto has plenty of cheap fertilizers. It also has about four months when the ground is frozen and the temperature is so low that composting cannot take place

Building a public composting plant, using temperature-controlled containers, is expensive. It would probably fail because the end product would be too expensive. Even if it was given away for free it would be difficult to get rid of it. It would probably have to be hauled to a special dump for disposal. Many homes in Toronto have developed a small backyard compost area. If the area is large enough it is easy. If the space is limited, plastic composters are available from the City for a small charge. It is possible, therefore, for a household using a compost system to reduce weekly garbage by as much as 50 percent.

INCINERATION AND WASTE HEAT RECOVERY

Before the Blue Box, Metro's waste composition was rich with paper, about 42 percent. This gave it a calorific or heat value of about 4,500 BTUs per pound, almost twice the value of other modern economies like Britain, Germany, Sweden, France, Japan, etc. In those countries, incinerators tend to be used as energy plants, using garbage as a fuel to produce electricity, steam and hot water. This also helps offset the enormous costs of importing oil and gas for those countries.

Incineration with heat recovery was viewed by council as part of the waste disposal solution in 1971. Metro Works Commissioner Ray Bremner was asked to find a site for such a plant. It should be near the downtown steam distribution system of the Toronto District Heating Corporation (now named Enwave), so that it could be easily connected. Bremner recommended that the City acquire a ten-acre site, owned by Gulf Oil, at Eastern Avenue and Cherry Street.

It was labelled the Refuse Fired Steam Plant, and Mayor David Crombie, in his 1973 inaugural address to council, highlighted it as one of his pledges for the new term. In 1975, council, having acquired the site, unanimously adopted Bremner's plan to build the plant. Bremner began, carefully and methodically, to steer the approval process through the various environmental and planning hurdles of the province. Everything was moving, but very slowly. Finally, 11 years later in 1986, when the decision came to actually build the plant, incineration — even with heat recovery — was no longer acceptable to local politicians. The opposition to incineration had gained so such momentum that the Refuse Fired Steam Plant was scrapped by city council — unanimously.

The decision to ban the energy-from-waste plant was a low point for politicians. It was based on fear and lobbying from people who thought they knew a lot about the subject but in reality knew very little. That fear and ignorance has dominated city councils for almost three decades, with the result that Toronto has become a "basket case" when it comes to handling its own waste.

ANATOMICAL WASTE

Although hospital and clinical waste is only a tiny fraction of total waste, a report prepared by the Love Consultants group in 1969 was used as a guide to control the haphazard way diseased tissue, dead animals and other hospital waste like needles and bandages, were disposed of. Among other things, the report proposed a small high-temperature incinerator. That incinerator was never built, but hospitals and clinics have organized a system to dispose of these wastes, without the involvement of governments. Diseased tissue — especially where contagious diseases are involved — must, by law, be cremated. Diseased body fluids have also posed serious disposal problems, particularly when contaminated blood samples have ended up in the sewer system. But health regulations are constantly reviewed for hospitals, clinics and funeral homes.

THE LIQUID WASTE PROBLEM

Landfill sites were used to dispose of everything until the end of the 1970s. Sewage sludge came from the sewage treatment plants daily. Liquid wastes — toxic, hazardous, all kinds — were emptied daily from tankers to percolate through the garbage.

These wastes seeped into the underlying aquifer and made their way in a constant migrating liquid plume of contamination. Many local wells would eventually be destroyed when the plume of poisons arrived.

One of my biggest battles was to get the province to introduce legislation to prevent liquid waste leaking from the garbage dump. At the time it was estimated that about 25 million gallons were dumped annually on Metro garbage dumps. I brought it up, time after time, in the Works Committee: something had to be done to recycle or dispose of these wastes in a safer way. Finally, I was able to get Chairman Paul Godfrey on side and eventually the province, in 1978, introduced new legislation governing the disposal of liquid waste.

THE ONTARIO WASTE MANAGEMENT CORPORATION (OWMC)

The Province had reasoned that it was all right to haul these liquids to the local dump, as there were no liquid disposal facilities available. They did not want it dumped in fields or at night along rural back roads. Hauling it to the dump gave the comfort of knowing where it was! The private sector had the resources and ability to take care of the liquid waste. All the Province had to do was introduce legislation to regulate its haulage, recycling and disposal. But the Province had grand ideas. It would solve all the waste problems. It set up the Ontario Waste Management Corporation (OWMC) to control solid and liquid waste. The government also decided it could handle liquid waste better than the private sector.

In 1981, Premier Bill Davis hired Dr. Donald Chant, head of the Zoology department of the University of Toronto and one of the founders of Pollution Probe, to recommend a location and design and build a liquid waste recycling and processing facility in Southern Ontario. In 1995, 14 years and $143 million later, the search for a site was shelved by Premier Mike Harris and the Ontario Waste Management Corporation was disbanded.

THE SEARCH FOR LANDFILL SITES

In the meantime the Toronto population had passed the 2 million mark and the two Metro dumps and two remaining incinerators were handling about 3 million tons per year. Metro was trying to locate at least one new landfill site, as the Thackery Road site was almost full and the final contours of the Beare Road site had to be revised upwards to squeeze out a few more years.

For the first time, in June 1976, Metro began to look outside its boundaries for a new landfill site. A site used mainly for the private sector waste haulers, owned by Disposal Services Ltd and Crawford Sand and Gravel Ltd., on Keele Street north of Major McKenzie, was the most likely to be approved. At the time, it was being processed through a provincial environmental assessment for use as a landfill site. It was targeted for purchase by the Metropolitan Toronto Corporation. Etobicoke Mayor Dennis Flynn and John Kruger, Paul Godfrey's executive assistant, led the negotiations. Godfrey excused himself from any discussion or involvement in the negotiations to acquire the Keele Street site as he had declared a conflict of interest. His mother worked for one of Norm Goodhead's companies. And Goodhead was a principal in Disposal Services, which had just been bought out by Waste Management Inc. (WMI).

I, too, had a conflict of interest. While out of politics between 1973 and 1974, I formed a consulting engineering company — Environmental Probe Ltd. — and began working on waste disposal. Later, I was back on Metro Council when my company acted for Crawford Allied Industries (CAI) in the environmental assessment and preparation of the Keele Street site. I was also on the board of directors of CAI.

Metro eventually bought the site for $38 million and named it the Keele Valley Landfill Site. Metro was also successful in purchasing a site on Brock Road in Pickering in the Region of Durham. It would serve the area east of Yonge Street, while the Keele Valley site served the area west of Yonge Street. Under new provincial regulations these two sites would be properly prepared and tightly controlled and monitored.

For the first time Metro was required to seal the pit areas so that no contamination or leachate from the waste would enter the underlying aquifer. Keele Valley used a plastic membrane, while Brock Road used a clay liner called "bentonite," imported from Wyoming. A sewer collection system captured the leachate from the garbage for treatment.

Public opposition to landfill sites had become so vocal that nobody wanted a landfill in their area — especially garbage from Toronto. Metro was a very open target. All meetings on the topic were held in public, so there was no way to get a head start on the "no dump" vigilantes. Every time a location of a promising site was mentioned "all hell broke loose in the area." Committees and organizations were formed to fight the slightest whisper of a landfill location. This was the beginning of the NIMBY attitude — "not in my back yard." Public meetings were filled with angry, shouting residents who did everything possible to stop the development of a landfill site. Eventually the proposed site was abandoned because of all the opposition.

It got so bad that, by 1986, none of the big waste management firms would dare apply for approval to use a site. First, the chances of being successful were almost nil. Second, the process would take many years. Third, the processing costs would be in the millions — not including the cost of land, environmental controls and other capital costs.

As all the privately owned landfill sites around Toronto were filled, and it was impossible to get a permit for a new site, Metro had the only two sites open for business — Keele Valley in Vaughan and Brock Road in Pickering. The private waste companies, hauling about 1 million tons of industrial and commercial waste per year, were now held captive to the Metro monopoly. And Metro soon raised the tipping fees to $150 per ton. This was like winning the lottery every week for the Metro treasury. Metro set up a special waste fund — to be used for waste management purposes. In no time the fund had $100 million, then $140 million. When Metro councillors found out about the bulging account, the fund was raided and depleted — the monies going to other pet projects of the councillors that had little to do with waste management.

INTERIM WASTE AUTHORITY

The Province of Ontario, in 1992, with Bob Rae as premier, recognized that obtaining a landfill site outside the boundaries of a municipality was beyond the capability of the municipality and set up the Interim Waste Authority (IWA). Its role was to search for, identify and rate potential waste disposal sites in Southern Ontario. The criteria required that the site have good road and railway access; not be prime agricultural land; preferably have an impervious clay base; and be isolated from dwellings. Over 60 sites were investigated, with the prime sites emerging through a rating system. But again, as potential locations were identified after all the site investigations, fierce local opposition formed and began to paralyze the process.

Ruth Greer, the Ontario Minister of the Environment at the time, had an understanding of the dimensions of the looming garbage crisis for Toronto. She asked Metro Toronto to redraw the final contours of the Keele Valley site to allow it to operate for another ten years. Metro then spent $5 million on new plans to extend the lifespan of the site to satisfy the Ministry of the Environment.

By the time all this was done Bob Rae had lost the election and Mike Harris became premier. In 1996, with Harris in office and expenditures totalling $110 million, the Interim Waste Authority was scrapped. And the $5-million Metro plan to alter the final contours of the Keele Valley landfill site was shelved.

Harris then announced that new criteria would be introduced to have a waste disposal site approved. It was entirely political — "there must be a willing host." That simply meant that if all the technical qualifications were met and the local municipality said "no" — that would be the end of the matter. Since it was apparent that no municipality in Ontario wanted Toronto's garbage, Toronto would have to look outside the province. To make matters worse, Al Palladini, now in the Mike Harris cabinet and the member representing the area where the Keele Valley site was located, made it abundantly clear that the site would close, as originally planned, on December 31, 2002.

Metro was in a panic with the closing of the Keele Valley and Brock Road sites looming in a year or two. It was now looking at potential sites outside Southern Ontario. A call for proposals was issued. Browning Ferris Inc., a large U.S. corporation in waste management, was awarded a five-year contract at $52 per tonne to haul a minimum of 250,000 tonnes per year to the Arbour Hills Landfill site in Michigan. This was the first time that Toronto garbage was disposed outside of Canada, although garbage from Halton Region and St. Catharines had been hauled to Buffalo for years for the refuse-fired power plant there.

Around the same time, Metro was approached by a company headed by Gordon McGuinty to haul all Toronto's waste to the abandoned Adams Mine site outside the town of Kirkland Lake, in Northern Ontario.

The newly amalgamated city council called for proposals on how to handle Toronto's waste. This was a long process and when it was over in June 2000, the Adams Mine site was the most favoured. It seemed that the proposal had the support of the majority of council. It was marketed to show that leachate could be collected and treated and would not pollute the aquifer in the surrounding area. And it could provide a dumping site for Toronto's garbage for the next 20 years. On top of that, the Kirkland Lake town council supported it. And Harris had indicated his support. But it had some organized local opposition in the Kirkland Lake area, as well as stiff opposition at Toronto City Council.

The Adams Mine proposal was finally approved, with some amendments, after a long and bitter debate by council on October 11, 2000. These amendments — designed to torpedo the deal — were adopted by Toronto council by a vote of 32 to 24. If the deal was signed, it would cost the city $51 per ton and amount to $1 billion over the 20-year lifetime of the contract. But the amendments were so difficult to meet and financially draining for McGuinty and his Adams Mine company that he could not accept them.

NOWHERE TO DUMP

With no help on the way from the provincial government and a curt reply saying that a proposal for an extension of the Keele

Valley site would not be considered, Toronto began to develop other plans. I had suggested to a few members of council that a concerted public effort should be made, with heavy emphasis on education, to reduce the amount of garbage going to landfill by 80 percent over nine years — three terms of council. The motion that eventually passed city council called for 100 percent reduction in 10 years — a feel good motion that severely damaged council's credibility. These were wishful words, not actions. Joe Citizen knew that a 100 percent reduction — meaning no garbage going to landfill — was ludicrous.

The only option available was to increase the amount of garbage going to the Michigan landfill site. A firm contract with Republic Services Inc., which operates the Carlton Farm Landfill site in Sumpter Township, 40 kilometres southwest of Detroit, assured Toronto of the disposal of its garbage. The price was $52 per tonne for the next few years or until Michigan was successful in blocking Ontario garbage from being dumped in the state.

As 2003 dawned over Toronto, between 100 and 120 red Wilson Logistics tractor-trailer trucks could be seen snaking their way along Highway 401, six days a week, heading towards the U.S. border to the 260-hectare Carlton Farms Landfill site at Sumpter Township, Michigan.

How long would this daily garbage-ridding ritual last, and what options would there be in the end for Toronto? To many, it has become the red ribbon of shame to the U.S. border. To provincial politicians, it was a godsend to be able to dump in Michigan and not make any long-term plans for the time when the nice folks in Michigan say, "We have had enough. Look after your own garbage."

It is embarrassing for any city to send its domestic waste to another country for disposal. It would be a blessing in disguise if Michigan could somehow ban the garbage. There is a flaw in the character of any government that has to rely on another country to look after such a basic service as the disposal of its garbage. It is only a matter of time before Michigan wakes up.

DEVELOPING A WASTE MANAGEMENT PLAN

With the expansion of populated areas in very confined and limited areas, it is not possible for a municipality to find vacant land within its jurisdiction for a waste disposal site. Consequently the senior level of government — the province — has to make sure that "outside the boundaries" lands are available for needed services. This should be an obvious simple requirement in the chain of command of good government.

Most people do not think about the garbage problem — throwing it out for pick-up on designated days is the limit of their involvement. If payment for disposal was by weight or by bag, then the public would be more aware of the seriousness of the garbage problem. But the Ontario Municipal Act requires that a municipality provide garbage pick-up services from the residential property taxes collected. It would be difficult for politicians to introduce a separate charge for garbage pick-up without a corresponding reduction in property taxes. There is no doubt that a restructuring of the system to place a specific charge on the garbage to be picked up at the curb would be of great value in making citizens become a greater part of the solution and less a part of the problem.

The concept of a willing host to accept Toronto's garbage is a simplistic and amateurish attempt to escape making decisions to help large municipalities. It directly affects the orderly management of the City of Toronto and portrays the Ontario's legislature as a government sadly out of touch with the real problems of its municipalities. I cannot see any municipality accepting Toronto's garbage without provincial help. Those who live near a city make their living on the amenities offered by that city. It is a two-way street. The role of the province is crucial in aiding the city outside its boundaries.

Toronto and the rapidly growing regions around the city need a long-term practical plan for waste management. That requires leadership from the Province in providing assistance so that a waste site or sites are approved expeditiously. Generally, all waste should be handled and processed near its source. All the work in rating landfill sites in Southern Ontario was already completed by the Interim Waste Authority in the early-1990s. It would be an easy approval system if all the criteria were met — an impervious clay base, effective leachate collection and treatment, easy access, rail and road access, distance from residences, etc.

The real wild cards in selecting sites are the NIMBY and political factors. They are unpredictable. A few years ago, I suggested to a government MPP that a waste disposal site meeting all the technical criteria, if located in an opposition member's riding, should be automatically approved. He did not know whether I was joking or serious. I could feel that it hit the right political button. But I knew that politicians would never contemplate making decisions that way!

Opposition parties make many useful proposals, but when they are in power the proposals are put aside and little is forthcoming. The story of Toronto and its garbage clearly shows the scale of political disarray at the local and provincial government levels.

Because of such bungling, not only Toronto but provincial taxpayers have paid dearly for the lack of real political leadership.

Just add up three projects over the last twenty years: Ontario Waste Management Corporation, $143 million; Interim Waste Authority, $101 million; Metro's expenditure to alter the contours of the Keele Valley landfill site (as suggested by the Province), $5 million. That's $249 million down the drain — clearly laying out in dollars and cents the cost of the leadership vacuum at Queen's Park and the chaos it has caused among many Ontario municipalities.

On this one municipal issue alone — waste disposal — the Province has shown a complete lack of understanding in its bumbling and incompetent attempts to help. With that type of help, Toronto's garbage problems will only multiply.

A WASTE HANDLING PLAN FOR TORONTO

1. To operate a successful long-term waste management plan, Toronto should seek legislation to amend the Ontario Municipal Act to provide the municipality with the option of charging residential buildings for disposal by weight. A corresponding reduction in property assessment would also be implemented. It would mean that the City set up a self-sustaining utility to operate and manage the pick-up and disposal of waste.

2. At least one energy-from-waste plant could be built in Toronto — preferably in the port lands area, to provide steam and electricity for the area. Modern technology has shown, through the many plants operating worldwide, that this is a practical and a preferred option for many modern cities. Bottom ash should be used for road building materials as well as the manufacture of solid blocks.

3. Two waste processing plants, within 100 kilometres of Toronto, could service the city and a large part of Southern Ontario. Environmentally, the energy used by trucks over long distances makes faraway sites unacceptable.

The ideal site should be about 200 hectares to allow room for storage, processing, composting, recycling and disposal. It would be labour-intensive, with at least one central conveyor belt system to carry the waste from the tipping floor. Cross conveyors would separate paper and paper products, wood, plastic, glass, ferrous and non-ferrous metals.

The residue at the end of the central conveyor system would be mainly organic matter for composting with a small amount of material left over for disposal.

A modern waste management plan should reduce up to 80 percent of the waste the city normally produces, with the remaining 20 percent — the stuff that is real garbage and nobody wants — going to the landfill area of the site. This means that about 200,000 tonnes would be land-filled annually. Separated material would be stored in specific locations to be sold when the market price is attractive.

4. Industrial and commercial waste offers enormous opportunities for recycling. Most of that material would not be land-filled. As an incentive, separated materials would get a discount while mixed waste materials charges would be much higher to reflect the additional costs of separation. But provincial legislation would be needed to ensure that separation and recycling occurs.

5. Compost would be sold or given away. City roads and parks projects would require, in the contract specifications, that such compost material be used as topsoil dressing. Excess compost could be stored in special compost farms. The waste processing and recycling plants would go a long way to reducing and solving Toronto's waste disposal problems for many years.

6. As part of the waste reduction plan, Toronto should develop an education program where "garbologists" would visit residents, on a house-to-house basis, and help develop a household reduction plan.

Three specific areas would be identified as a pilot project — a residential neighbourhood, old strip commercial/residential area and two or three high-rise apartments. A team of "garbies" would be responsible for the pilot projects. The garbage trucks for the study areas would be equipped with scales. The garbage from each house would be weighed before the project begins and three to six months after the project had been in place. The evaluation of the three projects would result in a blueprint for all to participate in the reduction of waste. It would be self-sustaining and would result in tremendous savings for the city. A reduction of 10,000 tonnes of waste would save $550,000.

7. Finally, Toronto should follow the lead of some European countries and take steps to ban all plastic from the waste stream. Plastic should be recovered for recycling. Plastic bags in landfill sites also prevent the predictable production of methane, as plastic bag filament tends to seal or lock in organic matter and prevent the breakdown process from taking place.

CHAPTER 15
Industry: Finding Jobs for the Citizens

Every city needs a variety of employment opportunities for its citizens. That means factories to produce goods for foreign and domestic sale, service industries and research and development in technology and science. And a city needs an efficient day-to-day service to make the whole system work.

The administrative structure of a city should have an industrial department — a lean, effective organization to make sure that the needs of industry and the creation and maintenance of jobs are a priority.

The old City of Toronto's industrial co-ordinating committees did a superb job in helping retain industries in older areas, which had a mixture of industrial and residential uses. The committees acted as referees between the residents and the industries. In the earlier years, divisions between industrial and residential areas were blurred. It was only later, after planning and political considerations, that politicians decided to separate industry from residential areas.

In the new amalgamated Toronto, the focus has been mainly on residential development, and the employment or jobs sector of the city's economy has been sorely lacking. The Planning Department has a surplus of staff that could be reassigned to cater to industry. And planning fits in very well with the attraction and promotion of industry. But it also requires sales skills to promote the city as a place for industry and manufacturing, as well as a place to live and play.

Commerce in the form of shopping plazas and office buildings is a broad-based service required anywhere large groups of people live. It cannot be compared to manufacturing, industry and research and development, which have special needs. When Metropolitan Toronto was formed in 1954, the outlying municipalities had taken a lot of vacant land — mostly farmland — surrounding the old City of Toronto into the new urban structure. With a new planning approach, which separated residential, commercial and industrial areas, new industrial areas were set aside — separate from residential areas. Commercial development very often became part of the buffer between residential and industrial lands.

The industrial lots were large and located near arterial roads and highways. The land was also inexpensive and became a magnet for industries from the old city — many of which needed to expand and modernize as well as escape the constant hassle and battles with residential neighbours. These expanding municipalities catered to residential, commercial and industrial uses in an attempt to provide a package deal for the new urban municipality. At the time, this new approach to urban planning was considered attractive, as it allowed the municipalities to segregate these uses in an organized pattern, with the urban amenities not far away. But it added to municipal sprawl, with mostly single-family homes in maze-like formations, called subdivisions, spreading ever outward in low-rise buildings. Industrial and manufacturing buildings, from a production point of view, justified low-rise buildings, as most activities were best carried out at ground level.

Toronto, from its earliest days, had a well-balanced but relatively unplanned industrial base. No one industry dominated. That provided for a good mix of talent for the workforce and a base for a healthy economy. But since the early days, city politicians took industry for granted. Some emerging municipalities had an Industrial Department, headed by a commissioner — a top sales-person whose sole purpose was to bring new industries to the municipality. But many older cities did not cater to changes in society and improvements in technology. And they did not notice the expanding municipalities around their borders, which little by little were wooing industries from the old city.

The earlier general view, though not publicly stated, was that industry was not glamorous. It had a dirty image, with many pollution problems — especially air pollution — affecting residential neighbourhoods. Promotional material for the old city showed many smokestacks from industry belching out black smoke from coal-burning furnaces. That was portrayed as a sign of progress.

In the early 1960s, the new gloss of modernism came with the development of the downtown area's box-like commercial sky-scrapers. Clusters of high-rise apartment buildings — also box-like

— sprang up around the outside of the downtown core. Plans for all these new buildings were presented at City Hall by the promoters — highlighting lots of open space, with trees and park-like amenities for strolling people. But in reality, these high-rise apartment buildings provided a lot of congestion, although the accompanying artists' sketches prepared for the developers and displayed at City Hall camouflaged most of that congestion.

By the middle of the 1960s, the movement of industries out of the city was significant. The adjoining municipalities of Etobicoke, Scarborough and North York were busting at the seams with the development of single-family homes, some high-rise apartments and industrial buildings. Even the outlying municipalities of Mississauga, Markham, Vaughan and Pickering were attracting industries — many from south of the border but some from the City of Toronto.

At the same time, the Ministry of the Environment began to recognize the increasing problem of air and water pollution. Slowly, tougher new environmental standards were introduced. Planning regulations were developed and rigorously enforced so that there would be a clear separation between land uses.

Many industries in the old city found it difficult to meet the new environmental standards. Many had to change by installing more efficient equipment to stay competitive and retain a fair share of their product in the marketplace. Many old industrial buildings did not have room to expand, and that provided another reason to look at the possibility of relocating to a larger, well-serviced site. For many industries it was just a question of time before the decision to move would have to be made.

LAND USE DESIGNATION

The modern approach to urban land use has to meet simple criteria that separate the various land uses. There are four basic uses — residential, commercial, industrial and open space. These can be further subdivided to meet the individual requirements of an area.

The designation for industry is quite broad. It varies from light industrial-related work, which may blend into commercial service activities, to heavy industrial — steel mills, heavy manufacturing, garbage processing, sewage treatment plants, outdoor storage for bulk granular materials, or loading and unloading of freight.

By the end of the 1950s the Canadian National and Canadian Pacific Railway companies had relocated and consolidated their freight facilities to new hump yards outside the old City of Toronto. The CNR built a new line around Toronto with a hump yard north of Highway 7 and west of Keele Street in Maple, while the CPR relocated its piggy back and all its freight handling to a new hump yard in Agincourt, in the northeast section of Scarborough. These were practical attempts to control and consolidate the movement of freight following the emergence of the piggy backs and the container system a few years earlier.

Some mixed industrial lands were prime candidates for change with the relocation of railway freight facilities. These areas would eventually become residential as many industries followed the rail facilities to relocate outside the old city. But there were also some large tracts of industrial land in the old city, separated from residential areas. The City had made strong commitments that an industrial base should be retained and these large areas should be safeguarded. Two areas in particular were earmarked for industrial use — the King-Strachan-Dufferin area in the west end and the Port Lands area in the east end.

THE MASSEY LANDS

With new pressures to rezone industrial lands to residential, the King-Strachan areas succumbed to the lobbying of the developers and the CIBC to rezone the old Massey Ferguson lands. This change in use from industrial to residential was a great victory for developers. It increases the value of the rezoned land by a factor of about three. And it provided small, minimum-type "affordable" housing.

The story of the King-Strachan area is probably the most interesting saga of all. It went through a creeping form of change from industrial to residential, beginning with the closing of the Massey Ferguson plant in October 1982. Massey

Ferguson had been in farm equipment manufacturing for more than 50 years — until about the mid-1970s. It had worldwide business interests and was proudly acknowledged as a great example of Canadian expertise.

The plant on King Street West covered 11 acres and at one time employed over 9,000 workers. The original Massey Harris head office, at 915 King Street West, was still standing, but senior management had moved to offices in the downtown core many years before. By the early 1970s, rumours began to surface that Massey Ferguson was in trouble. The company was not able to compete against the new farm equipment companies formed after World War II. Jobs began to be siphoned off and Massey Ferguson eventually announced it was preparing to wind up its business.

But the company owed many millions of dollars to the Canadian Imperial Bank of Commerce (CIBC). As part of the agreement, the CIBC would take over the Massey Ferguson properties on King Street West. When the last workers left the plant in October 1982, many industrial buildings lay idle. Massey Ferguson officials met with the city planners and politicians to look at possible future use of the lands. After almost three years of studies, meetings and reports, a plan was developed that was acceptable to the City and Massey Ferguson and bylaw #694-86 was passed. In called for:

- A portion of the land north of King Street to be zoned residential;
- The remainder of the land, especially south of King Street, would remain industrial and would be used for high-tech industries;
- The old Massey Harris head office at 915 King Street West would be restored as a historical building, with the ground floor used for community purposes;
- Massey Ferguson would participate in the cost sharing of the proposed grade separation, at the rail crossing at Strachan Ave, south of King Street;
- The five-storey, 35,000-square-foot building at 1071 King Street West would be turned into an "incubator" building to help small start-up businesses. The City would

own 10 percent of the property and would have a ten-year, rent-free lease on the whole building.

As the real estate market was hot, Massey Ferguson had no difficulty attracting buyers for the land. In no time the land was sold to developers for about $52 million — a success beyond expectations. The developers had visions of reaping fair profits in the sizzling real estate market. The CIBC was happy — it got more money back than expected from its investment in Massey Ferguson. The residential portion of the land, north of King Street, was built quickly, although a fire on the site destroyed some of the new homes, which had to be rebuilt. The CIBC parcelled out the land as demand increased. They were so happy that they even bankrolled the developers.

The CIBC decided to build an 800,000-square-foot data-processing centre south of the old Massey Harris building for its own banking operations to show its support for the development of the high-tech area. The bank filed plans at City Hall and began the building application process. Guarantee Trust also filed plans to build its own data-processing building at the southwest corner of King and Strachan. And Bell Telephone followed with its own complex on the east side of Strachan Avenue. It looked like the high-tech area was beginning to happen.

Massey Ferguson hired the architectural firm Kearns Mancini to draw plans for the restoration of the Massey Harris building. The plans were outstanding and Kearns Mancini was featured in the magazine *Architecture*. The City Library Board also retained an architect to develop plans for a public library on the ground floor.

The real estate buying frenzy became unreal as the market peaked in July 1989. Then, suddenly, everything fell apart. The market crashed and developers were left holding very expensive land, which nobody, now, seemed to want. Bankruptcies followed for many investors — speculators as well as developers. The residential component of the Massey Lands had been completed successfully. And Guarantee Trust built as planned — until they ran into financial difficulties and were taken over by another trust company. The Bell building also was well under construction.

But the CIBC decided not to build its data-processing centre, which was to have been the anchor for the high-tech area. It was a terrible disappointment and a death blow to high-tech plans to rejuvenate the entire area. The bank had other troubles with the lands. It had loaned money to the builders and developers, who could now not meet their payments. Bankruptcies were sure to follow. Once again the CIBC was stuck in a financial quagmire — the second time on the same lands. Developers walked away from their down payments and loans and the bank became the mortgagee in possession. The real estate crash cast a pall over the life of the business community. By 1992 the market was dismal. Building activity was at a standstill. The Massey lands were dead.

The construction industry was in dreadful shape, as many were out of work and the unemployment lines were getting longer. City planners, politicians and building officials tried to get some projects moving. Studies were begun in areas that might have some potential. Many scattered industrial and commercial buildings were vacant and in disrepair. Planners and builders suggested some of these old buildings could be converted into residential lofts, as the housing shortage was still severe. It was suggested that the applications could be processed through the Committee of Adjustment rather than through the standard planning process.

The Massey lands were now included in the general plan known as the "Garrison Common" area. It was named after the Garrison Creek, which was once a meandering creek through the lower end of the west end of Toronto — from Christie Pits, through Trinity Bellwoods Park and Stanley Park, to the lake. But the creek had long since been filled in and piped as the city began to grow in the early 1900s.

The development of industrial land — and that included land for high-tech — was dead. Or, at least, there was no one out front promoting the vast amount of industrial land available. Residences were needed and that was a sure winner for developers. The Garrison Common planning studies included discussions with local residents along the route of the old creek and many meetings with other adjacent resident groups. All this input allowed the planners to develop plans that highlighted the potential of the old industrial lands for residential use — with, of course, some properly designed open space. That was all the CIBC needed to hear. The lobbyists and developers talked to the politicians and the Massey Ferguson lands were again back before the planning process.

In a panic to get some housing started — and kick-start the building industry — pressure mounted to begin converting some old buildings in scattered industrial and commercial sites to residential lofts. The first few applications worked out all right. Lofts became trendy — an ideal location for people who had a small down payment and did not need a lot of living space. The development of the loft led to the rebirth of the residential market. Finally, in 1997, a new Massey lands agreement was reached. It is detailed in bylaw #1997-0521. It was a huge victory and a bail-out plan or the CIBC. The major differences from the 1986 agreement were:

- Residential uses would be permitted in all the industrial lands;
- The commitment of a financial contribution to a grade separation at Strachan Avenue was deleted;
- The Massey Harris building at 915 King Street West would be residential and the community ground floor uses were deleted.

After lying vacant for 20 years, by the end of 2002 the old Massey Harris historical building was in a terrible state. It has not been restored as proposed by the Kearns Mancini plan. The only real activity around the dilapidated building was the sales drive to market lofts. The lofts and low-cost housing were the foot in the door that developers needed. The lands would soon be developed to accommodate hundreds of lofts and "affordable" houses. It was the end of an industrial era at King and Strachan. The next big challenge for the developers to oust industry would shift to the Port Lands.

THE PORT LANDS

Planning, for any city with a port, has to include sufficient land to allow for industrial uses to keep the area vibrant and active in the manufacture, storage and movement of goods. Most of the land in the Toronto port area is publicly owned. The City, through the Toronto Economic Development Corporation (TEDCO), is now the largest owner in the area, with about 700 hectares, having added 163 hectares in a deal with the Toronto Harbour Commission in 1994. This left the Harbour Commission, later renamed the Toronto Port Authority (TPA), with only about 100 hectares.

The old Hearn Power Generation plant, now owned by Ontario Power Generation (OPG), which has been closed since 1982, owns 26.6 hectares. Another 2.56 hectares, mainly a 1,059-metre strip along the dock wall, 16.76 metres wide, is owned by the TPA and is leased to OPG for 999 years. Many potential buyers from overseas developing countries have looked at the old generation equipment. It is 1950s technology and in disrepair. And to a developing country seeking to buy cheap start-up equipment, it poses many problems. It is a 60-cycle electrical generation system, whereas most developing countries use 100-cycle systems. On top of that the costs of dismantling the equipment and shipping are horrendous. It would be much better to sell the equipment as scrap.

The Port Lands area is the only major industrial area left in the old city. It has the unsightly and basic industrial services every city needs — the sewage treatment plant; the garbage recycling stations; the oil storage tanks; concrete batching plant; sand and gravel storage areas; concrete and rubble recycling plant; salt storage areas and open storage areas along the dock walls. These may not be glamorous industries, but they are needed. There is also a lot of unused industrial land, vacant for many years, which could be used for the development of new manufacturing industries, especially for the export markets.

As the City pays no taxes on land it owns, there is no incentive to market the unused land. That could never happen in the private sector. Property taxes have to be paid or the property is seized and sold for taxes. Over the years the City has developed a policy of public ownership of the industrial port lands — all on the basis that public ownership would be financially profitable for the City. But the opposite has been true. Since the lands were City owned it was expected that industries would be attracted to leasing the land. But that did not happen. City politicians and bureaucrats have not been able to bring jobs and industries to the Port Lands. Plans have been announced from time to time about "great things coming." It is like the two tramps in Samuel Beckett's *Waiting for Godot*. We all know that Godot never came!

The port area of the waterfront — the last major industrial tract of land in the old city — has a practical appeal for industry. And the City has to acknowledge that the quality of life in any community depends on the provision of employment. A dynamic, proactive sales program to promote, entice, help and encourage industries is needed.

There are a few basic steps that should be taken to begin the process to attract industries. Here are some suggestions that could help. They would cost very little and would be a real boon to the people of Toronto:

- The vacant Port Lands properties should be sold to manufacturers and exporters. At least these owners would pay property taxes — and not let the land lie derelict and non-productive, as has happened over all those years.
- The City needs an industrial department to promote and attract industry and the provision of thousands of new jobs.
- The City should recognize the Port Lands as a major industrial asset and take steps to have it turned into a free trade zone.
- The City needs a vibrant and active port to enhance the commerce of the city. The Port of Toronto can be the industrial beacon of the city on the lake.

CHAPTER 16
On the Waterfront: The Making of a Port

Every city should be lucky enough to have a waterfront. I prefer an ocean lapping on my doorstep. It smells much healthier than the musty odour of a freshwater lake on a hot summer day. Since I grew up by the sea, I suppose my nostrils were more attuned to the salt-sea air and the constant roar of Atlantic winds. The *boreen* in front of our house was an old narrow road, meandering to the shore between two thick, mossy, limestone walls. At one time, over 200 years ago, it serviced 12 small thatched houses, at the end of the road, above the high-water mark. The families eked out a living as small farmers and fishermen. Only the four walls of the tiny houses now stand. The potato famine in the 1840s destroyed the community. In less than one generation, the homes were abandoned. Now the fox and badger find refuge in the high grass around the ruins, and seabirds nest among the bare stones of the crumbling walls.

As a young boy, I often wandered down to the sea, which was about 200 metres from our house. It had that eerie attraction for me. It was like leaving the human world and entering a place with haunting sounds — the cradle of nature — bathed in whispering winds, rolling waves and pounding surf. The shoreline was a rocky complex of limestone boulders — strewn around in haphazard formations by angry Atlantic waves. Here and there, little coves of yellow sandy beaches showed the more serene side of a wild seascape.

I could understand the classical world's reverence for the sea and for its god Neptune. I had enjoyed Virgil's *Aeneid* at school and I had no trouble conjuring up visions of the gods deciding who should have a rugged, rocky shore and who should have a golden, sandy beach. And I thought that maybe it was true that the raging storms and rock-strewn shore were created by a sadistic god to vent his anger. And perhaps the sandy beaches were the product of his better days.

Our house, the only two-storey building in the area, had a good view of a beach — called *loc an uisge* — meaning the "lake of water" in Gaelic. Once I got to know its rhythms and its personality, I felt at home there — in a more spiritual way than anything else. But physically, I was also part of the natural order of things — part of the land. I could read the runes of nature, from the wild plants and flowers that were rooted and grew among the rocks, to the seabirds and wild animals that constantly patrolled the edge of the sea.

The simple signs of nature, and the inclusion of all life, had a profound impact on my reasoning and understanding of the order of it all. As I sat on the shore, gazing out on the waves, I noticed the seagulls flying through the trough of the waves — almost touching the water. I knew that the seagulls were conserving energy and at the same time playing with the running waves. Then, as the wind blew stronger, I could see all the seabirds, resting on the short grass above the high-tide mark, facing into the wind, so that the aerodynamics were right for an efficient, fast takeoff.

The survival instinct also led me to the shore when the tide was out. I knew all the nooks and crannies, camouflaged by sea-weed, where I could collect big juicy crabs. And I knew where to get mussels, oysters and clams to add to the table for the evening meal. These gifts were another reason to feel at one with nature.

I could spend hours — alone — sitting on the side of a pool, with my bare feet soaking up the salty water. I could see all the different little fish and other crawly things enjoying a new respite in their lives when the tide was out. I was fascinated by the teeming life in these pools and began to understand the existence of a whole new microscopic world, carved out by the sea. Nature was wonderful. I wanted to know more — always inquiring and searching for ways to satisfy my mounting curiosity. I thought about becoming a marine biologist some day. But that was only a dream.

The constant west wind off the ocean had a power that could be kind and gentle, with soft breezes that sounded at times like fairy music. But when a storm blew, the fury knew no end. It was like the old devil himself, banging incoherently on a thousand kettledrums. But I thought of storms as the magnificent display of the power of nature — symphonies in the rolling clouds to be enjoyed while the wild winds were loose.

While I could not have all the material things that my friends had in the nearby town of Ballyvaughan or in the city of Galway, I had the panorama of a stretch of ocean as far as the eye could see — and further — to the coast of North America. And that panorama enriched my boyhood domain far more than the man-made streets or ancient walls of Galway town.

As a young engineer, I had my first real job with consulting engineers Sir Wm. Halcrow & Partners. I was part of a small engineering crew constructing sea defenses for the town of Seaforth, in Sussex, England. One night a terrible storm hit Seaforth. It smashed the concrete forming in an awesome display of power. I have never forgotten the first day after the storm — inspecting the broken timber supports strewn around like match-sticks and the tons of boulders washed away like little pebbles. It looked like a herd of mad demons, under the cover of darkness, had been unleashed by the gods of the wind and the seas. As I looked at all the damage, I remembered the historical accounts of the terrible storm that wreaked havoc on the 130 ships of the Spanish Armada in the summer of 1588 along the very same coast and north along the western coast of Ireland.

And when I arrived in Toronto, a thousand miles inland, my first impression of Lake Ontario was one of disappointment. I had thought that the Great Lakes would, indeed, be great. But I was wrong. The water did not have that refreshing smell — it was bland. There were no waves and no tides. It was only a lake, not the ocean. But in the end I became accustomed to the gentler and more predictable waters of Lake Ontario. It's not the sea, but it's the next best thing!

THE PORT OF TORONTO

Over the years, Toronto developed northwards from the shores of the lake. The lake served as the doorway to the town and its fledgling commerce and trade. But the early days of every frontier town were days of struggle to nurture the roots of a community. Toronto was no different. In the 1740s, the French voyageurs were the first Europeans to set up a trading post near the Humber

River. They called it Fort Rouille. The first cargo ship, a 50-ton French vessel, arrived at the fort in 1749.

During those years, the battle for control of territory was waged between the French and the English. And the native Indians were caught between those two European powers. After a few skirmishes and an attack by the English, the French set fire to the fort in 1759 and moved to Niagara. After the Treaty of Paris, following the defeat of the French in the battle of the Plains of Abraham, the English controlled the country. The Toronto Land Purchase, executed by representatives of King George III and the Mississauga Indians, was drawn up in 1787. The agreement was amended in 1805 to clearly define the limits of the purchase. When Canada was divided into Upper and Lower Canada in 1791, Colonel John Graves Simcoe was appointed governor of Upper Canada. He named the community around the harbour York — to honour the victories of the Duke of York against the French.

By 1803 the population of the town was 456. It began to grow slowly and the activity and commerce of the small port area increased. By 1834 the population had increased to 9,254. It was also during the early part of that century that the linking of waterways by canals became an integral part of transportation. The Lachine Canal in 1824, the Welland Canal in 1829, the Cornwall Canal in 1840, the Beauharnois Canal in 1845 and the Williamsburg Canal in 1849 — all were opened for business.

As soon as the canals were built, the steam engine appeared on the scene. By 1850 British North America had only 66 miles of railroad track. After 1850 interest in railways dominated the politics of transportation. It spurred the building of the railways, which had a tremendous impact on the movement of goods and people. Railroad building continued into the middle of the twentieth century.

After the turn of the century the area along the Toronto shoreline was a mish-mash of rickety wooden docks, wharves and swampy marshes with increasing human activity around the water's edge. And with the steady increase of global industrialization, Toronto was also swept up in this new approach to "progress." The clamour for the orderly development of the waterfront soon rose to the top of the public agenda. City council and the provincial and federal governments wanted to see some orderly control over development activities on the waterfront.

THE 1912 WATERFRONT PLAN

The Toronto Harbour Commissioners' Act of 1911 — a federal act introduced at the urging of the City — set the framework for the development of the waterfront. A master plan was prepared by engineers and presented to the Commission in November 1912. The engineers noted that the plan was to provide for "the proper treatment of the harbour both from a commercial and industrial point of view and also for the development of the aesthetic features of the waterfront." The plan was estimated to cost $19 million and would cover the waterfront from Victoria Park Avenue to the Humber River, split into three sections — east, west and central. The plan was developed with the view that the St. Lawrence Seaway would be built in the "near future" to open up the Great Lakes ports to ocean-going cargo vessels.

The recreational features of the plan included:

- Expansion of the beaches east of Woodbine Avenue and west of Bathurst Street;
- Protection of the shoreline by the construction of break-walls from Bathurst Street to the Humber River and from Woodbine Avenue to the eastern city limits;
- Provision for aquatic activities: rowing, boating, recreation and sailing;
- Expanding and reshaping the Toronto Islands by 894 acres;
- A complete waterfront system of driveways and paths.

The commercial, industrial and port facilities of the plan included:

- A new industrial district, in the vicinity of Ashbridges Bay, developed with the addition of 644 acres from the dredged material of the inner harbour;

- The harbour to be dredged to 24 feet to allow for larger cargo ships;
- Modern permanent stone or concrete docks to be built along the central port area to replace the old wooden wharves;
- New loading and unloading facilities, warehouses, freight sheds and factory space provided for goods and services and the needs of the port;
- A 6,800 feet shipping channel, 400 feet wide, to serve the new three miles of docks in the new industrial area;
- The mouth of the Don River to be diverted west into the harbour through the Keating Channel;
- All the dock areas to be serviced with railway lines and roads.

Once the waterfront plan was adopted, work began immediately. By 1930 most of the plan was in place. It began as a grand vision for the waterfront, which led to a remarkable period of planning and building — unparalleled in the history of the city.

The city had continued to expand as new immigrants arrived. And the railways continued to expand to link up with other cities and centres of commerce. All this activity helped shape the Port Lands area. The docks, as we know them today, were gradually built — thanks to the 1912 waterfront plan.

Generally, all the land — about 318 acres south of Front Street, from Bathurst Street to Cherry Street and the port area — is made from the garbage and rubble of the past. In 1820 there was so much garbage, rubble, cinders and ash being dumped in the marshy Ashbridges area that the City examined the possibility of using the Toronto Street Railway Company to take over the haulage. Eventually, council decided not to use rail-haul. They decided to stay with the horse and cart as the preferred mode of haulage. This continued until well into the twentieth century. And the dredging of the harbour from 14 to 24 feet, in the years 1914 to 1930, provided many more millions of cubic feet of dredged material to complete the filling-in of the Ashbridges Bay area. Between 1930 and 1950 very little work was done on the waterfront.

Over the years, since the beginning of the town of York, and in the absence of any rules or regulations, it was customary to dump sewage and all types of residential and industrial wastes in the marshy parts of the shoreline in the vicinity of Asbridges Bay or in the nearest gully. But the development of the port and the building of the dock walls finally put an end to the dumping of waste directly into the lake.

The areas behind the dock walls in the old city were filled with garbage, rubble and dredgate. The breakwall from around the foot of Bathurst Street, along the Western Beaches to the mouth of the Humber River, was built by the federal government between 1914 and 1925. It consisted of a wooden crib, anchored in the bottom sediment, filled with rocks, and capped with a poured concrete slab. It cost $5 million at that time.

Opening up the Great Lakes to large ocean-going cargo ships was always a dream of the cities along the lakes. A Deep Waterways Commission was set up in 1895 to examine this. It caused many a long-drawn-out debate over the years. Finally, in 1951 the Canadian government passed an act to set up the Seaway Authority. This was followed in 1954 by the United States with corresponding legislation — the Wiley-Dondero Act.

When it became evident that the St. Lawrence Seaway would be built and the Welland Canal would be improved (for the fourth time) to take larger cargo ships, the Harbour Commission began to complete the expansion of the port facilities.

In 1954, the final 52 acres of reclaimed land, between Yonge Street and Parliament Street, was added to the waterfront, making a total of 318 acres of reclaimed land in this area, with dock walls and open space for warehousing. Then, Marine Terminal #27, with 100,000 square feet of space, was added. In 1959, Queen Elizabeth II, while on a visit to Canada to open the St. Lawrence Seaway, visited Toronto and opened the Queen Elizabeth Docks and the Redpath Sugar Refinery, on Queens Quay East.

The railways — the Canadian Pacific Railway and the Grand Trunk Railway — played a vital role in the development of the waterfront. Having obtained large concessions from the governments of the day, the railway companies owned much of the land to service commerce and industry on the waterfront. The Toronto

Terminal Railways Company was set up by the two railway companies to have control of Union Station and the railway lands between Bathurst Street and Jarvis Street. The ownership of private, public and railway land was always an impediment to work on a large scale along the waterfront.

As an engineer, I worked for the Harbours and Rivers branch of the federal Department of Public Works in the spring and summer of 1957. I was assigned the responsibility of monitoring and calculating dredgate quantities for the Toronto harbour. McNamara Marine, Canadian Dredge and Dock and Russell Construction had dredging contracts.

The deepening of the Western Gap was completed at that time. It was carried out by McNamara Engineering to allow the large ocean-going ships into the Toronto Harbour from the west side of Toronto. The deepening was more difficult, as the bottom was mostly shale, which had to be broken up. A dragline was then used to load the dredgate to scows or dump trucks for disposal.

Dredging was carried out using either a suction system or a dragline. The suction system was used in the east inner harbour area, where the floating pipes carried the dredgate to a confined location in the Ashbridges Bay area. This material would form part of new additional land. At that time the docks along the inner harbour — east and west of Yonge Street — were used for shipping (cargo). At around the same time, the runway at the Island Airport was extended to its present length.

Dredging in the Toronto Harbour has not been a priority of the federal Public Works Department for almost 50 years. It is costly and fraught with jurisdictional and disposal problems, with little chance of speedy approval because of mounting environmental regulations over the years.

Dredging the lower Don River and the Keating Channel should be a priority. It is estimated that the Don River carries 40,000 to 45,000 cubic metres of silt to the lower Don and Keating Channel every year. And it builds up, year after year. After a heavy rainstorm, the lower Don River constantly overflows its banks and floods the Don Valley Parkway and local roads. The heavy rainfall in early August 2005 should have been a clear warning — the next time may be a catastrophy with the loss of many lives.

Over the years silt has also built up in the inner harbour. But it would not be practical to dredge all the inner harbour, as the depths for most of the harbour are adequate for navigation. But the lower Don and Keating Channel must be dredged.

Dredging the harbour is the responsibility of the federal government, as all navigable waters come under its control — under the Navigable Waters Act. Aquatic and fish life are also under the federal government through the Department of Oceans and Fisheries. There is no record of dredging the port area of any port unless silt build-up hinders navigation.

In the mid-1960s, with a building boom developing in and around Toronto, particularly in the downtown area, arrangements were made through the Metro Toronto and Region Conservation Authority to create parkland and marinas along the waterfront from all the excavated material. As a member of the Authority, I viewed the use of the fill as a practical and worthwhile way of creating new land.

The opening of the St. Lawrence Seaway was thought to be a real help to the ports of the Great Lakes. But as the years rolled by, with increasing seaway tolls and the advent of containers and huge container ships, inland ports were severely hampered. The Toronto port activities were dramatically affected and receded into a type of hibernation — waiting, as it were, for the ships that did not come.

But the port of Toronto has always been a vital component of the waterfront. And it can still play a very positive role in the industrial, manufacturing and export/import sectors of the economy. It has the three vital components of a transportation hub: rail services, highways and lots of dock wall for servicing ships. It has a 300-ton crane — the largest crane of any of the Great Lakes' ports.

In the early 1960s, the Harbour Commission, as owner of the lands on the south side of Queen's Quay between York Street and Yonge Street, decided to lease land for residential and commercial development. The Commission needed the money to balance the books. The agreement between the federal government and the City stipulated that if there was a shortfall at the Harbour Commission, the City would be required to pay it.

Robert Campeau, an Ottawa building contractor, built the Harbour Castle Hotel complex next to the Ferry Terminal dock. A convention centre for the hotel, on the north side of Queens Quay, was later added. High-rise apartments and condominiums followed west to York Street.

Opposition began to mount against the density and the blocking of the lake by such tall buildings. And citizen activist groups began to speak out against new residential buildings that were proposed in the place of commerce and the activities of the port. Shortly after all the turmoil with Campeau and his development, the city planners proposed to council that there should be no further residential developments on the waterfront and that all the land east of Yonge Street should be retained as industrial and for an active port. When it was enshrined in the city's plan, it was supposed to guarantee the untouchable status of the industries and the industrial lands east of Yonge Street. It also was a clear indicator that an active port was part of the city's plan.

As the city began to celebrate the hundredth anniversary of Confederation in 1967, the waterfront controversy was put aside. And members of city council thought that the future of the port lands and the port were guaranteed for industrial and export/import purposes. There would be no residential intrusions and the waterfront would be opened up for general recreation activities.

Late in the summer of 1972, prior to the federal election, the incumbent Liberal government promised that it would donate the waterfront lands, between York Street and Bathurst Street, for an "urban park." Mitchell Sharp, who was Minister of Finance and the cabinet minister responsible for the Toronto area, made the announcement. City politicians were delighted, as that strip of land was an eyesore with shacks and derelict buildings strung along that section of waterfront.

The Harbourfront Corporation was set up to oversee the development of the park. The only building that was worth retaining was the Terminal Warehouse at the foot of York Street. It was bought by Olympia and York and restored. It was a long and costly project, but when it was finished, it was a beautiful building with condominiums on the upper floors and stores on the first and second floors.

I had no idea that an "urban park" would mean a concentration of ugly high-rise buildings strung along Harbourfront! But that was what the city eventually got. I did not like what was happening and did not support it. It was a new definition of parkland. It fooled me!

The provincial government and its super salesman Stanley Randall, Minister of Consumer Affairs, had grand designs for building a beautiful state-of-the art recreational and entertainment complex to be known as Ontario Place. After an argument with Metro Chairman Bill Allen and some disagreements with Metro Council about the jurisdiction of the Ontario Place location, the matter was finally settled, with the provincial government having control of the property. Jim Ramsey, a senior official in Randall's office, was designated as the hands-on operations manager to make it all happen. It would be built on man-made islands and a sunken ship — jutting out into the lake, opposite Exhibition Place. There was so much excavated material from all the development in the downtown area that it did not take too long to build the islands. When Ontario Place was opened in 1971, it was lauded as the catalyst to bring the waterfront to life.

As the building boom continued, the excavated material was used by the Metro Toronto and Region Conservation Authority (MTRCA) for the development of additional lands for parks, marinas and recreation along the waterfront — east of Coxwell Avenue and west of the Humber River.

The ownership of the lands along the waterfront has always been a political jungle. The Toronto City Council, Metro Council and the provincial and federal governments all had a say in what happened. It was so mixed up at times that it was impossible to get anything moving.

THE WATERFRONT PLAN (2000)

When anything was about to happen or some plan or development was suggested, the waterfront was always a very confusing place — a bit of a plaything for developers and politicians. There has always been some type of plan floating around —

always, of course, promising a wonderful, open, recreational place for the people of Toronto.

The dawning of the third millennium saw the introduction of another new plan for the Toronto waterfront — but the new vision tended to trivialize and diminish the traditional industrial role of the port. Some Toronto politicians speculated that some of the port activities, like the bulk storage of salt for the roads in the winter, could be moved to Hamilton. One politician cynically blurted out that they might be able to move the Ashbridges Bay Sewage Treatment Plant to Hamilton, as well.

Over the years many dreamers — mainly planners and politicians — have presented visions of what the Toronto waterfront should look like. The latest waterfront plan was the dream of Robert Fong. I am sure he is well intentioned and wants to make a contribution. He is a successful businessman and friend of former prime minister Jean Chretien. Mayor Mel Lastman had been in office only a few months when Fong tabled his plans and visions of a magnificent waterfront to rival any in the world. The mayor became so excited with the plan that he went overboard with a verbal volley of his well-worn favourite superlatives.

As I listened to the first details of the plan, I saw it as an attempt to turn the waterfront into a kind of Disneyland with Venetian canals and lots of green space, with views of the water, trees and other delightful ingredients. The plan would be the bait to lure financiers and developers — all eager to take part in the projected profits and help the city "return the waterfront to the people."

The "Three Amigos," Mayor Lastman, Premier Harris and Prime Minister Chretien, travelled by boat to the Docks — an entertainment place owned by developer Gerry Sprachman. It was a sunny June day in 1998, and the three politicians vowed to make the new waterfront plan a reality. In the warm sun, with sailing boats in the background, they promised to work together to turn the port lands into the centrepiece of a bid for the 2008 Olympics. They would instruct their staff to work together to develop the plan and to work out the financial details.

The mayor urged the planners to work on it with all haste. Soon the enthusiasm for a magnificent waterfront had infected all who worked on it at City Hall. Many people believed that Lastman could pull it off. After all, he was "Bad Boy" — the great salesman. He had even sold a fridge to an Inuit and $2 bills for $1 at the corner of Queen and Yonge, in Toronto, before he became a politician. Selling a waterfront plan should have been a piece of cake!

The next meeting of the Three Amigos was on a bitterly cold November day in 1999 at Cinespace — a Queen's Quay building used for filmmaking by businessman Nick Mirkopoulos. It was the type of inhospitable weather that shrouds the waterfront most of the year. As the saying goes, it was "fit for neither man nor beast." There, in the indoor protection, the politicians, assembled on a stage that, ironically, had been used many times before to portray a make-believe world, announced that all three levels of government were working together to make the waterfront plan a reality.

They showed their commitment by declaring that each level of government would ante up $500 million to get the work started. That's $1.5 billion, but a small fraction of the $12 billion to build what the mayor had in mind. The three announced projects were:

1.   Complete the Union Station platforms to handle anticipated large crowds.
2.   Begin a clean-up of the contaminated publicly owned lands in the port area.
3.   Extend of Front Street west from Bathurst Street to link up with the expressway.

But who would provide the billions of dollars needed? There was a simple answer to that question, as well. The developers would line up to build thousands of apartments and condominiums in selected areas along the waterfront and over sections of the buried Gardiner Expressway. The air rights would be leased to them at top dollar. And the few inside developers who had already tied up some land in the port area would make a bundle when it was rezoned to residential.

As I listened to the Three Amigos throw superlatives around about their magnificent vision of the waterfront, I became a little suspicious of how easy it all sounded. There must be a catch somewhere. The planners had nice sketches with appropriate wording of how the waterfront plan would be a kind of gift to the people of Toronto. It would provide lots of green and open spaces, recreation and entertainment complexes as well as wonderful aquatic facilities for sailing, canoeing and other water-related activities. The pictures and sketches showed idyllic summer settings, which would be useful about four months of the year. There was no mention of the other eight months. I had the feeling that I had been through many of these news conferences before — and this one also appeared to be a candidate for the dustbin.

Then, after the news conference, I ventured outside into the penetrating cold to hurry back to my office. I knew, there and then, that something was wrong with the waterfront picture the planners had presented, as well as the political comments from Lastman, Harris and Chretien. They had forgotten to mention how this magnificent waterfront they planned would survive outside the summer season. I could understand that omission!

I have searched for some answers that may show why this massive waterfront plan is being promoted so vigorously, and the following observations always come into focus:

- The promoters will not have to pay — the taxpayers will pay … eventually;
- There is little understanding by politicians and planners of the role of climate;
- A group of property owners on the waterfront act as the lead promoters;
- It will rid the port area of industry and provide lots of affordable housing;
- Some city politicians want to close down the port and its activities.

The cost of the new waterfront was estimated at $12 to $17 billion. It would have lots of "affordable" housing — in nodules across the lakefront. Between these housing nodules there would be room for some commercial buildings as well as parks, trees and walkways. Beautiful sketches showed sailboats, rowing, flowers, families strolling through parks and water lapping shores — a tantalizing picture.

Obviously, the promoters of this new vision of the waterfront never asked why Ontario Place is only open for four months every year — and with limited success. The yacht clubs, canoe clubs and rowing clubs could easily answer that same question also. And the answer is simple: the waterfront, for eight or nine months of the year, is a bleak, inhospitable place, and no matter how much money is poured into it, it will still be a place controlled by our frigid northern climate. Ontario Place officials have tried hard to keep the "fun place" open after September 15, but when the cold winds begin to blow, Toronto folk abandon it, until sometime in early June the following year. It would be foolish to believe that the new waterfront would be any different.

City planners, at the urging of developers, visualize many thousands of apartments and condos in the port area. If, by any chance, a residential development is built, it would very quickly lead to a continuous fight with the industries in the area. Eventually, industry would be forced out, because only residents vote — companies cannot. But the "new" waterfront plan will never happen. Reality will take over after the chaotic first six years of the amalgamation of Toronto. Imagine what could be done with $12 billion to help the real concerns — such as meeting the transit needs of an expanded city?

THE GARDINER EXPRESSWAY

The Gardiner Expressway — especially since amalgamation in 1998 — has become a divisive element in the new waterfront planning. The proposal to demolish it is a "wouldn't it be nice" scenario. Built between 1956 and 1965 at a cost of $105 million, the Gardiner is a key component and a major part of the roads system — not only in the waterfront — but also as the entrance to the heart of the city. It carries 110,000 vehicles every day and its demolition would be a severe blow to the economy of the city.

The main argument against the Gardiner has been that it looks ugly. That argument is very subjective. Few people like sewage treatment plants, garbage processing plants, water filtration plants, railroad tracks and major road works. But the simple fact is that we could not do without them. It would be silly to demolish any major service simply because we do not like the looks of it. It would be foolish and a total waste of money. But then, on reflection, people have a tendency to spend other people's money on projects that would never merit a second thought if it were their own money.

The second argument is that it blocks the view of the lake, or in political jargon, "it separates the city from the lake." That does not make much sense either, as the walls of apartments and condominiums along Queens Quay, especially between Yonge Street and Bathurst Street, already block the view of the lake.

Tearing down the Gardiner Expressway and replacing it with an "at grade" road system would further separate the city from the waterfront. It would look like Highway 401, which now splits the northern parts of the city. It would look worse than the existing expressway and would have a devastating impact on the southern part of the old city. Most of the voices against the Gardiner are raised by those who know very little about the servicing of a city. And they know even less about setting financial priorities and the economic role of the Gardiner in servicing the heart of the city.

What to do with the Gardiner Expressway, has been the subject of many discussions for the last 15 years. It appears that the position taken by some active demolitionists will not change. To them, the Gardiner will always be an ugly barrier between the city and the lake. But others — I suspect most people in Toronto — will recognize that the Gardiner is vital and should stay.

Rebuilding the Gardiner over the waterfront railway tracks of the Toronto Terminal Railways Company — not in reinforced concrete but in structural steel — is the most practical suggestion for the replacement of the Gardiner. Using this route would not interfere with the operation of the present expressway. The space over the railway tracks, between the Skydome and the Convention Centre, would be the tightest squeeze for the expressway if that route were chosen.

The Railways Act requires that the distance from the base of rail to the underside of the expressway be 22 feet. This amounts to a structure of no more than three stories tall. And if it is decided that the air rights have some value, buildings could be built over the expressway in some locations. But practical solutions have no dream qualities. The demolition and replacement of the Gardiner is still many years away. Much depends on its rate of deterioration and the City's priorities.

As the expressway ages, the deterioration of the present concrete structure will become increasingly expensive to repair, as the concrete and steel reinforcing rods react to the salty road drainage of the winter. The annual structural maintenance costs up to 2002 were a minimum of $7 million annually. Those costs will gradually increase and eventually the Gardiner will have to be replaced.

The Waterfront Plan proposes to bury the expressway, or at least part of it, and lease parts of the right-of-way to developers. The finances raised through the leases would be used to rebuild a new underground expressway/road system. That of course would be enormously expensive, as a new underground expressway would be below the water table and much of it in the rubble of the past on lands south of Front Street. Also the new "on" and "off" ramps would require additional properties that may cause other location problems. The proposers of the new plan have stated that it would not cost Toronto taxpayers any money, as the developers would pay handsomely for the density rights. There are no studies or examples anywhere to back up that statement. If that is accurate, the tooth fairy is real and elephants can fly!

The plan to bury the Boston expressway is usually cited as an example for Toronto to follow. The total cost of that project has jumped from an original cost estimate of $2.6 billion in August 1985 to about $13.6 billion U.S. (about $18 billion Canadian) in 2004. That is much more than the entire Toronto waterfront plan. But the U.S. federal government is contributing about 80 percent of the Boston financing. It is doubtful that Ottawa would contribute one cent to the demolition of the Gardiner. There are other more deserving areas in need of funding.

And the idea of imposing a toll for those who use the Gardiner is an example of a lack of knowledge of the downtown. Tolls would kill the commercial heart of the city, which is already bleeding and bloody from the actions of governments with little understanding of business and industry in the downtown area.

Many Toronto offices — especially in the downtown area — are not fully occupied because of the enormous property taxes required to fund the city bureaucracy and the constant struggle to carry on business in an increasing unfriendly political atmosphere. These taxes are among the highest in North America.

A more practical plan for the Toronto waterfront is needed and the city should:

- set up an industrial department to promote and attract industries to the city;
- set up an industrial free trade zone for the Port Lands area, utilizing the adjacent rail lines, highways and shipping facilities, all of which are readily available;
- set up a Port Lands technical working group to process the easy movement of goods by rail and road to the port facilities;
- sell vacant industrial waterfront lands to industries, which would bring needed employment and pay property taxes;
- develop a practical plan for the future construction of the Gardiner Expressway over the railway tracks, with as little traffic disruption as possible; and
- petition the federal government to dredge the lower Don River and Keating Channel.

CHAPTER 17
Transportation: Getting Out of the Traffic Jam

The movement of people and goods is a key planning and engineering factor in every city. A good harbour or navigable river is an asset that boats, barges and ships can use. But a variety of wheeled transport on land is also essential. We are all familiar with the perennial cry for better roads. Early roads tended to meander haphazardly over the terrain. As G.K. Chesterton aptly put it, "The rolling English drunkard made the rolling English road."

The earliest recorded evidence of the use of the wheel comes from the area between the Tigris and Euphrates Rivers in the vicinity of Baghdad, around 3500 BC. It is the picture of a primitive two-wheel ox-drawn cart. It seems that tribes in central and Eastern Europe adopted the wheel a few centuries later. Some time later, the Celts adopted the wheel with enthusiasm and became superb craftsmen at wheel building. They added many innovations, including the one-piece wooden rim, spokes with iron tires and the metal-lined hub with wooden rollers to reduce friction for the axle. They also designed the front swivelling axle for the four-wheel cart, which became standard in all future four-wheel carts.

The Greeks, Persians, Romans, Assyrians, Chinese, Indians and many other peoples built their system around animal-drawn carts. Although the wheel was introduced in Egypt, the rulers of that country preferred the sledges because they were more movable in sand and sandy soil, in the absence of solid roads. But it was the Romans, adopting the innovations of the Celts, who took total advantage of the wheel, as they began to build superb roads to service their empire more than 2,000 years ago.

Roman road builders, unlike the English road builders who followed them, built their Via Appia highway straight north from Londinium — not so much for transportation reasons as to allow the army legions to march up to Hadrian's Wall to keep the rebellious Picts in check. The roads were solidly built with a top layer of mortared stone slabs on a layer of sand and gravel, resting on stone slabs set in a mainly clay foundation. The centre or crown was slightly elevated to provide proper drainage to the side ditches. All of the 80,000 kilometres of Roman roads were wide enough to accommodate at least a horse-drawn cart. The old roads also had a path on each side for pedestrians.

The old Roman town of Pompeii, just outside Naples, which was buried by volcanic ash following the eruption of Mount Vesuvius in AD 79, provides a good example of early city roads. Pompeii has been partially excavated over the last 75 years to reveal an almost perfectly preserved urban structure with streets, houses, stores and other amenities.

CANALS

Although navigable rivers had always been used, the idea of deepening rivers and connecting them with man-made canals opened up a new era. The Chinese were great canal builders, beginning about 200 BC. And they had perfected the use of locks many hundreds of years before the canal-building craze hit Europe. Their Grand Canal is a perfect example of their expertise — enabling vessels to rise 42 metres above sea level. And it is recorded that the Egyptians built a canal linking the River Nile to the Red Sea about 2000 BC, although there is no evidence of it today. The blowing desert sands over the centuries have obliterated any traces of that canal.

The first canal with a lock in Europe was built at Sparendam in the Netherlands in 1253. Soon, countries began to develop plans to link up navigable rivers and move goods and materials. These early canals had walkways along the sides so that horses could tow the barges. Many of these major canals had popular names, such as the Grand Canal or the Royal Canal. Some of them are still in use today.

Canal construction in the U.S. and Canada lagged Europe by about 50 years — primarily because of a lack of government funding and leadership from the business communities. Canal building in North America began about 1810 and for the next 50 years, great progress was made in linking many of the major water-ways to the ocean. In Canada, the canals included the Lachine Canal on the St. Lawrence River, built between 1821 and 1825 and enlarged between 1843 and 1848; the Rideau Canal, built between 1826 and 1832; the Trent waterway (1843 to 1848); and the Welland Canal (1824 to 1833), built to bypass Niagara Falls and the rapids, connecting Lake Erie to Lake Ontario. It was improved from 1842 to 1850, and again from 1873 to 1883, and for the fourth time from 1913 to 1932. The St. Lawrence Seaway was opened by Canada and the U.S. in 1959.

Building a canal required a large labour force to excavate and move the material for the new water channel, as well as guidance from engineers to lay out the most practical route. Sometimes a canal would require the construction of locks to raise or lower the barges to move through the canal. That required skill in hydraulics and building locks to move barges upstream and downstream. Many canals were in operation by the mid-1800s. As loading and unloading the barges required labour and factories needed a system for the transportation of goods, towns along the canals mushroomed into areas of industrial activity.

RAILWAYS

Thomas Newcoman, in 1712, developed the first reciprocating steam engine to pump water from mines. James Watt improved Newcoman's design and made the first rotary motion by crank and flywheel, which made it possible to use the engine for motion as well as pumping. By the end of the 1700s Richard Trevithick had further improved the steam engine to make it possible to develop the first railways. In 1804, for the first time, a steam engine moved passengers and goods, when a Trevithick-designed engine and car, carrying 10 tons of pig iron and 70 workers, went from Penydarren to Abercynon, in Wales — a distance of 10 miles — in just over four hours and five minutes. Trevithick won a wager of 500 guineas with that success.

The first public railway line, built between Liverpool and Manchester — a distance of 30 miles — began service in 1830. It carried goods and passengers and proved to be a profitable business for those who invested and saw a future in it. Railroads proved to be the real catalyst for the industrial revolution in England and Europe. Engineers and inventors began to design and build railroads — borrowing and improving all the time on the latest achievements in engineering and technology.

The first locomotive in North America was built by the West Point Foundry of New York for the Charleston and Hamburg Railroad (later the Baltimore & Ohio Railroad). The first day of operation, when public rail service began, was January 15, 1831. At speeds of up to 20 miles per hour, the train travelled for six miles from Charleston. By 1833 the line had reached Hamburg, a suburb of Augusta, Georgia, 135 miles away. It was a success and became very popular.

Building railroads in the United States was a mixture of business, politics and corruption. As business tycoons battled each other for right-of-ways, government help and support from politicians, many unsavory businessmen emerged and many shady deals were made. Arriving immigrants found work and adventure in pushing the railroad west. The work was hard and the conditions were rugged and demanding. Although European immigrants, especially from Central Europe, Ireland, Scotland and England, were attracted to this type of work, it also attracted characters from all over the world who contributed to the folklore and adventure of opening up the west.

The competition to link the east and west coasts by rail was fierce. The railway tycoons in California were wheeling and dealing in schemes to push the railroad east in a bid to meet a deadline to join the two lines at an appointed location. Chinese immigrant workers contributed most to that section of the line — at times under terrible personal abuse and appalling conditions. It took many years for the federal government to eventually clean up the mess and racketeering.

The Union Pacific and the Central Pacific rail lines joined at Promontory in Utah with the driving of the last spike on May 10, 1869 — linking the Pacific and Atlantic coasts. By that time, new federal guidelines and legislation to cope with political corruption were needed to bring order and respectability to the railways.

The building of railways in Canada lagged the U.S. by about 15 years, although the first steam engine appeared on the scene with the Champlain and St. Lawrence Railway Company opening a 16-mile rail line from Montreal's south shore to St-Jean-sur-Richelieu in 1836.

By 1850, British North America had only 66 miles of railroad track. After the 1850s, interest in railways dominated politics. It spurred the building of the railways across the country and had a tremendous impact on opening up the vast territories of the west. The first Canadian railway link to both Atlantic and Pacific coasts happened in 1885, with the arrival of the first train in Port Moody, British Columbia. As in the U.S., Chinese immigrants contributed greatly to the development of the Canadian railways. The building of the railways continued into the middle of the twentieth century.

The focus on the early railways has been on the design and modifications to the steam engine. But the laying and linking of the steel tracks on wooden ties, all resting on a solid foundation to carry the moving locomotive and rail cars, was just as important in ensuring that the system was reliable and worked safely.

The standard rail gauge adopted in England was 4 feet 8.5 inches, or 1.435 metres. There is no real explanation for that exact measurement, but it is about the width between the cart wheels for the old Roman roadways. Recognizing that the railways could be a great asset for the movement of armies and equipment, many countries decided on different rail gauges. In Europe, Spain, Portugal and Russia had different gauges that could not carry the standard rail cars.

In the early days of the railway in Canada, the major railway companies used a wide track gauge of 5 feet 6 inches (1.68 metres) but converted to the standard gauge in the 1870s. By the 1880s the narrow gauge tracks were also converted to standard gauge. Most of the northern U.S. states had used the standard gauge, while some of the southern states used different gauges. Eventually the standard gauge of 4 feet 8.5 inches became the accepted system in Canada and the U.S.

I remember going by train from Barcelona, Spain, to Geneva, Switzerland, in the summer of 1969. When the train reached the

French border, all passengers had to leave the train and transfer to another train for the journey to Geneva. At that time Spain had a different gauge from the rest of Europe. I also remember a July night in 1991, on the Soviet train from Leningrad (St. Petersburg) and Vilnius to Warsaw, having the same problem. When the train arrived at Grodno — the Belarus-Poland border — the axles and wheels of the train were actually changed for the journey to Warsaw, while the Soviet soldiers made sure that no passengers left the train during the three-hour changing operation.

I have always enjoyed the railways. They add a certain romance to travel. I worked as a bridge and building engineer and a track engineer for both the CNR and the CPR for two years in the early 1960s. I have never lost the fascination of that endless ribbon of steel.

By the beginning of the twentieth century, railway lines criss-crossed most countries in the world. Since many towns were built before the railway, they were not planned with adequate space for the rail tracks and related services. Accommodation had to be made to build a railway station to handle passengers as well as rail sidings, with storage buildings, to provide for the movement of goods. This often caused problems as the railway separated the town from the port area. But for a hundred years — from about 1840 to 1940 — the big steam engines, or iron horses, were the lifeline of North American towns and cities.

AUTOMOBILES — THE CAR

At the same time, the design and refinement of the bicycle made for a most attractive personal mode of transportation. By the early twentieth century, the bicycle began to replace the horse and donkey. But the horse and carriage and the horse and cart remained for a few more decades — until 1920 or 1930. And the bicycle is still very much a part of everyday life — even in competition with the car.

Henry Ford saw a horseless vehicle as the vehicle of the future after the development of the internal combustion engine. With three partners, he set up the Ford Motor Company in 1903. The

271

first automobile was the Model A. The company developed many models — going through the alphabet — each improving on the previous model and each having a limited success. But when the four-cylinder Model T was introduced in October 1908 it was an immediate success. They could not build them fast enough.

Ford decided to build a moving assembly line production system in 1913. It revolutionized manufacturing. The automated assembly line helped to mass-produce the Model T — the first automobile to be mass-produced. And it changed traffic and transportation forever. It also resulted in a significant change in the planning, design and structure of cities. In 1914 the Ford Motor Company produced 308,000 Model Ts. By 1923 the annual production reached 1.8 million. And by 1927 Ford had produced a total of 15 million. Seeing the success of the Ford Motor Company, other companies such as General Motors, American Motors and Chrysler were formed and began building automobiles. By 1929 there were 29 million vehicles registered in the United States.

The internal combustion engine was the key component. Other automobile companies sprang up in Europe — Austin, Peugeot, Renault, Fiat, to name a few. Very soon, millions of cars, trucks and buses were moving off assembly lines to meet the demand of an infatuated public. But there were not enough roads — vehicles clogged them, causing severe problems for the old towns, which could scarcely handle horse and cart transportation. The impact on the narrow streets of old cities in Europe was devastating.

Cities in North America fared a little better, as the towns and cities were laid out in square or rectangular grids and the streets were generally much wider. It soon became apparent that the automobile was dictating the planning and development of every urban area in the modern world.

The advent of the automobile had a devastating effect on the railroads. Up to the beginning of the twentieth century, railroads were the ribbons of steel, linking cities together. Business had been profitable for the many railroad companies.

Every city had a grand edifice for a railway station — and, just as in Toronto, it was usually known for its grand sounding name — Union Station, Central Station or Grand Central Station, etc.

But by the early 1920s, it was evident that the automobile was changing the passenger side of transportation. Gradually the railroad companies began to decline as competition for the passenger dollar increased.

After the Great Depression of 1929, North American railroads made a determined attempt to modernize and compete. Railway cars were built with lightweight steel. The steam engine was replaced with gasoline and then the diesel-electric engine. Some European countries, such as Switzerland and France, spearheaded the use of electric trains. The design of the train was also streamlined to reduce aerodynamic drag. This increased the efficiency and the speed of trains. But still it was a losing battle to capture the imagination of a more demanding and more mobile public.

When World War II broke out in 1939, it seemed that the railroads got a new lease on life. Some 90 percent of all military equipment and 95 percent of all military forces were moved by railroads. But with the end of the war the railroads went into a steeper slump. They just could not compete with the automobile and the newly designed passenger planes. By the 1950s, railroads — except in Japan and some European countries — had largely fallen into disarray. Their passenger services were hit by jet planes for longer distances and the more flexible and personal automobile for shorter distances. As the pattern of travel changed, with vacant train stations being replaced by ever-expanding airports, the automobile was clearly winning the battle on the ground and causing havoc for the railroads and the city landscape. New highways and expressways were built, weaving in and through the cities. The face of every city began to show the agony of that change, as politicians could not control the onslaught.

The grand rail stations became like vacant caverns from another era. Some were demolished, but many have been saved. They are some of the most beautiful structures in North American cities — monuments to the age of steam. Some are used as scaled-down railway stations and some are used for other purposes.

BUILDING ROADS

The earliest roads in Canada were made of wooden planks. Since wood was available and plentiful, it seemed like the best solution for roads that had to endure a rigorous climate. The right-of-way was cleared first and long wooden beams were laid, preferably in sand. Then cross planks were placed over them, with a small space between them, and nailed at right angles to the beams. Sand was then poured over the planks. A stretch of plank road, built east from Toronto in 1836, so impressed the city commissioners that they decided to plank many parts of Yonge Street north from Toronto in 1841. But as the roads became worn down with traffic, they became very uncomfortable, with a bone-rattling washboard effect. Still, plank roads were popular in the United States and Canada from the early 1800s to about 1850. Many of those early thoroughfares were toll roads, most operated privately. With a small population it was difficult to build and maintain any kind of road.

The standard road allowance of the nineteenth century was 66 feet — the length of a surveyors chain. As town planning developed and standards were set, municipalities adopted the 66-foot road allowance. This would be a publicly owned right-of-way that included a pavement of 28 feet to accommodate two lanes — one each way, with room for a sidewalk and a boulevard on each side. The new road surface was now tarmacadam, called asphalt — the development of Scottish engineer John McAdam. Asphalt is an ideal road surface — easy to make, relatively affordable, flexible, durable and easy to lay. As a road surface, it is difficult to beat.

Sewers — sanitary, storm or combined sewers — and water mains were laid under the travelled portion, while the other underground and above-ground services, such as gas, telephone, electricity, were relegated to the areas off the travelled road or wherever space could be found. In many cases, the underground was so crowded with utilities that it became a real challenge to build and maintain these services. With the arrival of the automobile, more traffic lanes were needed for some roads. These road allowances, called arterial roads, were designated 86 feet and 120 feet wide — depending on the volume of surface traffic.

But the narrowest local street was 66 feet wide. As a city politician, when attending to a constituent building problem, to find the property line, I would pace off eleven steps from the centre of the road. That gave me a fairly accurate location of the property line.

After that came highways and expressways, which were much wider and could carry eight to ten lanes of traffic or more. Wide ribbons of asphalt or concrete pavement crossed valleys, fields, mountains and rivers — improving the movement of people and goods but scarring the landscape. The U.S. interstates and inter-provincial highways in Canada are the main transportation links in North America. With a minimum of two lanes in each direction and no traffic lights, they are the cross-country ribbons of life, with gas stations, motels and small communities benefiting along their routes. The highways bearing the odd numbers run north and south, while the even numbers run east and west.

Cities did not fare so well with the arrival of the car. As autos, trucks and buses rolled off the assembly lines, the rush to own one became insatiable. In North America, a two-car garage became the symbol of the family home, located in new subdivisions outside the old city's boundaries. But it was inevitable that the automobile would lead to all-out battles in cities that could not handle any more cars without building new highways and expressways. And building expressways meant tearing down buildings to make way for the wide right-of-ways with enough space for "on" and "off" ramps. The battle between the automobile and segments of the population could not be avoided. As the vast majority of people had adopted it as a necessity for work and play, there was no doubt that the automobile would be the winner.

Governments had the problem of reconciling the economic importance of the automobile with its impact on urban areas, especially when seven of ten jobs in the manufacturing sector were provided by the auto sector. Making room for the automobile and maintaining adequate space for people to live and enjoy the city was not an easy task for planners. And it was too late for many cities. As expressways made cities look ugly and sterile, the holdouts who lived in the old inner cities could take it no longer. They fled to less complicated areas — away from the constant "zing" of traffic on the streets and expressways.

Between 1950 and 1985, every city in North America had to make room for the automobile — some more than others. In the beginning, planners and politicians, catering to the needs of the electors, worked hard and furiously to accommodate the automobile. But by 1985, many were beginning to question the destruction caused by the expressways and the health-related problems caused by the noise and pollution. The love affair with the automobile and the people was so complete, however, that few cared deeply about public transit until the end of the twentieth century, when planners and politicians started talking about other alternatives to the automobile. But for most North American cities, it was too late — so much damage had already been done.

Toronto was no different than other cities. It, too, had to make room for the automobile. And in 1962, as a project engineer with the then Township of Scarborough, I was responsible for the widening of Lawrence Avenue East, from Morningstar Avenue to Highland Creek. It was my first run-in with the Scarborough Expressway right-of-way. It was planned to cross Lawrence Avenue and I made no provisions for it, as inquiries to Metro Traffic Department indicated it would be a fly-over in its journey north to meet Highway 401. Besides, there were no details of the design for the expressway, as it would not be built for a few years. It would also be a few more years before a bridge would be built across Highland Creek — at which time Scarborough Township would hand over Lawrence Avenue to Metro Toronto as an arterial road.

The Gardiner Expressway — named after Metro Toronto's first chairman, Fred Gardiner — began at the eastern end of the Queen Elizabeth Way, just west of the Humber River. It began at ground level and became elevated east of Dufferin Street and proceeded as an elevated expressway over Lakeshore Boulevard to link up to the Don Valley Parkway. The Gardiner was built between 1956 and 1964 and cost a total of $106 million. This included the property acquisition costs. By way of comparison, rebuilding the bridge for the Gardiner and Lakeshore complex over the Humber River in the late-1990s cost $101 million.

At the Don Valley ramp one section of the expressway proceeded east for another mile, where it ended. It was supposed to proceed north from there into Scarborough as the Scarborough

Expressway to Highway 401 — but it never made it. Anti-expressway groups began to mobilize and Metro decided to defer making any further commitments to proceed. Forty years later, that section or stub of the Gardiner Expressway was finally demolished in 2001-2 at a cost of $42 million.

There were other plans on the drawing board for other expressways — the Crosstown and the Niagara — but they never saw the light of day, because people convinced the politicians that they should be scrapped.

SPADINA EXPRESSWAY

The Spadina Expressway was different. The land had been bought, some bridges were built and the grading and layout had been completed when the opposition against expressways suddenly exploded in 1969. Albert Campbell, mayor of Scarborough, had just been appointed Metro chairman. An anti-expressway group, led by Alderman Colin Vaughan and a few citizens, convinced him to halt any further development of the expressway and not pave the section that was laid out for paving. Premier Bill Davis also decided to withdraw the provincial subsidy of 50 percent, thereby, in effect, killing the expressway.

A few years later, Metro completed the unfinished section of the expressway between Highway 401 and Eglinton Avenue West. It is now known as the Allen Road — named after Bill Allen, another former Metro chairman. It was supposed to proceed south along the Northeimmer Ravine to join Davenport Road near Casa Loma and hook up with Spadina Avenue.

Fortunately, the right-of-way for the original Spadina Expressway included space to build a rapid transit subway line. This was built in 1979 from Union Station, under University and Spadina Avenue, along the Northeimmer Ravine and finally along the centre of the Allen Road north of Highway 401 to end at Wilson Avenue station. It was later extended by one more station — to Sheppard Avenue.

After the cancellation of the Spadina Expressway, Premier Davis advised Metro that the province would contribute 75 percent towards the capital cost of public transit. Unfortunately, Metro, at the time, did not seize that opportunity to develop a master plan for extending the transit system.

By the early 1970s, the era of expressway building was over. People were confused and shocked at the terrible physical changes that the car had inflicted on the city. It had staked out its role in our lives. The love affair continues, but there will be no more new expressways. During those years of road widening and expressway building, city planners continued to advise council to maintain sufficient parking for all new buildings. That was rigidly enforced — it was part of the requirements to get a building permit.

As an example, high-rise apartment buildings required a developer to provide one and a half parking spaces per apartment, plus parking for visitors. Since many tenants did not own a car, many of these apartment buildings had to close off the unused parking floors.

All these parking requirements made little sense to me. It appeared that we, as city councillors, were undermining the public transit system. Although there might be a streetcar or subway station outside an apartment building, the rigorous parking requirements were enforced or no building permit would be issued. I remember the old apartment building at the southeast corner of Church and Wellesley. It was built at a time when there were no parking requirements and therefore it had no parking. It was bought by Ken McGowen, the founder of Mac's Milk. It badly needed to be renovated.

McGowen filed an application for a building permit to renovate the building, but could not get it unless he provided parking for the building — if not in the building, then near the building. I did my best to help, but it was impossible to convince the bureaucracy to process the application. Eventually some arrangements were made for parking. At the time, the Church Street bus desperately needed passengers, or it would be cancelled by the TTC. Eventually the bus was cancelled. It appeared that one arm of government was destroying another — all in the name of "good planning" and progress.

The intrusion of the automobile has led to the decline of public transit. That is understandable, as a car is like a companion that takes us anywhere with ease, speed and comfort. And it has made us selfish, lazy, loud and fat. It is now an essential part of everyday life and to many, a necessary evil. To handle the increasing volumes of traffic, cities have resorted to other plans, such as one-way streets, street widening in some areas that did not involve tearing down buildings, computerized traffic lights and no parking during rush hours on some streets. Some cities have demolished buildings to widen streets to take more traffic. But Toronto has not followed that pattern, although widenings have been squeezed out to provide more traffic lanes. This can be seen on Avenue Road between Bloor Street and St. Clair Avenue, where splash guards had to be installed because the buildings were too near the travelled portion of the road.

At one time Metro had proposed to widen Bathurst Street, between St. Clair Avenue West and Eglinton Avenue West. But local opposition and the terrible impact it would have on the abutting buildings caused Metro to abandon the widening. The only evidence that it was ever contemplated is the widened Bathurst Street Bridge over the Northeimmer Ravine.

There is a constant worry that, as cities increase in population, permanent traffic jams will result. So cities are looking for solutions to get people out of their cars and into public transportation. Even an enticement for carpooling would be a step in the right direction. If cities are to rediscover their livable, people-friendly streets and neighbourhoods of the past, there has to be a truce with the automobile. And planners, politicians and people must work together to accept the automobile as the friendly intruder. The automobile is not going to go away. It is now the inanimate permanent part of the human family. For most it is treated like the family pet — a kind of dog or cat! So we have to make plans so that the relationship will be harmonious.

THE FUEL/ELECTRIC HYBRID

The recent development of the hybrid gasoline/electric engine has proven to be a major advancement in fuel economy and pollution control. The Toyota Prius, the Honda Insight and the Ford Escape are hybrids. They are fuel efficient — up to two times better than a standard automobile the same size. They produce very little pollution, especially in city driving where the batteries produce most of the power. The most effective way to get more of them on the streets is to provide tax and other incentives to consumers who buy them.

Ontario should take the lead by providing some form of matching investment to auto manufacturers to build hybrid vehicles in the province. That would not only cut air pollution but reduce the fuel consumed.

Toronto's mayor, David Miller, already knows about the problems of dirty air. He now uses a city hybrid car. But he and other political leaders need to begin political action for change. We complain a lot about dirty air, but seem to be incapable of doing anything. Some even look at the brown haze over the city as a measure of our progress in the modern world. Our health and our limited supply of fossil fuels cannot afford that picture.

Stop-and-go traffic, the bane of urban commuters, pumps out 10 to 12 times more air pollution than traffic that flows smoothly. That alone is the single biggest reason why Ontario should follow California in tightening regulations on auto emissions. Anytime a vehicle brakes to a stop and then accelerates, fuel is wasted and inefficiently burned. Multiply that by the hundreds of thousands of times that action takes place on city streets every day and it is easy to visualize the atmospheric air pollution concoction we produce and live in every day. We are vociferous in our support of mass transit, but that is a far as it goes. It is not possible in our democratic system to break the love affair with the car. The car is the vehicle of personal gratification — the ultimate mechanical aphrodisiac. Although many thousands use public transport every day, primarily because it meets their practicle and financial requirements, it is a sterile and cumbersome relationship.

Since Canada adopted the Kyoto Protocol on greenhouse gas emissions, in December 2003, it has not developed a clear coherent plan for the efficient use of fuels. It has focused on general solutions, which to most people are confusing when not detailed. One solution, like promoting the hybrid automobile as the ideal urban car, should be a simple example of how to reduce greenhouse gases. But it is probably too simple!

Since communities, towns and particularly cities are impacted most by air pollution from vehicular traffic and the inefficient use of fuel, it is only fitting that cities take a lead role in deciding the type of car favoured on urban streets. The California Air Resources Board (CARB) has shown the way. It has drafted regulations for automakers to reduce greenhouse gas emissions by as much as 30 percent by 2014. As usual, the automakers are objecting, claiming that the target cannot be reached. The Ontario government should follow the actions of CARB — there is much to gain and little to lose. Toronto, the largest city in the province, where the air is highly polluted by exhaust emissions, could work with the province and help develop new guidelines for fuel economy and emission standards.

The internal combustion engine is already a kind of hybrid — but in a small way. Although the engine primarily uses fuel to move the wheels, some electricity is generated to charge the on-board battery to provide the lights and the electric power for the inside of the vehicle. The development of the modern fuel-electric hybrid is a bold step to get the maximum energy from the fuel used. This is done by programming the engine with an improved battery complex, so that the smaller engine and batteries work in harmony to provide the maximum efficiency in fuel consumption The Honda Insight, the Toyota Prius and now the 2005 Ford Escape SUV have all shown that the fuel economy can be far in excess of that of the standard vehicle on the road today.

Litres/100 km	City	Highway
Honda Insight	3.9	3.3
Toyota Prius	4.0	4.2
Ford Escape SUV	6.6	7.0

From a public health point of view, the hybrid, in urban (stop-and-go) traffic, is a real winner, as exhaust pollution can be reduced by as much as 90 percent. That should be a blessing for the thousands of urban dwellers who live next to the heavy traffic of urban streets, where a constant invisible ribbon of poisonous exhaust emissions attack the lungs of everything that breathes.

The city should invite the provincial and federal governments to help develop legislation for the introduction of an urban car — based on the fuel economy and the emissions of hybrids — as a guide for the operation of vehicles. The involvement of these governments would be an enormous help, as environmental responsibility to meet the Kyoto agreement rests primarily with the provincial and the federal governments.

Here are some proposals for the automobile and our city:

- The City of Toronto should lead the way by setting the standards for an urban hybrid car. The City can seek legislation to require the basic urban car to have a fuel economy of 4.0 litres per 100 kilometres for urban driving. All other vehicles would require annual licence fees based on fuel economy. The City can also lead by calling for tenders on the city's fleet of cars to meet the basic specifications.
- Eliminate all speed bumps. They are costly and more of a hazard than a safety provider. And they slow down ambulances and fire trucks.
- Set up a carpooling/automobile-reduction office to expedite a decrease in the number of the single-occupant cars entering and exiting the city every day.
- Request the Province to provide 25 percent of the city's licensing revenues to the City to be used for the operations of the carpooling program.
- Develop an incentive monthly pass system for employers so that they can assist employees to use public transit rather than drive to work.

SUBWAYS FOR CITIES

As a young engineer I was fascinated with the subways of London and Paris. It was the way to get around these cities. What really hit me was the foresight of their city planners — long before the automobile had taken over.

The first streetcars in London were pulled by horses. But as the streets became busier with more people, more streetcars were needed to service the public. The feces from the horses became a constant smelly nuisance and a health hazard. Other cities at that time experienced the same problems. As soon as the use of electricity for transportation was proven, many cities decided to electrify their rail systems. Electricity was particularly appealing for underground trains, as no noxious fumes were produced by the trains. In 1857 London began tunnelling under the Thames River to build the first underground subway system. It was opened in 1863.

It was followed by New York in 1868, Chicago in 1892, and Paris and Budapest in 1898. An above-ground electrified railway system was demonstrated in Berlin in 1879 by Werner von Siemens, who, two years later, built the first electric streetcar system in that city.

North American cities developed about the same time as the automobile — setting up a relationship that let the automobile dominate planning. Automobiles took over the streets while public transit was neglected or relegated to a minor role in the movement of people.

Cities in the developing world were in a different category. Cars were expensive and few people could afford them. Overcrowded and uncomfortable, often carrying chickens, produce and goats, old rickety buses provided the transportation. Passengers clung to the sides and some climbed onto the roof. Many of the buses were the castoffs or used vehicles from the wealthier First World cities. But they provided a basic service in these poorer cities.

Toronto developed like most other North American cities. Public transit had to fight all the time for survival. Streetcars were introduced in the 1920s and became part of the image and identity of the city through the twentieth century. They are popular, but expensive, as track reconstruction and maintenance are very costly parts of public transit. Later buses were introduced and used on streets not serviced by streetcars. Buses were either powered by gasoline, diesel or later by natural gas. Electric buses, or trolleys, also formed part of the bus fleet.

After World War II, in the late 1940s and the early 1950s, the streetcar service on Yonge Street became so congested that planners and politicians agonized on various ways to remedy the situation. The proposed solution, in the early stages, was to bury the streetcars on Yonge Street. After further discussion and input from many interests, this was changed to build the first leg of the Yonge Street subway. The first section, from Union Station to Eglinton Avenue, opened in 1954. From then on, the subway extended north in incremental steps, until it finally reached Finch Avenue in 1984.

The next subway to be constructed was the Bloor-Danforth line — the east-west line. It was constructed in increments, as well, from Kipling Avenue in the west to Kennedy Road in the east. These extensions were extremely political as Etobicoke and Scarborough politicians vied for support for the next extension.

During the construction of the Yonge Street subway, it was decided that an east-west subway line would probably be built along Queen Street. At the intersection of Queen Street an east-west station was excavated and roughed in. When this was completed it was sealed off to await the Queen Street subway line. But the Queen Street subway was not built.

Another mode of transport — the light rail vehicle (LRV), a cross between between the subway car and the streetcar — was introduced in the 1980s. It ran on its own right-of-way and its capital cost was less expensive than the subway. The province at the time was promoting the use of cars built by a Crown corporation, the Urban Transportation Development Corporation (UTDC). Premier Bill Davis and UTDC guru Kirk Foley influenced Metro Chairman Paul Godfrey and Metro Council to use the system for the Scarborough line — a length of 6.5 kilometres. from the Kennedy Road station to Scarborough Town Centre. It was opened on March 22, 1985. As the LRV was Ontario technology, Metro felt obliged to use it. Besides, the provincial government was generous and paid 75 percent of the $19 million capital cost. Once in operation, it was used by the UTDC as a marketing tool to promote its use in other cities — at home and abroad.

I felt uneasy about it all. The engineer side of me told me the system was too small to meet future needs of an expanding urban municipality. The rail curves were too tight and could not be used by the standard subway cars of the Bloor-Danforth line. I regret not fighting harder against the LRT to the Scarborough Town Centre when I was on Metro Council. It should have been a simple extension of the Bloor-Danforth subway system.

I had visited the Swiss company working on the prototype for the UTDC in Schaffhausen in 1978. Although I thought the vehicle would fit into a new transit system, I was not convinced that it would fit into the existing Toronto transit system as a new added intermediate mode of transportation. That, I felt, would add another layer of costs to the already hard-hit TTC.

As we entered the third millennium, the TTC carried about 1,200,000 riders per day — using subways, streetcars, buses and light rail vehicles. And the city has been fortunate because there had been a close relationship between the central business district and feeder transit routes for over 100 years. As I look back over the development of our public transit system, the greatest mistake has been that we have not built on that relationship. There has never been any overall master plan for the development of a public transit. The process used was sporadic and entirely political.

As a member of the TTC in 1977 and 1978, I tried to promote the idea of a master plan for the expansion of the subway system to dovetail into the long-range projections of population increases. I got lukewarm support for the proposal at the time, and it was never really considered further.

The Yonge-University-Spadina subway line, also known as the Lampy Loop because of Mayor Allan Lamport's promotion of it, is an example of a subway built entirely on a political whim, with little positive planning support. It is used as a U line and extension of the Yonge Street subway. It runs from Union Station, under University Avenue and Spadina Avenue and along the ravine north of St. Clair Avenue to Yorkdale Shopping Centre, and across Highway 401 to Downsview Yard, ending up at the Sheppard Avenue station.

It was called "the line to nowhere," since it meandered through a low-density area and ended up in the vacant Downsview Airport lands, where the indecision of the federal government on the future use of the lands has also been a problem. Its only redeeming feature, at the time it was passed by Metro Council, was the contribution of $6 million by the owners of the Yorkdale Shopping Centre. That proved to be a real bargain for the success of the shopping centre.

In the early 1990s, a plan was developed to begin a subway along Eglinton Avenue West, beginning in the vicinity of Oakwood Avenue. It, too, was more political than anything else. About $85 million was spent when Metro Council had a change of heart and decided to fill in the tunnel and forget about doing any further work. At the same time, and on the other side of Yonge Street, plans for the Sheppard subway were begun. Although it had lukewarm support, the mayor of North York, Mel Lastman, was successful in getting it approved. The 6.4-kilometre Sheppard subway, from Yonge Street to Don Mills Road, was opened in the summer of 2002. With stations at Yonge, Bayview, Bessarion, Leslie and Don Mills, it has cost $940 million. That is about $147 million per completed kilometre and does not include any rolling stock.

But the actual cost of the tunnel itself for the Sheppard line was $148.1 million for the 12.8 kilometres of subway (two tunnels — side-by-side) or about $23.2 million per kilometre. That included $6.8 million for design, $99.7 million for construction, $15 for the two tunnel boring machines (TBMs) and $26.6 million for the liners.

SUBWAY MASTER PLAN

A subway master plan is not as inviting as the nice sketches and artists' impressions that show a waterfront plan in a tropical-like setting. The trees, parks, flowers and water activities — and strolling people with their children and pets — set a much more glamorous scene than an overall subway plan to move people. But the need for a long-range subway master plan to cater to the Toronto of tomorrow should be the cornerstone of how we grow, mature and stay together as a city in the next 25 years.

The following master plan is proposed on the basis that residential and commercial development densities will develop and depend on the availability of an efficient transit system. And, conversely, the economic viability of the transit system will depend on the number of people who live and work along its route. The key to a successful transit system is density.

The proposed plan would add 100 kilometres of subway to the existing 53 kilometres over the next 25 years. The proposed new subway lines, and extension of existing lines, are my preferences. But there are others who may have as much or more appeal — depending on planning and population densities.

1. The Circle Line — along Queen Street West, Roncesvalles Avenue/Parkside Drive, Keele Street, Eglinton Avenue, Victoria Park Avenue and Queen Street East — about 45 kilometres.

2. Yonge Street extension to Steeles Avenue — about 1.5 kilometres.

3. Sheppard extension from Yonge Street to Weston Road in the west and Leslie Street to Kennedy Road in the east — about 18 kilometres.

4. North Line along Steeles Avenue — from Weston Road to Kennedy Road — about 20 kilometres.

5. Bloor-Danforth extension to Mississauga Town Centre — about 10 kilometres.

6. University Extension to York University and Steeles Avenue — about 5.5 kilometres.

7. Replace the LRT from Kennedy Road to Scarborough Town Centre by extending the Bloor-Danforth line to Markham Road/Highway 401 — about 6 kilometres.

8. Integrate GO Transit with existing subway and railway lines.

Replacing the LRT to the Scarborough Town Centre and the connections to the GO system are not part of the presented financial plan. But if funds can be arranged they could be added to the 25-year master plan. The savings should be self-evident.

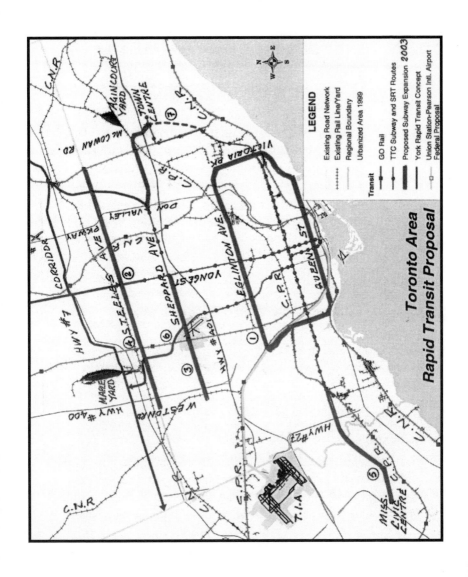

CAPITAL COSTS — WHO WILL PAY?

This is the most difficult and challenging part of any subway proposal. It is a constant headache for all cities to fund and build such essential services. Plans may be accepted and promises made, but on a project such as the building of the 100 kilometres of subways, the provincial and federal governments must assist in funding. I have tried to be innovative in my approach to planning and funding.

Part A

I have assumed an average cost of $35 million per kilometres of subway (two tunnels) over the 25-year construction period of the project, using two tunnel boring machines (TBMs), in a constant work program until the subways are complete. The cost includes design, supervision, the construction of the tunnel and liners and the disposal of the excavated material. It is assumed that the tunnel would be constructed in clay or shale, above the water table and not needing "under air" working conditions.

The three levels of government — federal, provincial and municipal — would contribute equally. At $24 million per kilometre averaged over the first five years, the cost should not be more than $35 million per kilometre over the length of the project. The project would require $96 million per year for the first five years to construct 20 kilometres of subway. That is $32 million per year from each level of government. The total cost of the tunnelling for the 100 kilometres is $3.5 billion.

Part B

The subway stations, tracks, electrical and related fixed equipment would cost another $30 million per kilometre, or $3 billion for the 100 kilometres. The real estate side of the project — especially the subway stations — should be a partnership of the public and private sectors. The subway line and train entrance/exit locations would be under the street or road allowance and below the services. This would not require any land expropriations.

It would be an opportunity for business to invest in the development of the subway. Subway stations would be connected to commercial and residential buildings and become nodules of activity. Buildings at the four corners of the subway station street would be owned by the private sector, with the TTC operating the subway station itself. The layout would be like the existing University Avenue line. The revenue from the station locations would offset the cost of building the station. This would greatly enhance the role of the TTC and its integration with the business and residential developments.

Part C

Assuming a headway of five minutes in the costing of new subway car requirements, at a cost of $2.5 million per car — or $15 million per train — this works out at $11 million per kilometre or $1.1 billion for the 100-kilometre subway, using the formula 54/H, where H is headway in minutes for cost per kilometre in millions.

The total cost for 100 kilometres of subway with rolling stock is therefore $7.6 billion. If the headway is three minutes, it would cost $700 million more, or $8.3 billion.

PLANNING PROCESS GUIDELINES

City and transit officials, together with area planners, business, industry, community groups and interested individuals, would participate in the preparation of the subway plans. Extensive research and public meetings would be held to determine the best location for the subway lines.

Road allowances vary from 66 feet for an old or local street to 120 feet for a major arterial road. Ideally the subway system should occupy the existing road allowance to ensure that no properties are expropriated. The subway would be deep enough that none of the other underground services (water, gas, sewers, telephone, etc.) are affected. Subway stations would be located at major intersections, with the buildings at each of the four corners of the intersection, having a "green door" entrance to the station. The station itself would have the ticket booth underneath the street.

The North line along Steeles Avenue would provide the kick-start to build a sorely needed east-west public transit system along the Toronto–Region of York boundary — to service an area that will see a population increase of at least 500,000 within the next 25 years. This section along the northern boundary of Toronto is the new gridlock area in the Greater Toronto Area.

The Region of York has already hired planners to examine the feasibility of developing a surface east-west transit system along the Highway 7 corridor with three north-south links to the Toronto transit system. And the adopted Toronto Official Plan projects a population increase of 540,000 by the year 2031. This is an opportunity for Toronto and York politicians to implement a long-range transit plan to service their common areas. But there will be greater increases outside the boundaries of Toronto — in Peel, Halton and Durham regions, on top of the expected increases in the Region of York.

DENSITY, PARKING AND MONEY

The construction of new subways must require a minimum density along the subway route. The density would be enshrined in the official plans of the municipalities and would be untouchable. There would be no exemptions to reduce those densities on commercial and residential zoned lands. Density should be based on a two- to four-minute walk to the subway station — or up to 400 metres. The route density (RD) around the subway station should be the highest coverage, tapering down to normal residential and commercial densities as the walking distances reached four minutes or 400 metres.

All development along the subway route must pay an annual transit tax, based on the floor area of the development. This could be structured at so much per square metre and tapering down at the edge of the RD area. An annual parking tax, per parking space, should be instituted throughout the development in the DR area — adjusted annually to the cost of living increase.

There cannot be a free ride for any subway station, like the Rosedale station on the Yonge line, which is under-used because no development has taken place around it. Local residents in the past have always lobbied successfully against any high-density residential buildings at that location. It is an excellent example of the success of the NIMBY syndrome. When the subway or section of the subway is officially opened the annual density transit tax, based on the permitted RD, would come into effect, whether the density is used or not. This would expedite development and use of the new subway.

Cities were not prepared for the mass migration of the 1950s — refugees after World War II and the flight of rural folk from the farms. It was an overwhelming experience most cities were not prepared for. There were no attempts to plan for the increase in population, so development took place outside the city proper without a long-range transit plan. This lack of a broad plan resulted in sprawl and the domination of and dependence on the automobile for transportation. Toronto, too, has become the victim of sprawl — around the outer limits of the old city. The rush to spread out and build single-family homes in subdivisions formed the basic planning approach.

Shopping centres or malls are haphazardly thrown into the overall sprawl and have consumed vast areas of prime agricultural land. It has been the constant pattern for development for the past 50 years. Public transit has not been a real part of the equation. Sprawl has been the dagger at the heart of transit — and California is probably the best example of that. Anyone who has been there is overwhelmed by the lack of transit and the proliferation of expressways.

The addition of 2 million more people around the fringes of Toronto in the next 25 to 30 years will turn the area into a perpetual traffic jam. We have to be a part of the solution — beginning now. If we do not begin to take action now, the traffic mess will be much greater as the city bulges to cater to all those extra people. There must be an action plan to develop an extended transit system to serve the needs of the expected population increase in the years ahead.

To develop an efficient, well-run transit system the following should take place:

- Adopt a 25-year master plan to build subways;
- Extend the Toronto Transit Commission to cover areas outside Toronto;

- Reduce the modes of transportation to three — subway, streetcar and bus. Eventually the streetcar system should be phased out. They are expensive to operate, as road reconstruction and road maintenance costs are enormous;
- Fuel-electric hybrid and/or fuel cell buses should eventually replace streetcars and all other buses.

CHAPTER 18
Planning, Politics and Election Mandates

The public perception of the city politician ranges all over the map — from the egomaniacal incompetent to the good and faithful servant with the sanctity of a St. Francis of Assisi or a Mother Theresa. Now and again, a city politician rises to the great occasion, as many New Yorkers felt Mayor Rudy Giuliani did after the World Trade Center disaster on September 11, 2001. But mostly the politician is looked on as a devious and slippery kind of character, a scheming Iago who will do anything to get elected. That description is unfair, as politicians represent a cross-section of the general population, where the good far outnumber the not-so-good.

Many disciplines mesh in the administration and government of a municipality. But the two blunt instruments are politics and planning. Politics is a strange world — not quite the "nasty, brutish and short" life described by the political philosopher Thomas Hobbes, but a world that can be confusing, contradicting and bizarre. It can also be dull and boring, as well as charming and lively — like the weather. But it is all part of our democratic system where we, the voters, choose who we want as our politicians.

And whoever is elected, every city needs a plan for orderly development. Politicians get elected for a variety of reasons — but mostly on the promises they make during election campaigns. Making those promises a reality depends on many variables and the advice of planners. On a broader scale, the planners guide the political system and evaluate all proposals, whether made by politicians or outside interests. In Toronto, as in every city, planners are now a key part of operations. At one time, the planning department had a few people on staff to process small projects and co-ordinate the independent consultants hired for major projects. Now the City's planners are part of the municipal workforce and have replaced outside consultants.

There can be no change without input from planners. All projects end up being processed through the planning department. Projects are seldom contracted out — unless specialists are needed. And the annual cost to maintain a full planning department is staggering. Hiring outside planning consultants on a project-by-project basis should be part of the running of an efficient city. It would reduce the annual planning budget considerably.

THE URBAN SPECIALISTS

There has always been a rivalry between engineers and architects. These two professions depend on each other. In the municipal world, engineers take the lead in the building of services such as communications, airports, roads, bridges, water supply, power generation and distribution, sewers and sewage treatment and general engineering works.

Architects design and supervise the erection of buildings. Working for the architect, the engineer's responsibility is to make sure that the structures designed by the architect stand up. In its simplest form, architects design structures — mainly buildings — and engineers have to make sure they are structurally sound. Both engineers and architects are licensed under provincial legislation to practise their professions.

Engineers and architects have made enormous contributions to the building of the city. Theirs is a quieter contribution, with a mix of rivalry and co-operation in building the basic services and infrastructure of the city. Planners, on the other hand, are interpreters of the political mood. Since it is not an exact science, the planners have much more flexibility to act as the front line troops of the people in charge of change — the politicians. The planners also attempt to read the mood of local interest groups that may be affected by a proposal. But it is difficult for a planner to be objective and independent. Although planning expertise is expected, it is always clouded and shortchanged by the political realities of the moment. To perform their role as planning advisers, they must be prepared to tap into the prevailing moods.

Planners live in a different world — a grey world somewhere between the public, politicians, promoters and developers. Their real job is a thankless one. I think of them generally as being the tea leaf readers of the times and also as a liaison between the people and the politicians. In the absence of strong political leadership, the opinion of the planner becomes more important and the city's agenda slips under the aegis of the planning department.

It is doubtful that politicians would ever reduce the number of planners on staff. It is a perfect out for any politician to refer a problem issue to the planning commissioner for review and then report back. This little sleight of hand can take any politician off the hook and into the lap of the bureaucracy. It has saved the life of many a politician and put troublesome issues on the back burner — maybe never to return, or return when they are no longer front and centre issues of any consequence.

Then there is always the opportunity for the politician to influence the direction of the planner's report. Some politicians are better at this than others. Getting a planner to tailor a report to fit the real wishes of a politician is an art unto itself. Planners, unfortunately, because of the nature of planning, can support most of the views of a politician. But it would be unfair to blame them for the ills of a city. They take political direction — and they are often in a no-win situation, where they have to be politically flexible to survive in the muddle of municipal politics.

PLANNING FOR EXPANSION

Toronto, after World War II, was the magnet for most newcomers to Canada. Many came from the displaced persons camps of Europe or fled the cauldron of conflict in Asia. The old city could not accommodate this new influx, so development began to spread to the surrounding municipalities. It was chaos, with haphazard development and little or no planning or infrastructure to handle the explosion in population. Sewers, roads, water, electricity, etc. — all the basic services — needed to be provided.

Gravel roads, individual septic tanks and wells for water supply serviced the existing farmhouses, the crossroad cluster of buildings and the few rustic hamlets. The countryside around Scarborough, North York and Etobicoke consisted mostly of green fields and sectioned-off farms.

With a population of 750,000 and little room to expand, the old city of Toronto could not handle much of this new influx. In the built-up areas of the city, the only way to expand was to demolish older houses and low-rise buildings to build new high-rise apartment buildings. This took time and money. Many were looking to locate in newer and quieter surroundings and the green fields of the adjacent municipalities looked inviting.

The provincial government recognized the problem and set about establishing guidelines for development. Planning, zoning, financing and orderly servicing was essential. New sewers and sewage treatment plants as well as an adequate water supply system were needed as were paved roads, parks, schools and electric power. In the existing streets of the outer municipalities, septic tanks were to be replaced by sewers and piped water would replace individual wells. All this would be carried out under the Local Improvements Act, where the benefiting homeowner was assessed separately for the actual cost of the installed services.

The Department of Municipal Affairs was responsible for planning through the Planning Act. The Ontario Water Resources Commission (OWRC) and the Ontario Municipal Board (OMB) were the two main provincial agencies, with total control of all development in the municipalities. The OWRC controlled water and sewer services, while the OMB had the final say in handling public input and keeping a watchful eye on municipal financial matters.

By the mid-1950s, new provincial guidelines required that all sewage piping would be separated. The sanitary sewer — the one that collected human and organic wastes — should go to a treatment plant, while the stormwater or rain runoff should go to a separate sewer and into the nearest watercourse to be carried to the lake. The idea here was simple: it was easy to calculate the piping for sanitary sewage but the capacity of the storm sewers depended entirely on the weather. The general guidelines for storm sewer design were based on rainfall records. Later, in the mid-1960s, the OWRC directed that all upstream sewage treatment plants in and around Toronto should be phased out and bigger plants should be built on the shores of Lake Ontario.

All these guidelines provided a new opportunity to the developing municipalities. They also began to take a lot of pressure off the old City of Toronto. Sprawling new subdivisions began to change the face of the countryside as bulldozers, scrapers, shovels, graders and paving machines worked the green fields into ugly urban landscapes. Municipalities were inundated with requests from developers to expedite the planning process to obtain building permits.

All development of raw land was processed under a plan of subdivision. An agreement between the municipality and the developer or subdivider outlined that all the lots were provided with basic sewer and water services as well as sidewalks, curbs, gutters and roads — all to the standards of the municipality and the relevant provincial agencies. The municipality also extracted hefty lot levies from developers — which were unilaterally set by the local municipality. These levies were supposed to be used by the municipality to help in the maintenance and servicing of the newly constructed development.

All these new levies were deposited into the general account of the municipality. The new homeowners paid property taxes like every one else. Some years, many municipalities made so much money in these lot levies that they were able to boast that through "good management" there would be no tax increases. While encouraging new residents, municipalities had found another source of funds to placate long-time residents by keeping the taxes down.

In the meantime, carrying out what was considered to be orderly planning and zoning, municipalities allowed the development of residential, commercial and industrial sectors — all of it on the spread-out or sprawl system. The only redeeming feature was the use of buffer zones to separate these uses.

Although I had worked for the Township of Scarborough as a works engineer, I was not happy with the shape and density of residential and commercial development. I had no say in planning. My role was to design and install the basic services requested by the politicians. The subdivision sprawl was an eyesore — and in most cases inefficient and a waste of land. Strip commercial, along the main roads, with a hodge-podge of cheap ugly stores and plenty of front parking, looked worse. And, a little later, new shopping centres, with acres of parking, began to siphon off business from the downtown. That was later followed by the huge box-type stores — Price Club, Home Depot, etc. — all driving another nail in the coffin of the strip commercial and the old downtown shopping streets.

The new municipalities had no core or downtown — no heart — in more ways than one. They were basic dormitories for the old city — a place where people went after work. These areas were sterile — like a chaotic Salvador Dali tableau. They lacked the togetherness thar I found so charming and alive in old European cities.

Even the old City of Toronto had a lot of variety and cramped charm, a great sense of community and a real downtown with a variety of arts and entertainment. It was a relatively young city — the halfway point between a London or Paris. And although the old city core still has that compact presentation, newer developments along the outside arterial roads have generally destroyed the landscape with stringy, ugly, low-rise, uncoordinated street development. Anyone who drives along Lawrence Avenue or Eglinton Avenue in Scarborough will get that feeling of ugliness and the impact of that sprawl.

Maze-like residential subdivisions, where one- and two-car garage houses set the standard for residential living, have gobbled up what used to be productive agricultural land. At the time, these developments were considered the best way to provide housing for an expanding population. In reality they became the standard housing for the families of young working people. Tragically North American cities have made little attempt to grow in an orderly way. Although older cities followed the European urban concept, all new cities tended to accept sprawl without a real identifiable centre.

When I worked as a municipal engineer, first with Town Planning Consultants, then with Fred Schaeffer & Associates, and later as a municipal engineer with the Township of Scarborough, I was following the guidelines laid out by the municipality and the province. And although I did not question the overall planning rationale, nevertheless I was part of the system that developed sprawl. I felt uneasy when I had to design and lay out a subdivision from the Elms Golf Course in the Islington Avenue/Rexdale

Boulevard area. I looked on it as the evolution of the North American way of living. Besides I had no opportunity to inflict my views on municipal expansion. But it did arouse some basic feelings I had about the destruction of lush green fields with a meandering stream. I did not know any of the local politicians. I was not interested in local politics, at the time. But the Elms got my political instincts aroused.

Development was linked to transportation. It was, and still is, the view of planners that one of the first requirements for development is transportation. That meant roads and automobiles — and to a lesser extent, public transit. The automobile easily won out. It provided an easy and convenient way to move around. The new urban conglomeration was planned and built for the automobile, just as the Old World city was built for the horse and buggy.

The in-between mode of transportation was the railway. It was the backbone — and it led the industrial revolution in the 1860s. The hub of the city became the train station, and it was logical that local public transit would evolve from the railways. But the automobile led to the physical destruction or strangulation of many of the old cities.

The new city has been geometrically simplified with little creative thought. It is presented as a sterile impersonal jumble of developments — usually without a heart or core. Mississauga is a good example of such a city. It is continuous sprawl. And I used to get a chuckle every time Mayor Mel Lastman spoke about "downtown North York — the city with a heart." Scarborough and Etobicoke were also good examples of the new city — cities without a heart.

Perhaps it is my fondness for history and for old cities and towns, but I feel every city should have a main square and a vibrant downtown full of shops and people. That's why I love the charm and warmth of the cities of the Old World — although sadly, squeezing automobiles into those cities has led to the erosion of the quality and fabric of life. The Spanish, for example, were great city builders. The beautiful old cities of Spain, with a little Moorish influence, have so much warmth and character — Salamanca, Toledo, Grenada, Cordoba, etc. Some examples of Spanish planning and city building can also be seen in many old Central and South American cities.

The real problem with modern North American cities is that they have such extremes — very high densities downtown and very low densities everywhere else. London, Paris, Madrid, Amsterdam and other great cities have shown that balanced development with sub-centres can enrich a city. But in our cities, the development of mini-cores or sub-centres has not been promoted. Indeed, it has been popular for residents to fight the introduction of higher densities when it is in their backyard but to support high densities when it is someplace else — particularly in the downtown.

The most troublesome area for our cities has been the need to develop and improve public transportation systems. This does not mean that we should chart an extreme course and ban the automobile. It does mean that we must develop a long-range plan — an investment in the future — for subway construction.

Engineers and planners must now address the role of the automobile for the next century. Automobiles are part of our industry and culture. They will not disappear as many of our politically correct politicians might wish. But the depletion of our oil and gas resources will demand a more fuel-efficient vehicle. A small hybrid automobile will be the city car of the future — not the big gas-guzzler on today's city streets.

Density is also an issue. I find it hard to believe that the Sheppard subway line in North York was built without any enshrined requirement to increase the density along the route. Such lack of vision lays the groundwork for economic failure. Surely, the enormous amount of public funds being spent would require that many more people would live along the subway line.

On the railway lands alone, in the vicinity of the CN Tower, between 1967 and 1997, close to $50 million of public and private funds went into planning studies, lawyers and hearings.

In the city, there was another problem as well. With so many employees on the planning staff there was always the need to have them doing something. It was impossible to downsize, once they became permanent. So politicians used them to prepare reports and more reports — reports on anything. Many planners were first employed as community organizers in the period 1973 to 1980, when it was decided the communities needed help to organize. In the early 1970s the small development department was included in the planning department. And the new planning department ballooned to a staff of 172 when community organizers assumed planning duties, even though few, if any of them, had a planning education or expertise in planning.

THE BATTLE OF THE BANKS

The big banks and trust companies have always dominated the financial district — the centre of downtown. The competition for the tallest building began around the centennial year, 1967, when the Toronto Dominion Bank began to build the three-tower bank complex King and Bay streets. Its first 54-storey tower was complete in 1970, making it the tallest building in the city.

The next bank to reach for the skies was the Canadian Imperial Bank of Commerce — across the street on the east side of Bay Street. The much earlier bank building, the tallest building in the city when it was built in 1928, was incorporated into the new bank complex. The Bank of Nova Scotia, with developer Robert Campeau, decided to build a taller development on the north side of King Street between Bay and Yonge. The competition between the banks was intense. Then Olympia and York — the Reichman Brothers — teamed up with the Bank of Montreal to build the 72-storey First Canadian Place complex on the northwest corner of King and Bay. In the 20 years between 1968 and 1988, the skyline of the downtown changed immensely, with the CN Tower capping it all off as the world's tallest free-standing building.

The Royal Bank — the last of the four banks, and financially, the biggest — built a smaller and much more practical building complex at the northwest corner of Bay and Front streets. This building reflected real value with its gold-coloured glass windows.

Generally, all these bank buildings are considered as big average period buildings, boxlike in shape with little planning or archectural imagination. Many people today would call them ugly and sterile. But each era has its own pronounced building shape and presentation. The only bank building that could fit in with today's architecture is the Royal Bank. It has a little more variance in presentation than the others.

HARBOURFRONT PLANS

Harbourfront is an example of planning gone wrong. It was a sliver of land along the waterfront between York and Bathurst streets, mostly owned by the federal government. During the federal election of 1972, the Liberal government promised to give the land as a gift to the city for an urban park. But the planners, developers and politicians loaded up Harbourfront with high-rise buildings from Bathurst Quay to York Street. Thirty years later, these waterfront buildings offer a permanent barrier to the lake. They provide waterfront views — but only for those who live by the water.

That section of the waterfront was a collection of old warehouses, sheds and an assortment of dilapidated buildings, which spoiled the otherwise tranquil view of the Toronto Islands and Lake Ontario. The largest building was the Terminal Warehouse, which was totally renovated. All the other buildings were demolished to make room for Harbourfront.

The next 20 years redefined the meaning of "urban park." Harbourfront turned out to be a huge, mixed-up jungle of high-rise buildings of questionable design and quality. The Harbourfront Corporation was set up to run the urban park and provide recreational programs for Toronto citizens. The annual grant given by the federal government was not enough to finance the operations. So Howard Cohen, a former city planner, was hired by the Harbourfront Board to oversee the management and development.

Cohen, as I remembered him, was an up-and-coming member of David Crombie's planning team at City Hall. I regarded him as somewhat anti-development. And he was intelligent, persuasive and articulate. He was also plugged into the roller coaster ride of urban planning at the time. He had more understanding of the changing political winds than any planner I knew. But I felt uneasy by the action and role of the anti-development city planners. So

Howard Cohen and the Harbourfront urban park made little sense to me.

Still, planning matters at the local government level gave me a clearer view that it was all a part of the political process. Some buildings were considered magnificent when completed, but later became a blight on the urban landscape. Some will argue that planning is entirely a political process. Planners give advice to politicians to conform to accepted trends and what they perceive as advancement for the municipality. Planners act as a cushion between the people and the politician. But politicians make the final decision.

Cohen set about selling off sections of Harbourfront land to developers to supplement the limited grant money from the federal government. And so the building boom began to gobble up the land and fill in the urban park. Crombie, as mayor, was able to muster enough votes to have the overall plan for Harbourfront approved. With the support and co-operation of the chief planner, Steve McLoughlin, the plan did not have very much opposition.

I had a difficult time participating in the Harbourfront plans, as I just did not believe in all the high-rise redevelopment for the waterfront. If we were to have development, I had reasoned, it should be upscale and complementary as a marine road drive. I could not see any cheap-looking buildings cluttering up the water-front. But the arguments about who should live in Harbourfront dragged on for four years at City Hall. The left wing of council fought against condominiums but supported rental and other low-cost housing programs, as long as some of it was subsidized and "affordable." And the city ended up with some ugly buildings that did nothing to enhance the waterfront.

The railway lands, some 190 acres bounded by York Street, Front Street, the Gardiner Expressway and Spadina Avenue and owned by the Canadian Pacific and Canadian National, presented a development plan to the City in 1968. After more than 35 years of wrangling with planners, politicians and the owners of the land, and the expenditure of many millions of dollars in public money on planning — and many more millions from the owners of the land — development has taken place haphazardly, with no resemblance to what was originally planned and approved.

LOBBYING THE POLITICIANS

Getting a plan for a project approved at City Hall can be a monumental obstacle course. This is where the lobbyist comes in, operating in the twilight zone of politics. Since the beginning of organized government, the lobbyist has been a fixture in the political system — the hired gun to ensure that his client's interests are looked after in the rough and tumble of political decision-making. In Washington, D.C., lobbying has become a multi-billion-dollar business, with senators and congressmen entertained, dined and swamped with funds from organizations attempting to strengthen their influence. In Ottawa, the scenario is much the same, but on a smaller scale.

At the city level of government, lobbying is more personal. There are fewer large national corporations and organizations. It is much more local. Lobbyists have to be more flexible, as the roles of politicians are more intertwined with those of senior administration staff. It means more work for the lobbyist. Finding the right button to push is key for the developer wanting to build a high-rise building or for a corporation trying to get the City to contract out municipal work. Proposing to build a new sports centre, leasing Union Station, treating sewage sludge, leasing computers are just the type of projects that attract lobbyists.

Lobbying is legal and part of the democratic process, but there are certain rules and regulations. A lobbyist cannot offer money for a vote, and a politician cannot accept money for voting a certain way. That is bribery and corruption and is a criminal offence. The lobbyist can contribute funds, work for a candidate, and collect funds, like any citizen under the regulations governing elections.

Being a good lobbyist is an art, which lawyers seem to easily fit into their profession. But non-lawyers can also be effective. It is all a matter of convincing politicians to vote for or against a particular proposal — depending who is paying the bill. I see the lobbyist as a type of salesman — like a car or appliance salesman — who never stops trying to pitch his product. As an example, take the redevelopment of a piece of property that requires rezoning. Let's say it is adjacent to an old single-family residential area. The developer has put together a team to plan, design and process the project through the municipal system. The lobbyist, who is probably a lawyer with considerable experience in municipal law, begins the process of steering the project through. The lobbyist speaks to the local councillor and the planners for the area and canvasses the local area residents to get a sense of the support and opposition.

After the preliminary assessment has been made and it is decided to proceed with the process, the touchy question of density — the number of units or the number of square metres — is discussed. It is the most important factor for the developer. The developer has a good idea of what the lowest density should be to break even. Anything above that makes the project more attractive. Anything below that means there can be no project. The plans are drawn with the supporting backup material. The density or number of units is probably twice what the developer needs to break even. The package is filed with the appropriate committee at City Hall. At the committee meeting, deputations may be heard for and against the project. The committee usually refers the project to the planners for a preliminary review with instructions to report back to the committee at a specified later date.

By this time the lobbyist is working hard on the proposal. He contacts the planners to make sure there are no unanswered questions. Then the lobbying of the committee members begins in earnest. But what does the lobbyist have to do to get the politician's vote? Here's where it can get messy. As well as being a salesman, the lobbyist is also a kind of psychologist, banker and campaign worker. Some politicians may have no problems voting for the proposal, as it fits into their announced policies. There may be some minor alterations, perhaps a comment on reducing the density, but the lobbyist is assured of the vote. The councillor expects a financial contribution at election time.

At the other end of the scale, a number of politicians may have an intense dislike for the development as a matter of policy. They would not vote for it under any condition. Here, the lobbyist will not waste much time, but will go through the motions of calling on each one to see if there is any hope of getting their vote or if they have any suggestions. The idea here is to muffle the opposition as much as possible before the project comes through the system and on to the council floor.

Other politicians may have little interest in the project, but that is where the lobbyist earns his fee. If the proposed development is not in the politician's ward, it probably is not an issue for that politician. But that vote may be up for grabs. The good lobbyist has a reading of every politician. After every meeting, lunch or dinner with the politician, he has a few more little notes to add to his rating card.

Eventually, a deal for the vote is within reach. It may end up with the lobbyist making a simple contribution to the re-election campaign; soliciting his clients to make contributions by buying tickets or tables at a fundraiser; working on the political campaign; or doing something specific to aid the quest for re-election. But in the long run, it depends on what the lobbyist can do for the councillor — it is that simple.

Now that all the lobbying has been done the hardest work is ahead — making sure that all the committed politicians turn up for the vote. This is the most vexing time for the lobbyist. Getting the vote out is the acid test. On the other side, people or organizations against the proposal also lobby politicians. A committed politician, for whatever reason, may decide to jump ship and vote against the project. The defecting politician will be sought out to see what has gone wrong. If the lobbyist can entice the politician back to the fold, it will be worth the effort; if not, he will attempt to convince him or her to take a walk — go to the washroom or leave the chamber before the vote is taken.

I have tried lobbying on a few projects since leaving politics, but I do not have the stomach for most of it. I am probably not a good salesman. It is not for me!

DRAINING THE SWAMP

To the lobbyist, the bureaucrats are part of the target group. And a good lobbyist has to be able to gain the confidence and trust of the key people in that group. Bureaucrats are often used to handle the patronage side of the party in power. This is a tightrope act for many bureaucrats, but it is something that is built into the system.

It falls apart now and again and hits the headlines if something goes wrong. And lately, many things have gone wrong.

Many compare politics to the ecology of a wetlands — a system where stormwater, flowing through the aquatic vegetation, maintains the healthy status of the wetlands. If the water is contaminated by illegal dumping of toxic wastes, the wetlands will begin to die and eventually rot. When that happens it becomes stagnant and a breeding place for mosquitos. The wetlands have now become a smelly swamp. Restoring it back to health may require the swamp to be drained and the contaminated material hauled away for treatment.

In the case of contracts for advertising and promotion in the federal government's program to convince Quebec to stay in Canada by the Chretien forces, all eyes have been focused on the Gomery Commission — trying to follow the trail of how many millions of dollars was moved around, laundered and squandered. It can get nasty at times and the taxpayer will pay dearly for the antics of some slippery characters in and around government.

When Brian Mulroney was prime minister, his government awarded a large construction contract to the Matthews Construction Group for work at Pearson International Airport. Matthews was a strong supporter of the Conservatives. When Jean Chretien became prime minister, he cancelled the airport contract on the grounds that it was patronage. The Matthews Group sued. That little caper cost Canadian taxpayers many millions — about $350 million to the Matthews Group — after some court proceedings.

A different type of case is now troubling Toronto taxpayers. It is all about a bridge to the Toronto Island Airport that was approved in 2003 after a lot of studies, discussions and meetings over the preceding three years by the then Toronto City Council. During the discussions, the debate centred on whether it should be a bridge or a tunnel. Council eventually supported a 400-foot bridge across the Western Channel. It was estimated to cost $22 million. Contracts had been awarded and some work had begun.

David Miller, a lawyer, in his campaign for mayor in November 2003, made the cancelling of the bridge one of his many election promises. When he was elected he mustered enough votes in the new council to cancel the bridge. Council went along with the mayor as he promised that cancelling the bridge would "not cost a toonie." But I doubt if many of the supporting councillors would have embarked on this venture if they thought it through or if it was their own personal financial responsibility.

When the dust had settled, the cost of cancelling the construction of the bridge had been underestimated by the mayor. After some lobbying, the federal government agreed to honour the wishes of the new city council not to build the bridge. It provided $35 million to the Toronto Port Authority in May 2005 to pay off the legal costs for cancelling the construction. The outgoing city council supported the building of the the bridge at a cost of $22 million and the incoming council scrapped it for $35 million. It is hard to know which level of government is more stupid. But it is only money. And it will be spread out a little more, courtesy of the federal governent, so that all Canadian taxpayers can share and enjoy the cost of this little caper!

Then there are the Order in Council appointments, where the federal cabinet makes individual appointments to various agencies, boards and commissions. It is the gravy train for loyal party workers and friends — and, oh yes, the odd person or member of another party is appointed from time to time, just to show that there is no patronage! But the prime minister, without any hearings or debate, makes the juiciest appointments of all. The ability to appoint friends and supporters to the senate and the Supreme Court and to the positions of the governor general and the lieutenant-governors is part of the prime minister's bag of goodies.

It does not matter which party is in power, the results are always the same. In handing out plum jobs, contracts and favours, the process is designed to accommodate the friends of the party in power. It is a corruption of the democratic system that we have all accepted. If the Liberals are in power, favour is shown to their friends and contributors. We accept it without a murmur. The same results occur when the Conservatives or another party is in power.

At the provincial level of government, patronage works much the same way. The premier does not have as many appointments to hand out — but here again, the friends of the party in power get the vast majority of the appointments. It is the accepted way. The general rationale is that people who are appointed should be competent and should support the policies of the party. It is an added bonus if they are party members and have contributed to the party.

At the municipal level of government, the system works the same way, but on a much smaller scale. The mayor does not have the power to make the big patronage appointments, like those handed out by Ottawa or Queen's Park, but he can still orchestrate things in such a way that council accepts his recommendations.

The amalgamated city, in its first two terms, lifted the veil a little. The antics of Mayor Mel Lastman and his administration opened up Pandora's box — a glimpse of how those close to the mayor benefited and those outside that circle were frozen out. The image of a disoriented mayor, with little idea of the operations of the city, emerged through the MFP computer leasing inquiry. During Lastman's first term his immediate staff shielded him. He was not a people's mayor, but a mayor for a select group. Only those who were on that list had access. The stage was set to manage and control. Those who had the ear of the mayor in that first term of the new council laid the groundwork for the spoils waiting to be picked. These friends and lobbyists did extremely well. The key to their success lay in the appearance they gave to the councillors and the senior bureaucrats that they were acting with the support of the mayor. If a company wanted to do business with the city, that company needed special assistance. And who was better able to help than a friend of the mayor? It was like taking candy from a baby — and the fees were staggering. It did not matter whether it was a city contract, a development proposal, a rezoning application, or a business trying to get the ear of the mayor.

But the way governments are run — all governments — depends entirely on the degree of political honesty and the competence of the bureaucracy. Politicians make policy decisions and the bureaucrats ensure those policies are acted on. Politicians rarely make decisions on major issues without first asking senior staff to report on all the ramifications.

By the time the second term of city council began in January 2000, the process was well and truly in place. But cracks appeared in the system. Budget chief Tom Jakobek was no longer around

— he did not run for re-election. David Shiner — a leftover from Lastman's days in North York — became budget chief.

Lastman was intoxicated by all the media attention he got after winning the mayoralty in November 1997. He set his sights on winning the 2008 Olympic Games for Toronto. He began to focus on the Port lands area as a stage for the Olympics and the rebirth of the waterfront. That, of course, made property in the area the target of many developers who had visions of making a fast dollar. The City owned much of the land in the area, mainly through the Toronto Economic Development Corporation (TEDCO).

Knob Hill Farms, owned by Steve Stavro, operated a large grocery store on prime waterfront land owned by TEDCO. The lease had seven years to run. On the advice of Eisen, TEDCO decided to write a new 20-year lease for Knob Hill Farms to cover a larger land area. The land would greatly increase in value as plans for the area steamrolled ahead. At the same time the City was attempting to impose a moratorium on any development on the waterfront until the plans for the Olympics were finalized. When the news broke about the new lease to Knob Hill Farms, the chairman of TEDCO, Fred Eisen, resigned. Stavro would not back down and proceeded to hold the City to the new lease agreement.

But it was councillor Bas Balkissoon, chairman of the audit committee, who finally pried open the lid of how business operated at City Hall. He began to ask questions about a computer contract that council had awarded to MFP Financial in July 1999. He noticed that the contract had ballooned to $82 million from $43 million, without discussion or approval by council. After much acrimonious debate, the City decided to hold an inquiry. Council earmarked $2 million to carry out the inquiry and Justice Madame Bellamy was appointed to preside.

The inquiry began in December 2002 at the East York civic building. It opened the proverbial can of worms. By the beginning of 2005, the cost of the inquiry amounted to almost $20 million. It was a galling price to pay to show how wasteful the whole system had become and how incompetence and cronyism had prevailed. Mayor Lastman's summed up his testimony in a few words: "I knew nothing." Many knew that the mayor, in fact, was telling the truth. He really knew nothing. His trusted staff was in charge and did everything. He was really not plugged into the management of the city at all.

But there was much more to come as the inquiry proceeded. As witness after witness paraded through the witness box, it showed that few remembered many details. Amnesia was part of the problem as trips, entertainment tabs and phone call details were discussed. As the inquiry proceeded, it appeared that MFP had been able to convince the bureaucrats and a few of the top politicians that the City had a great computer leasing agreement and that all the contract agreements were duly authorized and signed by the appointed signing officers at City Hall. There was nothing illegal about the contract. MFP had done a great sales job. The City staff and council bought the deal.

The inquiry provided a glimpse into the role of the politicians and senior bureaucrats who had been handling the affairs of the city. It also showed that the mayor knew little about the day-to-day operations of the city and seemed oblivious of the mess in the city. People began to see the mayor as a modern-day Nero fiddling while Toronto burned.

The MFP inquiry lifted the lid a little off the confused and incompetent system of government that a botched amalgamation plan had spawned. The over-expenditures and questionable practices have been anything but businesslike — just an ongoing strain on the bewildered, hard-pressed taxpayer. Drastic changes must come.

At one time, when municipalities had financial difficulties — and many went bankrupt — the Ontario government set up the Ontario Municipal Board to oversee the borrowing of municipalities. It has worked well, as all municipalities must now submit their annual debenture program to the OMB for approval. Although Toronto does not need that type of board, it could do with some outside professional business advice from time to time.

The City needs an independent financial advisory board — a few independent outside experts to advise on funding and contract arrangements. They should be available, when called on, to advise city council if there are any doubts or hidden financial implications for the City in any deal or proposal.

CHAPTER 19
Culture and Tourism in the Modern City

When I arrived in Toronto in 1956, as a 23-year-old immigrant, I was a stranger to a new country and to a city where I knew no one. It is said that first impressions last longest. I remember on the first Sunday, sitting on the side of my bed in a small rooming house, counting out the sum total of $17 — my last few dollars after the journey across the Atlantic. Counting the money was a desperate attempt to review my options — to see if I could get away. The city closed down on Sundays — so dull for a young person alone — no Sunday paper, no movies, no taverns or stores open. The saying of the time for Toronto on Sunday — "The Protestants are in bed, the Catholics are in church and the Jews are in Miami" — was half in jest, of course, but had some kernel of truth. Toronto was dull.

But since those days after World War II the city has come alive with the impact of hundreds of thousands of immigrants from all over the world who have made Toronto their home. It is this immigrant base, with its attendant cultural and artistic ingredients, that has enhanced the life of the city and made it one of the best in the world.

Cities derive a significant portion of their wealth from culture and tourism. In the past that was so — travellers flocked to the old capital of Changan in imperial China, to Baghdad in Mesopotamia, to Alexandria in Egypt, to Athens, Rome, Constantinople and Marrakesh. They were entertained by musicians and snake charmers, acrobats and strongmen, actors and storytellers. Often, great cities hit their apogee in an intersecting orbit with the richest periods in art, architecture, learning and literature — Venice under the Doges, St. Petersburg under Peter the Great, Florence with the Renaissance and the Medicis, London in the age of William Shakespeare.

Try to imagine the economies of London, Rome, Paris and New York — where ten major airports play host to many millions of tourists — without the casual visitor in search of the ambience of a city of culture. Sometimes it is just its streets, its clubs and restaurants and its intangible feel. But take away those visitors and you have the problem Toronto found itself in when SARS drove overnight stay statistics down by 12 percent in 2003. That translated into half-empty hotels, taxis battling for passengers and restaurants where the staff outnumbered the patrons.

But what did Toronto have to offer to counter the effects of SARS? It has no singular attraction — except perhaps the CN Tower as a landmark — to make it a "must" destination for tourists. Unlike the Ontario capital, much smaller cities can thrive on a single clearly focused attraction — Chartres has its cathedral, Pamplona its bulls, Galway its oyster festival, Nice its Riviera, Rio de Janeiro its carnival, Cleveland its orchestra, New Orleans its Mardi Gras, Havana its faded Spanish architecture, Ravenna its Byzantine mosaics, Liverpool its Beatles. Even an artificial, concocted beachfront city such as Cancun can benefit greatly from its Mayan cultural hinterland.

What Toronto and its tourist czars seem not to have understood is that cities rise or fall on the integrity of their civic culture. Some cities have survived entirely because they retained their cultural integrity. Kyoto in Japan — the capital city before it was moved to Edo (Tokyo) — might have become a flattened and fire-bombed ruin in World War II if a senior diplomat in Washington had not realized that its wood-framed temples and houses represented some of the most perfect examples of Buddhist architecture and culture in the East. Kyoto survived, and today it still presents the Noh theatre in the unchanged and rigorously precise style of the fifteenth century. Gaijin tourists flock to Kyoto's ryokans and to the Golden Pavilion. And millions of Japanese come too, speeding from Tokyo and Nagoya on the bullet trains.

Cultural tourism is thriving also in medium-sized European cities such as Dublin and Edinburgh — good examples of outposts of empire that have overcome their provincialism and retrieved their status as significant European centres of learning and literature. Dublin, once the second city of the British Empire, is filled with tourists, some of whom come simply because Joyce lived there, and Bono still does. The U2 frontman rewards them by letting them stay in his hotel for $500 per night. Edinburgh, too, has its castle, its memories of Mary, Queen of Scots, and its enormously successful summer festival of theatre, dance and many other fringe activities. Even Glasgow, once a hard and grimy industrial city, has been transformed by great museums and by its recent status as a European City of Culture.

Even smaller cities create cultural watersheds around high art. Think of the elegant Provençal cities of Aix-en-Provence, Avignon and Orange, each with flourishing summer festivals of opera and theatre, or Salzburg with its Wagnerian ring cycle — soon to get a full staging in Toronto's new opera house. More recently we see the transformation of the dull Basque port city of Bilbao into an architectural mecca for tourists drawn to Frank Gehry's titanium-clad Guggenheim museum. Another Spanish city, Barcelona, has turned itself into a major tourist destination by creating a heady mix of culture and architecture, led from the grave by the great Catalan genius, the nineteenth-century visionary Antonio Gaudi, whose Holy Family Cathedral is only now being completed.

And if Canadian cities have been less successful than their European and American counterparts in drawing large numbers of tourists, it may be because much of Canada's early resource-based wealth did not go into creating strong indigenous cultural landmarks. Instead, the money flowed "home" to the imperial capital, where it helped the development of rich institutions such as the British Museum, the National Gallery, the Tate, the Victoria and Albert — and also the royal palaces. In America, the War of Independence helped sever those colonial ties, and the wealth stayed in the burgeoning U.S. cities.

Canada cannot match the sheer plethora of low and high art brought to the American cities by the buying power of the barons of banking and industry. No city north of the Great Lakes comes close to the treasures of the Metropolitan or Modern Art museums in New York, the Boston Fine Arts Museum, or the incomparably endowed Getty Museum in Los Angeles. At the other end of the scale, no Canadian city has the drawing power of the cultural artifacts of the Hollywood studios, nor of the Disney characters who turn indifferent cities such as Orlando into some of the most popular tourist traps in the world.

While most tourists from Europe and Asia fly south of the border, Canada has had to rely on smaller cultural attractions, some of them difficult to quantify in terms of drawing power. The Japanese are lured by the schoolgirl charms of Anne of Green Gables, the Americans by the Gallic flare of Montreal and Quebec City, the English by the faint colonial tang of Ottawa and Toronto.

In general, nature is a far greater draw than cities for tourists coming to Canada. There is the *de rigueur* visit to the somewhat unique charms of Niagara Falls, the east coast shoreline, the Cabot Trail, the spectacular Gaspé and the Perce Rock, the beauty of the Rockies and the interior of B.C., the great sweeps of forest and lakelands in central Canada, the Arctic, cowboy treks in the Prairies, Lake Louise, skiing in winter in Whistler, Banff and Calgary.

That is not to say that Canadian cities do not have their cultural attractions — the Montreal Museum of Fine Arts, the National Gallery in Ottawa, the Royal Ontario Museum in Toronto, the Winnipeg Ballet. But on the whole Canada has been unlucky to have spent so much of its history with its back turned to its urban centres. Perhaps it is not surprising that the cities are not well-funded, especially when it comes to the arts and culture. A nation with an artificially located capital, stranded on the border between Upper and Lower Canada, is unlikely to create a centrist cultural powerhouse such as London or Paris. In addition, Canada has had a largely rural, provincial genesis. It is a country built on remote trading posts, where for the first two centuries, according to the chronicler Peter Newman, the Hudson's Bay Company took millions of furs out of the north for shipment to London, without ever inviting a Canadian tailor to work on a fur coat.

But some of the colonial trappings are coming off. Montreal and Quebec City are proudly francophone, no longer mere outposts of Parisian culture. Quebec theatre and literature, the Montreal Symphony, the films and poetry, can stand with anything in the French-speaking world.

And in Toronto, finally, there is a sense that something is about to happen in a relatively prosaic cultural milieu. The old Hogtown is benefiting from the influence of post-colonial arrivals — world-class writers like Michael Ondaatje, born in Sri Lanka, and Rohinton Mistry, born in India. It is also generating a home-grown flowering of internationally acclaimed opera singers, architects, engineers, musicians and filmmakers.

But "culture" is still something of a dirty word in many of the English cities in Canada, perhaps because of the dreary provincialism imposed by the strict Victorian and Edwardian values of the mother country. That dreariness, which was reinforced by the Calvinist values of many Scots and Ulster Protestant settlers, is slowly giving way to the many cultural influences of the Mediterranean — particularly Italian, Spanish and Greek — and also to the refined aesthetic of Asia, represented initially by its food, but increasingly by a much broader sense of style and sophistication.

In architecture, Toronto has a chance to lead the way, despite losing the opportunity for the major redevelopment that might have flowed from a successful bid for the 2008 Summer Olympics. Vancouver will benefit from redevelopment driven by the 2010 Winter Olympics. Toronto was shut out of the 2012 Olympics — did not even apply — by the much greater spending power of Paris, London, New York, Moscow and Madrid. It is a measure of how the wealth of cities can shift that Moscow has 34 billionaires, three more than New York, while Toronto has only a handful.

In terms of scale, too, a single New York sports franchise, the National Football League's Jets, has boosted that city's Olympic prospects by announcing plans for a green stadium complex that will cost $1.4 billion U.S. The New York Sports and Convention Center dwarfs Toronto's overall expenditures on an entire group of highly touted cultural developments. The south facade of the new stadium will contain 25,000 solar collector tubes and the walls will be topped by 34 wind turbines, each 40 feet tall. That should make it the most environmentally correct building in the world. The windmills alone will generate almost all of the energy for the facility when it is being used as a football stadium and about 25 percent when its retractable roof is closed for conventions, exhibitions and other events. The budget for the new West Side stadium is about three times the cost of Toronto's retractable-roofed Sky Dome, which seemed like a miracle of reinforced concrete when it opened on June 1989. But it now carries with it the decaying odour of a sarcophagus — a baseball stadium without grass, and precious little open air. It was resold in December 2004 for $25 million — a little over 4 percent of what it cost to build 15 years earlier — and renamed the Rogers Centre.

ROYAL ONTARIO MUSEUM EXTENSION

Not everything is being downscaled in Toronto. The Royal Ontario Museum — Canada's largest — is spending $200 million to commission the Polish-born architect Daniel Libeskind to create a striking glass extension that will provide 220,000 square feet of renovated space, including 40,000 square feet of new galleries. The Bloor and University building will house everything from Alberta Badlands' dinosaurs to a new acquisition, a fossil of the world's largest sea scorpion, seven feet long and more than 400 million years old.

The renovation of the ROM — and it is a rebuild rather than a renovation — is a bold and innovative move for a conservative institution that should easily top 1 million visits a year when the new space comes on stream. The improvements are a major step forward. Just forty years ago, a visitor would have been struck by the casual dowdiness of the place. A curious child could gaze at eye level at a long table of prancing Tang dynasty horses, standing *en plein aire* without benefit of holding cases and only minimal security. Other Chinese and Asian masterpieces were everywhere — and there was much to be said for the casual approach to displays. Some of the improvements of recent years amounted to little more than a change of packaging — neat little glass-enclosed displays looking very prim and educational in the best minimalist way. But what they revealed was how much was lying unseen in the basement.

The Chinese collections make the ROM one of the world's great resources for Sinophiles. And although relentless new archaeological digging across China has uncovered countless artifacts, including a standing terracotta army in a vast Xian burial chamber, the ROM deserves better space for the chinoiserie and the great stone carvings so quietly added to its 5 million objects.

To open up its collections — and its mindset — the ROM has needed to spread its wings and provide space and access to its collections. Sometimes a little untidiness, the jumble of things you might discover in an old attic, is better than the feeling that all the objects are trapped in tiny spatial boxes, as if the curator were saying to the child, "Look, look, look at this, and only this, it's precisely what I want you to see." At last, the ROM seems to understand this — and as major renovations got underway, it was conducting daily tours, led by volunteers, boldly inviting visitors to "Come See the Mess."

The new-found openness helped the ROM to successfully solicit community support — and also funding from philanthropists such as Galen Weston and Christopher Ondaatje. Openness is central to Libeskind's design. The proposal to open up the Bloor Street facade to public view by creating huge new crystal extensions got some criticism from Toronto's legions of conservatives, but what it amounted to was a turning of the museum inside-out. Where Toronto had been a closed city for much of its short history, it was learning to be more European, to let the street go inside and the institutional and domestic interiors go outside.

This idea was espoused forty years ago by a Toronto visionary, Marshall McLuhan, who brought the idea of the global village into his tiny Centre for Culture and Technology — little more than a cottage on the University of Toronto campus. Europeans go outside to be public and to entertain, McLuhan said, while North Americans stay home. The corollary of this is that the European town square is a place of entertainment and commerce and the North American square tends to be empty. Hence we get the hideous Dundas Square off Yonge Street in downtown Toronto — a space planned more for advertising than for people.

But still, Toronto has changed. European, Asian and Latin immigrants have slowly reversed attitudes sufficiently to take citizens out from behind closed doors and into their urban spaces, to outdoor cafés and parks with summer theatre, to street carnivals embracing many cultures, to rock concerts and public entertainments ranging from Ed Mirvish's Christmas turkey giveaway, the Toronto International Film Festival and the Hispanic Fiesta to the Gay Pride Parade, St. Patrick's Day Parade and the huge Caribana Carnival.

ONTARIO COLLEGE OF ART AND DESIGN

If people can get out onto the street, so can art. And if Libeskind's ROM design was visionary in its approach to the aesthetics of the streetscape, Will Alsop's $42-million building-on-stilts for the Ontario College of Art and Design embraced McCaul Street and the future with a chaotic, pop-art style. It worked brilliantly if you were a fan of artistic flamboyance — but as some critics on Internet chat lines said, it might also be the "worst building ever." Still, the idea of hoisting the building 15 storeys in the air on multi-coloured steel stilts was not merely calculated to make a polka-dotted fashion statement in the sky. The architect's rationale called for opening up the building's underpinnings to allow the existing Grange Park, at the rear of the Art Gallery of Ontario, to flow under the OCAD lecture rooms.

The technical feat of mounting the 90,000-square-foot Sharp Centre for Design on top of slender steel pillars was considerable. The Alsop engineering team had to factor in the effects of high winds acting as an uplift on the building and countless other stresses. The importance of getting the calculations right was heightened by the collapse of a futuristic year-old terminal building at Charles de Gaulle airport in France.

ART GALLERY OF ONTARIO

The new Ontario art college building is just behind and across the park from the staid old Art Gallery of Ontario, where one of the leading architects of the day, the Toronto-born Frank Gehry, released plans for a post-modern titanium and glass facade with a rebuilt interior. Gehry's plans for the $195-million rebuild were greeted by a flurry of protest, in part because it seemed that the titanium facade was planned around a mere squiggle, an elongated sketch of how the old rectangular limestone front of the building would be covered up and attenuated horizontally along Dundas Street. Those who liked the plan could see the sense of bringing a glass front-piece to the building, opening up some exhibition space to pale northern light. But Toronto's more conservative burghers saw it as mere exhibitionism. In the end, Gehry reworked his plans, changing parts of the facade from titanium to wood and backing away from gutting parts of the interior. He could easily have walked away from the whole project, but it was just around the corner from the street where he was born.

Ironically, the gallery could have opted for an entirely new building on donated waterfront land, which might have allowed Gehry to work his magic with a titanium and glass structure facing south towards the lake. But the AGO trustees, after some discussion, insisted on staying put. Gehry said coolly that he had been given neither the money nor the space to do a Bilbao in Toronto, so he had to work with what he had.

But his experience in his native city contrasts sharply with what he did for Chicago's new Millennium Park, a $700-million waterfront extravaganza that opened in 2004 on a 10-hectare site. The two cities had the shared reality of grey Great Lakes' waterfronts, but while Chicagoans built themselves a showcase for great architecture, Toronto merely drew up plans for empty parks and found a way not to carry them through. Gehry's particular contribution to the Chicago park is an outdoor concert hall capable of seating 13,000. Its enormous stage, trimmed with steel and aluminium, will be capable of showcasing everything from rock acts to the city's symphony, one of the world's greatest orchestras.

How did Toronto move so far from its world-class pretensions? In 1967, the centennial and the year of the Montreal Expo, Canada had a young population, a baby boom in the making. It had its highest intake of immigrants; the dollar was high and the natural resources of the hinterland unlimited. Toronto had a hippy village in Yorkville, bright new cafés facing the street, new community colleges to educate hundreds of thousands of students, and a flush of civic pride that flowed in part from Viljo Revell's stunning City Hall, whose half clam-shell wings seemed to clasp the municipal space below in a warm embrace. It also was getting a superbly cool modernist masterpiece, the stark black towers of Mies van der Rohe's Toronto-Dominion Bank Centre. And soon, the CN Tower would reach as high as corn in Oklahoma, a visible calling card for an up-and-coming city.

But then came hubris, highlighted most tastelessly when Mayor Mel Lastman shot down what was left of the city's Olympian dreams by saying that he feared going to Africa because he might be boiled in a pot. It was a frightening fall from grace for the former North York mayor, who had so blithely backed his suburban values into a newly amalgamated metropolis. And so, nearly 40 years after the mid-1960s flush of energy, Toronto found itself in decline. Its immigration, like the dollar, was slumping, Yorkville and its environs was a lifeless condo-ville, the waterfront was still a blight, and the tourist image was shattered.

THE CULTURE OF CHANGE

When Lastman exited the civic scene and the infinitely more radical mayor David Miller took over in 2003, the city was ready for change. Miller had fought his election in part on blocking plans for a bridge to the underused Toronto Island Airport. The new mayor and some of his constituents on the city's west side did not care to face the prospect of dozens of flights a day, and possibly some business jets, over their airspace. Miller clashed on the issue with the Toronto Port Authority, the federal agency that controlled the commercial side of the port as well as some of the port lands. Toronto was, once again, caught in an old dilemma: how could it redevelop the waterfront and enhance its cultural heritage without full support from the provincial and federal governments and their agencies? That battle played itself out with a new prime minister, Paul Martin, the Toronto-educated Liberal lawyer whose party had swept all 48 Greater Toronto ridings in the 2000 election, but who in the 2004 election faced a growing tide of dissent across Canada's largest metropolis.

There was hope that the city and its new mayor could salvage something from the wreckage left by Lastman and his predecessors. City council's own publicity machine proudly announced that there were 125 museums and public archives in the Greater Toronto Area, more than 50 ballet and dance companies, six opera companies, two symphonies and one of the broadest ranges of theatre experiences in the English-speaking world. The library system, however starved it was for funds to buy books, had a superb Reference Library building, the work of Canadian-born Raymond Moriyama, and the libraries were the most widely used in North America — Los Angeles was twice as large, but Toronto had more book borrowers.

Then there was Hollywood North, which was hit hard by SARS and even harder by a provincial government decision to cut back on tax breaks for filmmakers. Still, Toronto was the third-ranked city in North America for TV and film production, and second as an exporter of TV programming. What the PR story did not mention was that filmmakers were hampered for many years by the lack of the large sound stage needed for Hollywood blockbusters, which had to go to Montreal or Vancouver instead. Detailed plans to build a new 10-hectare film "city" were finally unveiled in early 2004, but faded as the year ended.

The waterfront has also been enhanced by the Distillery District, saved because 44 old buildings near the rundown Parliament and King Street area were so dismally located that they were not deemed worthy of knocking down for redevelopment. The Distillery Building, built 140 years ago with limestone blocks shipped to its own dock from Kingston, is one of the city's older structures — most of those built in wood were burned down in major fires. The Distillery District has cobbled streets paved with old bricks, art galleries, restaurants and stores. It needed more of a sense of habitation and of connectedness to the lakefront, but at least it had survived. Its owners, Cityscape, stressed the need to make it into an art district, like Chelsea in Manhattan, but they clashed with their principal investor about the direction of the project. Until artists could actually live and mingle there, it seemed unlikely to become the success it might otherwise have been, or indeed to be fully integrated into the city and its waterfront.

Other critics of waterfront development had made the point over the years that the only way to revitalize the city's southern littoral was to build low-rise residences and small commercial properties to create an "urban streetscape" that connected directly with the lakefront. Most plans called for parks, which unfortunately were doomed to be empty in winter, and for condos, whose owners had virtually nowhere to go if they stepped out from their front door. But the port lands area could serve another basic purpose — a modern industrial park to provide jobs, exports and research for a diverse population.

And so artists stayed away from the bleak and unfriendly waterfront. In fact, it was the impoverished Parkdale area in the west end that saw an artistic revival driven by low rents. Galleries and antique stores clustered along Queen Street West, and a retro boutique hotel, the Drake, became one of the city's trendiest destinations. Painters and poets moved into old Victorian homes that had once been the abodes of wealthy suburbanites drawn to the coolness of the lakefront village. Many of its better villas had been demolished, especially along Jameson Avenue, to make way for ugly apartment blocks, but enough Victoriana survived to give the area a reasonably authentic nineteenth-century feeling.

THE OPERA HOUSE

All great cities need an opera house — even Manaus, the Brazilian city in the Amazon River jungle has a famous one, from the by-gone days of the colonial rubber barons. Berlin has several, Milan has La Scala, London has Covent Garden, New York has the Met. Paris has the stunning new Paris Opera, built in the 1990s by a Toronto-trained architect, Carlos Ott. The nouveau riche Hollywood honchos in Los Angeles have the flamboyant Walt Disney Concert Hall, built with a curving titanium facade for $275 million (U.S.) by none other than Frank Gehry.

Unfortunately, Toronto did not hand Gehry the contract for its new opera house, but at least it did manage to scrounge some land from a reluctant provincial government, and it got enough money together to create a complex — topped off with a residential tower at the busy corner of Queen Street and University Avenue. It might not be a thing of great beauty, but opera buffs would be happy enough if the acoustics were not as awful as they had been in Arthur Erickson's nearby Roy Thomson Hall, home of the Toronto Symphony. That hall had been so acoustically dead — at least until a 2003 restoration brought resonant wood surfaces into its concrete interior — that the Irish flautist James Galway vowed he would never play there again (and at least until the restoration, he had not). The architect fought hard against the acoustic changes, but in the end music was deemed more important than the cold and bear concrete surfaces of the round building.

Other cultural buildings were being reconstructed to suit post-modern tastes. The Distillery District was to get a new theatre school and performing space for George Brown College's drama students, who would work closely with a professional theatre company. And young ballet dancers, for years one of the city's greatest artistic triumphs, would learn their skills in a rebuilt National Ballet School.

And if enough of Gehry's vision can survive at the Art Gallery of Ontario, the Ontario capital might at last have an art space that would not only house the billionaire Thomson's $300-million art collection but also herald a new culture and tourism boom in the modern city.

CHAPTER 20
Education: The Key to Caring for Planet Earth

Many of the developed countries have demonstrated that they have the willingness and ability provide leadership in global peacemaking, through the United Nations, over the years. They can also provide leadership on energy and environmental education, particularly in the developing world. Led by First World countries, a volunteer Green Planet Corps, with a hands-on commitment to developing countries and the backing of an environmental professional educational package, would make an enormous contribution to providing the basic necessities for life in the villages, towns and cities where help is needed most.

SHARING A SMALL PLANET

When we went to school, we were taught the basics — reading, writing and arithmetic. These were the first steps in education. But the world has changed so much since the beginning of the industrial revolution in the mid-1800s that we can no longer get by with just basic education. As more and more people crowd the planet, and life expectancies increase, the human drive for a better quality of life impacts the natural environment in a way that has damaged the very basic elements of nature that we depend on for survival.

The human species — and all living things — are nurtured by a thin ribbon of atmosphere around our planet. The waters of the earth, which support all life, allow nature to blossom to its fullness and then die, to be born again in an endless cycle of life and death.

But nature on its own, without anthropogenic involvement, can also display awesome cataclysmic and destructive powers. On December 26, 2004, an earthquake in the Indian Ocean spawned a tsunami, with waves speeding out from the epicentre, bringing death and destruction to the shores of Sri Lanka, India, Thailand, Indonesia, ocean islands, and even, seven hours later, as far away as the east coast of Africa. More than 200,000 people died and many more thousands were left homeless as costal cities, towns and communities were just wiped out. And down through the ages, natural disasters of every conceivable type have caused havoc, destroyed properties and killed millions.

These enormous disasters point out the need for more knowledge and education of nature and the physical world. We, as global citizens, can become the leaders in this field of education. In the 1960s the United States developed the Peace Corps. It was a great idea — full of promise and goodwill — to assist and raise the living standards of poorer countries. But it got derailed along the way, and the U.S. now has reversed course, with billions of dollars consumed by a war machine. They have abandoned their leadership role of helping developing countries understand the fragility of our natural environment.

We now have an opportunity to step in with on-site personnel to bring environmental leadership to the world. This would involve setting up the "Green Planet Corps," a team of environmentally committed people, fanning out all over the world. It is a logical next step, following the first small steps of the Kyoto agreement, as we wrestle with the problems of global warming, declining non-renewable fossil fuel resources, poverty and ever-increasing populations in developing countries.

The Green Planet Corps would be backed by an educational package of high-quality documentaries dealing with environmental and energy issues. These documentaries can be a great tool in the education field. Documentary filmmakers would produce fourteen 60- to 90-minute films, in video and DVD formats, whose main purpose would be to provide a basic education for the youth of the world so that they would become practising, caring and knowledgeable environmentalists.

The documentaries would provide a broad education that would lead to a better understanding and life-long commitments of caring for the planet we share with other living organisms. It could be called a "good housekeeping" recipe for living in harmony with our natural environment.

There are more than 3 billion young people in the school-age category and most of them are living in developing countries. They are the decision makers and leaders of tomorrow — and they could benefit from a basic energy and environment education. And there are hundreds of millions of young people, mostly in developing countries, who cannot get that basic environmental education. These young people will inherit the mess that this and the past few generations have inflicted on planet earth. We must provide them with basic education tools to overcome the problems we have caused.

A NEW ROLE FOR DEVELOPED COUNTRIES

Promoting the energy and environment cause worldwide does not seem to be high on the agenda of any developed country. The Stockholm and Rio de Janeiro conferences, in the latter part of the last century, have shown how little has been achieved. Most countries are too self-centred to pay much attention to what is happening in poorer countries. And most governments are too blind to see much beyond their own borders and the next election. Inaction is leading to the incremental destruction of the natural environment — unless developed countries begin to act.

A litany of studies and polls has shown that these issues are high on the list of concerns of people all over the world. But that is as far as it goes. Action on most of the issues — even the simplest action, at times — takes years, if it happens at all. But, more often, it falls between the cracks or slips from being a priority.

Most people — young and old — have little or no understanding of how we should live in harmony with the natural environment. Developed countries should take the initiative and fill a leadership vacuum in a worldwide drive for education on energy and environmental issues. It would not be difficult to find people from all walks of life to participate in this new "helping hand" education, energy and environment program.

SERIES FORMAT

Each subject will be a documentary-style video/DVD, with voice-over narration to dub into English, French and other languages. Working with recognized experts from around the world, location shooting and stock footage — ranging from highly advanced experiments in the biosphere to the negative examples of overflowing garbage dumps of world cities — the documentaries would blend history, geography and technology. Graphics would also help highlight the details.

Each documentary would be supervised by a team of experts for technical accuracy, educational content and location examples to explain local and broader ramifications. The documentaries would be visually interesting, challenging and informative to reach the young people of the planet.

ROLE FOR FILMMAKERS

The world has many distinguished filmmakers who would gladly accept the challenge to develop the feature-length documentaries. Given the challenge, these documentaries could be award-winning films with many far-reaching consequences in the education field as well as recognition for the filmmakers. As an added feature, these documentaries would be backed up by a package of teaching material.

The 14 Documentary Subjects:

1. Water supply — the source of all life on earth.
2. The air we breathe — keeping it clean.
3. Waste management — production, disposal and recycling.
4. Sewage collection and treatment.
5. Food and population growth challenges — helping feed the hungry.
6. Traffic and transportation — moving people and goods.
7. Ozone depletion and climate change.
8. Lands and forests — looking after the land and managing forests.

9. Electric power — its development and use in our daily lives.
10. Fossil Fuels — diminishing supplies of coal, oil and natural gas.
11. Solar, wind and water energy and other alternate energy sources.
12. Nuclear energy and nuclear medicine.
13. Endangered species and the future of our species.
14. Natural disasters — earthquakes, hurricanes, floods and tsunamis.

Arrangements could be made with film distributors to ensure that virtually all young people will view the series. In many countries, the television channels, public broadcasting and education networks would help. A series like this would be distributed internationally, where documentary material of this kind is considered prime-time television. But the value of these documentaries would be enormous in the poorer areas of the developing world, where millions of young people can get a better understanding of our fragile planet.

COSTS AND MANAGEMENT

The overall production budget for each of the fourteen documentary programs, including expenses involved in raising corporate sponsorship, is estimated at $1.5 million. This does not include the costs of dubbing languages other than English and French.

The board, agency or corporation in charge of the production would solicit suitable business sponsors to participate in the funding. Foundations, financial institutions, engineering, environmental and manufacturing companies would be ideal sponsors. Sponsors should receive closing credits in the documentaries as well as visual/casual name recognition of products used where applicable, and in study guides, posters and other collateral material distributed to educational markets with the series. Sponsors would see an opportunity to display their skills or products internationally, and such a sizable market would make sponsorship very attractive.

Because of the extensive research and planning needed to produce the series, work on the project would take about three years.

Without doubt, rich countries have feasted on the bountiful resources of this planet over the last 200 years. It is time, at least, to pause and look at our insatiable and squandering ways. We can make amends and become leaders for the rest of the world by becoming part of the solution through education and not a constant part of the problem.

With an ever-increasing world population, cities have become magnets for the uneducated rural poor. Heavy concentrations of poverty, population, pollution and industries have made many cities unmanageable and in many cases unhealthy places for life and living. Indeed, many cities are now examples of the extent of the pollution of our planet, as the impact of more people and poverty destroys the urban landscape.

Telling the full story of the environment of the planet, in a compelling educational manner, so as to promote practical remedial action, will be a real achievement.

THE "GREEN PLANET CORPS"

As a companion to the documentaries, the federal governments of developed countries should set up the Green Planet Corps. This would tap into the vast pool of young people who are developing skills or have developed skills as teachers, engineers, planners, etc.

Employment would be voluntary and on a contract basis of from one to three years. It could be administrated by a governmental or non-governmental organization with the help of professional organizations such as those for teachers, nurses, medical doctors, engineers and planners.

I have not attempted to develop a budget for this, as it would depend entirely on the project's scope and size and the overall commitment by the government or governments and the financial participation of the related specialist organizations.

The Green Planet Corps, at the "grassroots level" in developing countries, would be a helping hand from friends to help people to help themselves. It is much better to send people with teaching, energy and environmental skills than soldiers with tanks and guns.

Taking a leadership role in producing the educational documentaries and developing the Green Planet Corps would be an ideal role for a country or group of countries in the European Union. The governments of these countries are much further ahead in understanding the impact of human activities on the natural environment and the need to be prudent managers of the resources of the planet. Working through existing NGOs would be more effective and more productive than setting up new organizations.

Following the July 2, 2005, Live 8 concerts to combat famine, and with the involvement of young people, I am convinced that the leadership of people like Bob Geldof, Bono and a host of other artists will have a greater influence on the next generation to change the stale, sterile and selfish attitudes of traditional "weapons of war" politics of the developed world and lead to a more caring and sharing world of the future.

APPENDIX
Notes on Conversion Factors

UNDERSTANDING QUANTITIES

It is impossible for an ordinary person to understand all the different terms and quantities for fuels, electricity, power and energy. It is complicated by the mixture of the imperial, U.S. and metric systems. It would be much more practical and understandable if only one system is used. That should be the metric system — for all measurements.

Measuring energy — in its many forms — is further complicated by the unwillingness of many people working in the business to accept international standards. We often read or hear of an oil field producing so many barrels of oil, an engine being so many horsepower, coal having so many British Thermal Units per pound (BTUs), or the temperature being so many degrees Fahrenheit. It would be so much simpler if fuels and energy measurements were in metric and temperatures in Celsius.

Large quantities of solid and liquid fuels should be measured in metric tonnes. Generally, gases should be measured in cubic metres. The capacity of an electric power plant should be rated in megawatts (MW) and the use of electric power should be measured in kilowatt hours (kWh).

Length
1 inch = 2.5400 centemetres; 1 centremetre = 0.3937 inches
1 foot = 0.3047 metres; 1 metre = 3.3281 feet.
1 statute mile = 1.6093 kilometres; 1 kilometre = 0.6214 miles

Area
1 acre = 0.407 hectares; 1 hectare = 2.4710 acres
1 hectare = 10,000 sq. metres; 1 sq. kilometre = 100 hectares
1 sq. mile = 2.899 sq. kilometres = 640 acres
1 sq. kilometre = 0.3861 sq. miles = 247.1 acres

Weight
1 lb = 0.4536 kilograms; 1 kilogram = 2.2046 lbs
1 tonne = 1,000 kilograms = 2204.6 lbs
1 Imperial ton = 2,240 lbs = 1.0161 tonnes
1 short ton (US) = 2,000 lbs = 0.9072 tonnes

Volume
1 cu. foot = 0.0283 cu. metres; 1 cu. metre = 35.3147 cu. feet
1 imperial pint = 0.5682 litres; 1 litre = 1.7600 imperial pints
1 imperial gallon =1.2009 U.S. gallons = 4.5461 litres
1 U.S. gallon = 0.8327 imperial gallons = 3.7854 litres
1 barrel = 42 U.S. gallons = 34.97 imperial gallons = 159 litres

Energy
1 kilowatt hour (kWh) = 1.34 horsepower = 1.98x 106 foot lbs =
3.412 BTUs = 859.845 kilocalories (kcal) = 3.6 megajoules (MJ) = 0.034 therms
1 terawatt hour (TWh) = 1x10^3 gigawatt hours (GWh) = 1x10^6 megawatt hours
(MWh) = 1 x 10^9 kilowatt hours (kWh)
1 gigajoule (GJ) = 277.78 kilowatt hours (kWh)

Power
1 kilowatt (kW) = 1.34 horsepower (HP)
1 gigawatt (GW) = 1x103 megawatt (MW) = 1x10^6 kilowatt (kW)
1 kilocalorie (kcal) = 4.187 kilojoules (kJ) = 3.968 BTU
1 kilojoule (kJ) = 0.239 kcal = 0.948 BTU
1 British thermal unit (BTU) = 0.252 kcal = 1.055 kJ
1 kilowatt hour (kWh) = 860 kcal = 3600 kJ = 3.412 BTU

Caorific Equivalent (Approx)
1 tonne of oil = 10 million kcal = 42 gigajoules = 40 million BTU
= 1.5 tonne of hard coal = 3 tonnes of lignite = 12 MWh electricity
106 tonnes oil = 4,500 gigawatt hours = 4.5 terawatt hours (power plant electricity)

Temperature
1 degree Kelvin = 1 degree Celsius = 1.8 degrees Fahrenheit
°C = (°F - 32) x 5/9
°F = 9 (°C x 9/5) + 32
0° Kelvin (absolute zero) = - 273.15°C

Conversion between fuels (rounded figures)
1 tonne crude oil = 7.3 barrels (Average) = 256 imperial gallons = 301 U.S. gallons
1 barrel per day = 50 tonnes per year (Average)
1 tonne of Motor Spirits = 8.45 barrels (Average)
1 tonne fuel oil = 6.7 barrels (Average)
1 tonne of oil = 1.5 tonnes coal = 3 tonnes lignite = 1.11 cu. metres of natural
gas = 12,000 kWh = 43,000 therms = 40 x 10^{12} BTUs = 10 x 10^6 kilocalories
= 43,000 MJ
1 kg. kerosene (paraffin) = 11.94 kWh/kg = 43 MJ/kg
1 kg. natural gas = 12.50 kWh/kg = 45 MJ/kg
1 kg. coal = 7.78 kWh/kg = 28 MJ/kg

1 kg. wood (oven dry) = 5.55 kWh/kg = 20 MJ/kg
1 kg. wood (air dry) = 4.16 kWh/kg = 15 MJ/kg
1 kg. dung or agricultural residue (air dry) = 3.30 kWh/kg = 12 MJ/kg

Natural Gas conversions

The gas industry accepts 1,000,000 BTUs (MMBTUs) = 1,000 cu. ft = 1 GJ. But in reality, 1 MMBTUs = 0.948 GJ. That is a 5 percent difference. It should also be recognized that the BTU value of natural gas varies from 920 to 1,000 BTUs per 1,000 cubic feet. The industry has been selling gas at prices based on 1,000 cubic feet (Mcf), but is moving to sell the product in BTUs or in gigajoules (GJ). To further confuse the buyer, the price of natural gas to the residential customer is based on a cost per cubic metre (m^3).

The conversion factors are provided mainly for easy references in the change over from British/American imperial units to metric units. Conversion factors between fuels are averaged and are based on statistics compiled by British Petroleum and from Gerald Foley's book *The Energy Question.*

The weight of sludge is based on information provided by the Toronto Works and Emergencies Department. As the water content of sludge at the Ashbridges Bay Sewage Treatment varies between 70 percent and 75 percent, I have used 28 percent as the amount of solids in a wet tonne, with the other 72 percent being water.

ABOUT THE AUTHOR

Tony O'Donohue's twin career paths — as a civil engineer and civic politician — have given him an intimate and unique understanding of the troubling issues confronting the urban environment and an expanding world city. He is concerned that Toronto is in decline, because of its collective inability to understand our relationship with our less fortunate fellow human beings and with nature itself. This could have frightening implications for the city, and also for Ontario and Canada.

He has worked on many major engineering projects and has seen at first hand how political incompetence and waste can lead to serious problems in administration. He has seen Toronto go from a clean city to a relatively dirty one — and from a rich city to a relatively poor one, mostly as a result of the botched introduction of amalgamation in 1998. He has immediate concerns about the wasteful use of our dwindling fossil fuels and our gluttonous use of electricity — highlighted by the August 2003 blackout; the long-term implications of dumping urban waste in the United States; and the cost of the political miscalculations — as much as half a billion dollars to be picked up by Toronto taxpayers for boondoggles in computers, sludge, the waterfront, the bridge to the Island Airport and other major issues. He worries, too, about the risk of maintaining a disabled and degraded nuclear power plant on Toronto's doorstep. "There is no DIY manual for repairing Pickering," he says in this important book.

O'Donohue graduated as an engineer from University College Galway in Ireland, and part of this book is a memoir contrasting two entirely different worlds. His father built a wind turbine on the rugged Burren coast to power the only wireless radio for miles around, which brought news of the bombing of Hiroshima and Nagasaki.

O'Donohue has devoted much of his time to environmental issues — water, sewage, transportation, waste, recycling and the efficient use of electricity. In city council, he persuaded Toronto to set up the Toronto Atmospheric Fund, led the drive to become the first city in the world to enact an ozone protection bylaw and set up the framework to combat global warming at the local level.

He received the Citizenship Award from the Ontario Association of Professional Engineers for his "substantial contribution to humanity."